THE 1970S

Kelly Boyer Sagert

American Popular Culture Through History

GREENWOOD PRESS
Westport, Connecticut • London

Library of Congress Cataloging-in-Publication Data

Sagert, Kelly Boyer.
   The 1970s / Kelly Boyer Sagert.
         p. cm. — (American popular culture through history)
   Includes bibliographical references and index.
   ISBN 0–313–33919–8 (alk. paper)
      1. United States—Civilization—1970–   2. Popular culture—United
States—History—20th century.   3. United States—Social life and
customs—1971–   4. Nineteen seventies.   I. Title.   II. Title: Nineteen
seventies.
E169.Z8S24   2007
306.0973'09047—dc22   2006031201

British Library Cataloguing in Publication Data is available.

Library of Congress Catalog Card Number: 2006031201
ISBN-10: 0–313–33919–8
ISBN-13: 978–0–313–33919–6

First published in 2007

Greenwood Press, 88 Post Road West, Westport, CT 06881
An imprint of Greenwood Publishing Group, Inc.
www.greenwood.com

Printed in the United States of America

The paper used in this book complies with the
Permanent Paper Standard issued by the National
Information Standards Organization (Z39.48–1984).

10   9   8   7   6   5   4   3   2   1

This book is dedicated to the memory of my two grandmothers, Berneice and Beatrice, affectionately known as Gramma B and Nana.

Gramma B loved to recall stories from our family's past, and she shared them in a way that was both fascinating and entertaining. Nana cherished reading, and she helped instill in me the joy of delving into a book to find just the right answers— and then discussing the multitude of possibilities.

I hope that I've absorbed some of what they tried to teach me, and I hope that this book does their abilities and talents some justice.

Contents

Contents

Preface

Pop culture serves as shorthand for "popular culture," which is the culture of the people, the study of which mirrors the attitudes and beliefs, entertainments and activities, challenges and stumbling blocks of a particular time and place. The choices, often mundane, that we make—in our cooking, in our clothing styles, in our reading material, and in our musical preferences—combine with the political, social, economic, and religious framework of an era to form its unique climate and to brand it with the swirls and whorls of its own recognizable thumbprint.

The study of pop culture differs from other types of scholarly observation, research, reporting, and analysis. Researchers focus more significantly on commercial and media-related influences on society. Because of the development of mass media—television, film, and the Internet, among others—Americans can simultaneously participate in (or at least witness and observe) mutual leisurely pursuits; because of the intense financial motivations of those involved in commercial endeavors, even our advertisements—think of Super Bowl commercials—bond together a significant percentage of Americans.

Who among us that watched the 1977 Super Bowl, for example, can forget the Xerox commercial in which a humble monk, Brother Dominic, duplicates an ancient manuscript for his superior; he then learns that 500 more sets are needed. Slipping through a secret passageway, Dominic returns to his modern-day shop that boasts the Xerox 9200, a marvelous machine that can create two copied pages per minute. When he returns to the monastery with his completed task in hand, the head monk proclaims Dominic's work "a miracle!" Named the fourth-best Super Bowl commercial, ESPN credits—or perhaps places the blame on—this commercial for all subsequent ones that "push the envelope."

Pop culture, although still a babe in the woods when compared to other academic pursuits, is now studied at many universities in the United States. These educational facilities offer courses that range from broad pop culture overviews to the microscopic review of one niche aspect—whether film or music or fashion. After studying a particular segment of American society, pop culture advocates often extrapolate greater societal meaning. The rise of the disaster movies during the 1970s, for example, led some to suggest that average citizens identified with the impending crises portrayed in these films because of the Vietnam War, Watergate, and the oil embargo—and that they felt a sense of relief, of catharsis, when the hero finds an innovative way to survive a nearly impossible situation. Perhaps they too, then, can survive their own tough challenges.

The American Popular Culture Through History series breaks the pop culture of the United States into discrete segments, and then analyzes what societal movements, trends, fads, and events propelled an era in the direction that it did. Chapters focus on the everyday experiences of Americans, both adults and youth, along with the influences of advertising, architecture, fashion, food, leisure activities, literature, music, performing arts, travel, and visual arts associated with that era. Although not every American was influenced in exactly the same manner by each of these facets of life, the simple act of collectively looking back places an important time of U.S. history into context and allows all of us to determine how prominent attitudes, beliefs, and customs affected daily life—ours and those of others. We may even feel a sense of solidarity, of standing on common ground on a platform of shared experiences as fragmented events start to merge into a particular—and occasionally quite peculiar—cultural identity.

Introduction

The field of pop culture analyzes collective experiences and group influences during a defined period of time, placing societal movements, trends, and situations into context.

Although pop culture is inextricably connected to politics, economics, religion, and other weightier topics that have long been considered suitable subjects for scholarly study, the more newly defined field of pop culture also delves deeply into more "common" subjects that are typically considered part of everyday life experiences; these might be considered "folk culture" or part of the mass-media movement—a more "low-brow" or commercial foci. Scholars involved in the study of pop culture might, for example, discuss topics as diverse as "tattoos to horror movies, from 'leather and lace' to the Three Stooges, from the cultural significance of bourbon to the relationship between Darth Vader and the legend of King Arthur"[1] in a typical pop culture conference setting.

To study contemporary pop culture, researchers may hang out at a Denny's restaurant or a honky-tonk bar, listening to conversation and jamming to music, watching what people enjoy eating and what they prefer to drink as they socialize. Information collected and observations recorded might then be handled in one of two ways. Perhaps the observer is satisfied with simply documenting these behaviors and preferences as a reflection of contemporary pop culture; other researchers and scholars would go further, extrapolating those behaviors to determine underlying themes and values of a particular time period.

Interestingly, and counterintuitive to researchers and historians for whom accuracy and verification are twin virtues of scholarship, many of those studying pop culture believe that inaccuracies—perhaps found in a popular movie or best-selling novel—provide value in the interpretation of an era; these may even become the focus of a particular study. As one pop culture aficionado explained, there is the sinking of the ship Titanic … and then there is the movie of the same name. The two are not identical. Why? What "wrong" film elements added value and viewer satisfaction in this particular era of moviegoing?

When watching an historical movie or while living through a particular decade, most of us don't spend our time wondering in which pop culture development we are currently participating; rather, we live out our lives, and then, in retrospect, we attempt to fit our experiences into that era's developments. "Oh, yes," we might say, "I remember doing/watching/wearing that … " For those who lived through the 1970s, you may find yourself doing just that as you read this book. You might remember who watched Saturday Night Fever with you; if you were a younger teen in 1977, you might also recall what tricks you used to sneak into this R-rated film—or into the 18-and-up discothèques, complete with flashing lighted floors and a silvery disco ball dominating the center of the hall. Perhaps you recall the original host of Saturday Night Live, as well, who tongue-in-cheek informed viewers that, "I'm Chevy Chase … and you're not." Maybe you still have a pair of glitter-encrusted platform shoes hidden at the back of your closet or some satiny hot pants that you'll never wear again—which is fine, because they don't fit, anyhow.

Movies, television, music, dance, and fashion styles are all covered by the American Popular Culture Through History series, as are trends in food, groundbreaking advertising, and much more, including the fads of the decade—and the 1970s, in particular, can certainly be remembered for its fads. According to journalist Dolores Barclay, "The 1970s were a giant cauldron of fads, fancies and fetishes … trendy times."[2] From the tongue-snapping pop rocks to the passively owned pet rocks, and from the introspective mood rings to the exhibitionistic fad of streaking, Barclay's observation holds true. The 1970s, they were trendy times, indeed.

That said, the prominence of the trendy and commercial aspects of pop culture should not be allowed to overshadow the inclusion of information gathered via more traditional disciplines; economic, political, and social data are extremely important to the overall pop culture of an era. During the 1970s, economic challenges certainly were on the forefront. Americans wrestled with the confounding economy of stagflation that combined dual challenges of rising prices with sluggish, lower employment rates. During the 1970s, an economist invented the term misery index to indicate the depths of the country's economic distress, and, at the end of the decade, this index was at an all-time high. Americans also had to reluctantly swallow the bitter pill of Watergate as they lost trust in their government and as they watched the televised investigative process with anger and resignation. They shuddered at the horrifying body count as American soldiers fought in Southeast Asia and at the deadly clash between the Ohio National Guard and students at Kent State University. Furthermore, although many felt freer from societal chains because of the civil rights, gay rights, and women's rights movements, others despaired of—or were simply baffled by—the rapidly shifting cultural mores.

How we felt during the 1970s—or how we perceive its events in retrospect—cannot, of course, be reported in a strictly objective manner. Whereas some disciplines—mathematics, for example—have neutral standards against which to measure formulas and statistics, no pure analysis of pop culture exists. Events and movements are filtered through the lens of experience, and how one feels about or discusses the 1970s will be colored by one's value systems. How one interprets women's lib and the Stonewall Riots, for example, will differ dramatically for those who identify themselves as feminists—or not; or as gay, lesbian, or bisexual—or as wholly heterosexual. The emotions attached to a discussion of the 1970s' civil rights movement will, overall, fluctuate significantly according to a person's racial identity. As yet another example, no matter how dispassionate one attempts to be, Democrats and Republicans will never perceive the Kent State shootings or the Watergate break-in exactly the same way.

The 1970s were also a time of significant contrasts. Dubbed the "Me Decade" by journalist Tom Wolfe, it saw the self-absorbed EST movement, wherein one's personal emotions were paramount; the quirky pet rock, which was extremely popular, in part because it did not require any effort on the owner's part; and a plethora of first-person songs that focused on individual feelings—all of which certainly bolstered Wolfe's claim of me-focused society. This decade, though, also served as a time of selflessness, as many men marched in favor of women's rights and voted for the Equal Rights Amendment that would constitutionally negate gender favoritism. Not everyone fighting for civil rights was black or even a minority, and heterosexuals as well as gays and lesbians believed in the rights of all, regardless of sexual orientation. Not one of these actions focused solely on "Me."

The 1970s also served as a symbol of persistence and the hope for a better day. The notion that the postwar United States would continue to have a strong and burgeoning economy was shattered. The idea that an elected president would serve out his term until completion—unless he died—was negated, and the Vietnam War left young protestors as well as soldiers bloodied and battered. Yet, America survived. People adapted, and they put the pieces back together again—but, whenever old ideals splinter, the reconstructed framework is never exactly the same as the original, and so it was—or perhaps so it especially was—for the culturally dissected and somewhat fragmented picture of the 1970s.

We all search for meaning in life, and, if you lived through the 1970s, you will surely see bits and pieces of your own still burning bright within the pages of this book. Looking back at an era, though, is somewhat like a group of people all staring at a prism; although we would all be gazing at the same prism, we each would see differently refracted images reflecting back—and that is exactly as it should be. Enjoy your view.

Timeline of the 1970s

1970

Richard Nixon sends U.S. troops into Cambodia.

Four Kent State University students are killed by the National Guard after a protest of the bombing of Cambodia.

Black Sabbath debuts, playing heavy metal; ZZ Top joins the Allman Brothers (debut 1969) in launching "Southern rock."

Two prominent rock singers—Janis Joplin and Jimi Hendrix—die of drug over-doses.

An estimated 20 million Americans participate in the first Earth Day commemora-tion.

The Environmental Protection Agency (EPA) forms.

Monday Night Football premieres on ABC.

Childproof safety caps are introduced.

California becomes the first no-fault divorce state.

Lithium is approved as a treatment for depression by the Food and Drug Admin-istration.

Big Bird of *Sesame Street* appears on the cover of *Time* magazine.

Postal reform laws make the U.S. Postal Service self-sufficient.

1971

Swann v. Charlotte-Mecklenburg Board of Education: the U.S. Supreme Court upholds school busing as a tool to correct racial imbalances in schools.

Jim Morrison of the Doors dies of heart failure; drug overdose speculation occurs.

Andrew Lloyd Webber and Tim Rice's musical, *Jesus Christ Superstar*, debuts on Broadway.

In *Reed v. Reed*, the Supreme Court rules that laws discriminating against women are illegal under the 14th Amendment.

The first word processor, the Wang 1200, is invented.

Cigarette advertising is banned on radio and television.

NASA Mariner 9 circles Mars, the first time a spaceship orbits another planet; Apollo XIV lands on the moon.

Pentagon Papers, which describe U.S. war activities in Vietnam, are released to the *New York Times* by Daniel Ellsberg; *New York Times* publishes them.

Richard Nixon imposes a 90-day wage and price freeze to combat inflation.

All in the Family, starring Carroll O'Connor as Archie Bunker, debuts on television, changing the direction of programming dramatically.

Prison riots in Attica, New York, last four days, with more than 40 inmates and guards killed.

MRI (Magnetic Resonance Imaging) technology is first used on humans to detect medical issues.

Charles Manson and three female followers are convicted of murdering Sharon Tate and sentenced to death.

Congress passes the 26th Amendment, which lowers the voting age to 18.

1972

Title IX bans gender discrimination at educational facilities that receive federal funds.

David Bowie's album, *Rise and Fall of Ziggy Stardust*, ushers in the era of glam-rock.

The Equal Rights Amendment (ERA) is adopted by Senate; state ratification needed.

Richard Nixon visits Moscow, and the U.S. and the U.S.S.R .agree to freeze nuclear weapons at current levels; he also visits China, another historic event.

Five burglars are arrested after breaking into the Democratic National Headquarters; this becomes known as the Watergate break-in.

Gloria Steinem launches *Ms.* magazine; *Life* magazine ceases weekly publication.

Arabs terrorists storm the Olympic Village and kill 11 Israeli athletes at Olympics held in Munich, Germany, after their demands are not met.

The Godfather, starring Marlon Brando, receives 10 Academy Award nominations; it wins Best Picture, Best Actor, and Best Adapted Screenplay.

Nike shoes debut, contributing to the fitness craze.

The Supreme Court declares the death penalty as cruel and unusual punishment; sentences of Charles Manson and his followers are commuted to life in prison.

President Nixon wins his reelection bid by the largest margin since Franklin Delano Roosevelt won in 1936.

Atari's Pong begins the video game craze.

HBO launches its cable subscription service in New York.

Alabama Governor George Wallace is shot while campaigning for president; he survives but suffers from paralysis.

1973

Richard Nixon orders a cease-fire in Vietnam after peace talks begin in Paris.

The U.S. draft is abolished, and an all-volunteer military begins.

Vice President Spiro Agnew resigns after being charged with accepting bribes and falsifying federal tax returns; Gerald Ford begins serving as vice president.

OPEC enacts an oil embargo against the United States because of the military aid provided by the U.S. to Israel during the Yom Kippur War.

The Supreme Court hears *Roe v. Wade;* it overturns prohibitions on first-trimester abortions and eases restrictions on second-trimester ones.

American Indian Movement seizes Wounded Knee for 71 days as a protest against the government for its treatment of Native Americans.

Billy Jean King defeats Bobby Riggs in tennis's "Battle of the Sexes."

Congress passes the Endangered Species Act.

UPC bar codes are introduced, allowing retailers to scan in information about purchases; this simplifies inventory tasks.

The Exorcist, a horror film, receives five major Academy Award nominations.

1974

Publishing heiress Patty Hearst is kidnapped by the Symbionese Liberation Army.

President Richard Nixon resigns because of the Watergate scandal/impeachment threat; Gerald Ford becomes president and he pardons Nixon for any Watergate crimes.

Hank Aaron hits his 715th home run, breaking Babe Ruth's record.

The first programmable pocket calculators become available for sale.

Naked students "streak" across college campuses; Ray Stevens's song "The Streak" becomes popular.

Eight former White House aides are indicted for conspiring in Watergate cover-up.

The U.S. Merchant Marine Academy becomes the first U.S. service academy to enroll women.

The first black model—Beverly Johnson—appears on the cover of a major fashion magazine (*Vogue*).

The Supreme Court orders Little League to allow girls to participate.

Women are ordained as Episcopalian priests.

1975

The precursor to the home computer, the Altair, debuts; assembly required.

Lynette "Squeaky" Fromme, a Charles Manson follower, attempts to assassinate Gerald Ford.

Unemployment reaches 8.9 percent, the highest since 1941.

The FBI captures Patty Hearst, who now goes by the name of Tania.

Joshua Reynolds invents and begins marketing the mood ring, a fad that sold millions.

Gary Dahl packages the Pet Rock and becomes a millionaire within a year.

Catalytic converters are introduced in cars, mitigating air pollution.

The U.S. government passes the Metric Conversion Act, stating that metric measurement is the preferred system, but people ignore its passage.

After scoring a perfect 800 on his math SATs, William Gates drops out of Harvard University to write software programs for a small computer company, Micro-Soft.

Saturday Night Live debuts on late-night television, satirizing politicians and other social phenomenon.

Teamster union leader Jimmy Hoffa disappears after meeting suspected mobsters at a restaurant.

1976

On April Fool's Day, Apple Computer launches its first product, selling it for $666.66.

4.8 million people apply for a CB license; it is estimated that only half of CB users actually apply for one.[3]

The New Jersey Supreme Court allows Karen Ann Quinlan's parents to remove her from life support after a long coma.

The first stand-alone Betamax VCRs are put on the market.[4]

The United States celebrates its Bicentennial; the U.S. mint issues commemorative coins and President Gerald Ford gives a nationally televised speech.

Jimmy Carter is elected president in November after the Democratic National Convention selects him as their candidate on the first ballot.

Chicago writer Saul Bellow wins the Pulitzer Prize for his novel *Humboldt's Gift*.

The U.S. Supreme Court reverses its 1972 decision and legalizes capital punishment.

Journalist Tom Wolfe gives the decade the nickname that sticks in "The 'Me' Decade and the Third Great Awakening."

More than 200 people attending a Philadelphia convention for ex-service personnel become ill with Legionnaire's Disease; 34 die from the disease.

1977

King of Rock and Roll, Elvis Presley, dies at age 42; heart disease named as the cause.

John Travolta stars in *Saturday Night Fever*, furthering the popularity of disco, and *Star Wars* also debuts in theaters, with its phrase, "May the force be with you."

The Alaskan pipeline is completed, providing the U.S. with 15 percent of its oil supply.[5]

Jimmy Carter is sworn in as president after parking his limo and walking down Pennsylvania Avenue.

President Carter grants unconditional amnesty to most of those who evaded the draft—the "draft dodgers"—to avoid serving in the Vietnam War.

The country deals with "stagflation," an economic condition consisting of continuing inflation, and stagnant business activity with its corresponding high rates of unemployment.

ABC airs the hugely successful television miniseries, *Roots*, based on a book written by Alex Haley.

"Son of Sam"—David Berkowitz—is arrested after a 12-month, 6-person killing spree in which he believes a black "demon" dog was instructing him to murder.

President Carter signs the Panama Canal Treaty and Neutrality Treaty, which relinquishes U.S. control of the canal by the year 2000 and guarantees its neutrality.

President Carter halts development of the B-1 bomber in favor of the development of the cruise missile.[6]

Billy Carter, the brother of the president, starts selling Billy Beer; he appears on the cover of *Newsweek* holding a can.

1978

The birth of the world's first successful "test-tube baby," who was conceived through in-vitro fertilization, serves as a focal point of the science vs. religion debate.

President Carter, Egypt's Anwar Sadat, and Israel's Menachem Begin meet at Camp David to discuss peace in the Middle East.

Love Canal, New York, was declared a federal disaster after the chemical wastes dumped beneath the town leak; rates for cancer and birth defects are extremely high.

American cult leader Jim Jones of the People's Temple persuades hundreds of his followers to commit suicide in Guyana, most by drinking poisoned Kool-Aid.

Congress extends the deadline for ERA ratification, changing it from March 22, 1979, to June 30, 1982.[7]

A sniper shoots *Hustler* publisher Larry Flynt, leaving him paralyzed.

In the *University of California v. Bakke*, the U.S. Supreme Court rules that the use of quotas is not permissible in affirmative action programs.

The former president publishes *The Memoirs of Richard Nixon.*

The first arcade game, Space Invaders, premieres in Japan.

Dallas, an evening soap opera starring Larry Hagman as J.R. Ewing, first airs on CBS.

1979

A near nuclear disaster occurs at Three Mile Island near Harrisburg, Pa.; fierce arguments over the safety of nuclear energy ensue.

Militant Islamic students in Iran storm the U.S. embassy there, taking more than 90 people—65 of them Americans—as hostage; they hold 52 of these hostages for 444 days.

Fundamentalist preacher Jerry Falwell forms an organization called the Moral Majority; its aim is to reestablish traditional religious values in the nation.

The U.S. and China formalize diplomatic relations.

The first gay and lesbian rights march takes place in Washington, D.C.; Falwell responds by praying and saying that "God made Adam and Eve, not Adam and Steve."

The U.S. mint issues the Susan B. Anthony dollar; the coin approximates the size of a quarter, confusing many consumers.

The Sony Walkman is introduced in Japan.

The U.S. government awards the Sioux Nation $105 million in land claims.

President Carter delivers his "Crisis of Confidence" speech, telling the American people that he shares their pain.[8]

Francis Ford Coppola's movie about the Vietnam War, *Apocalypse Now*, wins the Academy Award for Best Picture.

PART ONE

LIFE AND YOUTH DURING THE 1970S

THE 1970S

1

Everyday America

INTRODUCTION

In the 1970s, Americans dealt with a decade of sweeping social, cultural, and political changes as best as they could. Few conventions were left unchallenged; perhaps this decade could be best summed up as the years of no sacred cows. Minorities continued their efforts to effect change and to institute laws that protected their civil rights. Countless women, many of them inspired by the courage and dedication of those fighting for civil rights, marched for their own freedoms, including economic, political, religious, social, and cultural gains; the near ratification of the Equal Rights Amendment symbolizes the controversy that this movement created. Meanwhile, the gay and lesbian cause gained momentum, with its advocates also experiencing heartbreaking setbacks. Moments of celebration and rejoicing alternated with other moments of anguish and gnashing of teeth for all of these groups that so desperately fought for change.

The 1970s were also a decade of disillusionment. Too many Americans lost their jobs during an era of stagflation—a combined economic disaster of inflation, when wages did not keep up with the increasing prices of goods and services, with stagnation, when the economy remained sluggish. Two oil embargoes, a festering yet still-bloody war in Southeast Asia, and some of the worst political scandals to ever hit the White House contributed to the sense of malaise that spread through the country.

Contradictory yet true, the decade that pushed forward some of the most liberal causes was also weighted down by a sense of hopelessness and apathy. Near the end of the decade, President Jimmy Carter addressed the latter condition, to the horror of many who felt that he had just admitted to the political pink elephant in the room.

To add to the troubles of the era, crime rates continued to increase, including murders; the use of illegal drugs also escalated. Experts were increasingly attributing the causes of crimes to failures of society, and tax dollars were therefore poured into social reform and rehabilitation efforts. Nevertheless, this decade contained spectacular and brutal crimes.

Changes in the family structure echoed those of the overall society. Divorce increased and birth rates dropped. People experimented with living together before marriage, and, when they did marry, they often wrote their own vows and created their own ceremonies. In increasing numbers, Americans left mainstream churches to seek spiritual answers elsewhere, perhaps in the growing Evangelical Christian movement, perhaps in a religious group dubbed a cult by the mainstream, or perhaps through New Age avenues of enlightenment.

Throughout the tumultuous 1970s, the people, the government, the courts, and the social institutions tackled the taxing issues first raised in the 1960s, and they fought to make sense of the contradictions and challenges before them. This was not an easy task.

THE ECONOMY AND HEALTH CARE
The Economy

The 1970s witnessed an economic slowdown after a period of significant postwar growth. After World War II ended, Americans had come to expect a stable job market with low inflation and a steady growth of the overall economy. If and when economic recessions or unemployment issues arose, they were fairly brief and easily remedied.

By the summer of 1970, though, industrial productivity had begun to decline, while unemployment rates were increasing. Interest and inflation rates were on the rise, and economists expressed concern over trade deficits that would reach $1.1 billion; unbalanced budgets and growing deficits were also warning signs of a troubled economy. In August 1971, President Richard Nixon instituted a 90-day price and wage control program, something unheard of during peacetime, with the hope that this policy would curb inflation. It did not, although many economists supported Nixon's plan at the time.

This economic slowdown was more than surface deep. According to statistics cited by Paul Krugman in *Peddling Prosperity: Economic Sense and Nonsense in the Age of Diminished Expectations*, the productivity of an individual worker averaged 3 percent from the end of World War II until 1973 and then it dropped to about 1 percent, where it remained throughout the decade and beyond.[1] Why, specifically, this happened, no one can say for certain, although many theories abound.

To understand the impact of these economic changes, it is important to dissect the downward cycle that was affecting Americans during this era.

In 1973, prices of consumer goods were increasing by about 8.5 percent per year; although other Western countries were dealing with inflationary rates that were much higher, this inflation was still quite challenging to the pocketbooks of those living in the United States.[2] Furthermore, because of the prosperity of the past 28 years or so, people had become accustomed to consuming products at an accelerating rate. Plus, there were record numbers of births during the Baby Boomer generation, and these rising population figures meant that the needs of more people had to be met during a time when the average individual was consuming increasingly larger quantities of products.

To put the increased population growth into perspective, consider that about 2.6 million births occurred in the United States in 1940, the year before the country entered World War II. In 1957, 4.3 million babies were born. Fast-forwarding to 1973, America as a society therefore had large numbers of teenagers needing financial support, while young adults on the brink of starting their own lives, sans parents, were struggling to find employment. So, at a time when prices were rising and jobs were uncertain, the young adult population had increased significantly, which meant that even more product consumption was occurring—leading to an almost surefire recipe for economic crises.

Another factor existed. Although the United States had satisfied much of its own oil—and therefore gasoline—needs through 1950, the increasing amount of oil and gasoline consumption during the 1960s and 1970s caused the American government to import more of these products. By the early 1970s, 85 percent of America's workers drove to their jobs every day and many of these workers lived out in the suburbs, away from their place of employment, and so they needed to purchase more gas to drive to their workplaces. This was only one factor that led the United States to import 35 percent of its oil by 1973.

Much of this oil was exported out of Middle Eastern countries that had formed a cartel, the Organization of Petroleum Exporting Countries (OPEC), more than a decade earlier. The combination of this collaboration among Middle Eastern countries and the increasing oil demands of people in the United States and other Western countries gave OPEC significant bargaining power and left America in a vulnerable position. By 1973, the petroleum reserves of the United States were nearly gone; Nixon placed controls on the reserves, but the situation was already on the brink of disaster.

Then, on October 6, 1973—Yom Kippur, the holiest day of the Jewish calendar—Arab forces attacked Israel on more than one front. With the support of the United States and other Western European nations, Israel was able to rebuff these forces and a ceasefire agreement came about the following month. However, on October 17, in the middle of this short war with far-reaching consequences, OPEC enforced an oil embargo on the

United States, whereby Arab countries stopped selling oil to the United States in protest of its support of Israel during the Yom Kippur War. The United States, plus the Netherlands, was particularly pointed out as supporting Israel, but OPEC also raised oil prices for Western European countries by 70 percent, which increased the price of a barrel of oil from $3 to $5.11, overnight. In January 1974, the prices were raised much further, to $11.65.

This oil embargo drastically affected those living in the United States, many of whom paid little to no attention to the Arab-Israeli situation; even if they had, many citizens struggled to understand the correlation between prices at their gas stations and a religious war, far away from North America. The United States, accustomed to buying oil in the quantities needed, suffered from this economic retaliation, and government officials had to ask citizens to turn down their thermostats, car pool to work, and otherwise limit their consumption of oil products. Gasoline prices increased from 30 cents per gallon to $1.20, which severely curtailed discretionary income. Gas stations were eventually limited to 10 gallons of gasoline per transaction and Sunday sales of gasoline were forbidden.

When oil stocks are removed from the calculations, the stock market fell about 15 percent in just one month—from October to November 1973—and by 45 percent over the next two years. OPEC lifted its punitive embargo on March 18, 1974, but significant damage to the United States economy—and the disruption of daily lifestyles—had already occurred.

In a bid to regain some independence from OPEC, Nixon pushed for the completion of the Alaskan pipeline, which would pump oil for the United States and thereby decrease the amount of imported oil purchased from OPEC. Construction of the pipeline began on March 27, 1975, and the project was finished on May 31, 1977. Just three weeks later, oil was being transported through its pipes. This solution, though, was somewhat chicken-and-egg. When citing reasons for the economic troubles of the 1970s, some experts pointed to the costs associated with the increasing environmental regulations put in place to prevent more despoiling of nature. Not surprisingly, some of the strongest criticisms of the pipeline came from environmentalists. Yet, the Alaskan Pipeline was the solution, which some say was unavoidable, to sidestep future control by OPEC—thereby freeing up more funds to protect the environment.

Economists generally point to a couple of other reasons for the change in the economic picture during the 1970s. First, the scientific and technological advances that boomed throughout the country, postwar, had already had their effects in speeding up productivity. Therefore, the effects of the postwar boom had simply run out of steam, which would be a natural and unavoidable consequence.

Conversely, others suggest that it was America's inability to keep up with the technological advances of other countries—most notably Germany and Japan—that hurt the U.S. economy. Because the United States did not invest in enough research and development, they say, the productivity of American workers did not increase along with their wages. Therefore, the prices of American goods either stayed the same or increased, but their quality did not, and so people began purchasing imported goods to a greater degree. Some manufacturers began moving their operations overseas, where cheaper labor could be found, which meant that many American workers, especially in the Midwest, lost their jobs. Plus, with a lower household income, because of unemployment, Americans searched out lower-priced goods—which were frequently made overseas. In particular, the oil crises of 1973 and 1979 caused many Americans to purchase smaller, foreign-made cars that were more economical. For the first time in the twentieth century, in large part because of the downward spiral just described, the United States imported more goods than it exported.

Moreover, politically conservative experts believed that the anticapitalist lifestyle that surfaced during the 1960s—with its accompanying increase in drug use and crime rates—damaged the country's work ethic, leading to an economic downturn. Although social conservatives also expressed the opinion that women in the workforce helped cause this downturn, it is also logical to assume that rising gas prices and other inflationary trends actually pushed many women into the workforce, to ease their family's tight budget.

Economic troubles did not end after the oil embargo ceased. Hourly wages, which included benefits, rose only 0.5 percent during the decade, and unemployment rates generally hovered over 6 percent. In May 1975, the unemployment rate was a staggering 9.2 percent.[3] Meanwhile, the gross domestic product growth slowed to 2.8 percent throughout the 1970s.[4]

By 1975, the U.S. economy was clearly in a state of "stagflation," a newly coined word that ominously told of rising prices (inflation) at a time when the economy was stagnating, with high unemployment rates and an economic recession. In response to this stagflation, President Gerald Ford proposed a moratorium on any new federal spending programs, and he capped both Social Security raises and federal employee pay raises at 5 percent. He also proposed a one-time $16 billion tax cut. Congress did not acquiesce with the cuts in spending, however, appropriating more funds and further increasing the deficit. Later that year, Ford proposed yet another combination of a massive tax cut and spending ceiling; again, Congress agreed with the tax cut but ignored the ceiling. In 1976, though, spending limits were enforced, and, that year, prices rose only 4.8 percent and four million more people were employed than were in 1975.

In 1979, a second oil crisis, smaller in scope yet still damaging to the economy, occurred. By this time, the phrase *energy crisis* was in common usage—and this energy crisis was precipitated by the revolution in Iran. After the Shah, Mohammad Reza Pahlavi, fled this Middle Eastern country, the Ayatollah Khomeini took control. Although the Ayatollah did resume the sale of oil to the United States, the volume was reduced and so the relative scarcity of product meant that prices once again increased. OPEC nations filled in much of the gap, but the volume of oil in the United States was still down 4 percent. Panic ensued, along with the proliferation of conspiracy theories about oil companies holding back petroleum to artificially set higher prices.

President Jimmy Carter had been warning the country about another potential energy crisis, but the country was suffering from a "crisis of confidence" and responded to his warnings with apathy and resignation, rather than with energy and enthusiasm. Beaten down by a war in Southeast Asia, shaken by political scandals such as Watergate, and barely recovered from the oil crisis of 1973, the American people simply did not believe in their leaders the way they once did. Nevertheless, on July 15, 1979, Carter delivered yet another energy-related speech, one that is still analyzed and debated. In this speech, he proclaimed that the country's problems were much deeper than an energy crisis and an overdependence on foreign oil. The real issue, Carter stated, was the country's moral failure to consider the good of all humankind over personal fulfillment.

Health Care

In 1971, our neighbor to the north, Canada, introduced a government-run health care system; some U.S. politicians hoped to do the same, but perhaps the economic situation in the United States was too complicated at that time and too entrenched in challenges for a push to be fruitful. Nevertheless, in 1973, Congress passed the Health Maintenance Organization (HMO) Act, which provided grants to employers who offered HMOs to their employees. HMOs provide care directly to the patients, and so were seen as a lower-cost alternative to health care funding. In the HMO system, physicians who participate receive fixed annual payments to service its subscribers, rather than receiving a fee for specific services provided. Those insured were not always pleased with HMOs, though, as they needed to select doctors and hospitals that participated in the program; this meant that many Americans needed to leave their longtime family doctors if they wanted to continue to be insured.

During the 1970s, mass media focused attention on four main problems of the U.S. health care system. First was the undeniable fact that health care costs were soaring out of control. Next was that, even though the government now provided insurance for the elderly and those on welfare, far too many Americans remained uninsured. Also, the ever-increasing number of malpractice lawsuits against doctors and hospitals brought the quality of medical care into question, and, finally, bureaucratic controls caused many patients to complain about the loss of humane medical treatment.[5] None of these problems were solved during the decade.

In 1977, Congress formed the Health Care Finance Administration, which restructured the way in which the federal government paid doctors and hospitals in its Medicare program. This is the bill that created reimbursement methods such as "diagnosis-related groups" and "relative value scales." This bill broadened the powers and influence of the federal government in health care and continued the trend wherein Medicare served as a tool to control reimbursement costs rather than to insure care.[6] Medicare, as a political tool, continued to propel the growing "gray lobby" of aging Americans, and it also was used as a leverage tool of the government to enforce its antisegregation and antidiscrimination policies.

Other than these two initiatives, the creation of the HMO bill and the expansion of Medicare, national health care did not surface as a political issue during the decade, even though health care costs were rising at a rate of two to three times of the overall economy.[7] In fact, some have noted that health care legislation, as a national political issue, is noteworthy during the 1970s only because of its lack of priority.

During the 1970s, the term *holistic* became part of many people's vocabularies, usually in conjunction with their health. In holistic health care, the entire mind, body, and spirit triage is considered when diagnosing and treating problems—and, perhaps even more important, in the prevention of diseases that could be avoided by careful choices of consumption: what healthy foods and vitamins, for example, should be consumed, and what substances—alcohol, nicotine, drugs, and so forth—should be avoided or limited. Moreover, alternative treatments, including acupuncture, meditation, herbal ingestion, and so forth, found new followings during the 1970s.

Robert D. Johnston, in *The Politics of Healing: Histories of Alternative Medicine in Twentieth-Century North America*, traces the resurgence of holistic health treatments in the 1970s to one single influential magazine article. Called "Homeopathy: A Neglected Medical Art," it appeared in the February 1969 issue of *Prevention*, and its effects reverberated through the 1970s and beyond.[8]

Although much of what holistic healers advised was mere common sense and/or compatible with more traditional care—the avoidance of nicotine, for example, or the importance of rest—other suggestions relied on more ancient philosophies and beliefs. In the *Holistic Health Handbook*, as just one example, women who wanted to avoid unnatural forms of birth control were told to sleep under low-wattage lamps during the middle of their ovulation cycle and in darkness during the rest of the month. This was called "lunaception," and it attempted to regulate women's menstrual and ovulation cycles to match the moon, to imitate and re-create the highly predictable menstrual cycles that happened naturally to women who slept outdoors in traditional villages, long ago.[9]

Increasing numbers of Americans also turned to exercise during the 1970s. Jogging was a prime pursuit, while fashions, which included warm-up suits and designer running shoes by Nike, both aided and were influenced by this trend.

POLITICS AND POLITICAL LEADERS
Richard Nixon

Mention the name of Richard Milhous Nixon and the word "Watergate" almost inevitably follows the reference to this former president of the United States. Watergate is the scandal—perhaps better described as a series of scandals—that ended the political career of Nixon and many others in Washington, D.C.; it is named after the hotel that served as the center of corrupt activity. Ever since Watergate occurred and was thusly named, other political scandals have traditionally had the suffix "-gate" attached to their names.

Richard Nixon rose to national political prominence after serving for three years in the House of Representatives (1947–1950) and another two in the Senate (1951–1953). He then served as the vice president for two terms under Dwight D. Eisenhower (1953–1961). In 1960, he easily obtained the presidential nomination of the Republican Party and challenged John F. Kennedy for the office. From a religious standpoint, this was an interesting race to watch and analyze, as a Quaker (Nixon) ran against a Catholic.

Losing that close race by only two-tenths of a percentage of the popular vote, Nixon then ran for the office of California's governor, also losing that contest. Nixon seemed bitter after those two losses; after telling reporters that he was leaving the world of politics for good, he told them that they wouldn't have Nixon to kick around any more. Contrary to that statement, he then ran against Hubert Humphrey in the 1968 presidential race—and this time, he won the popular vote by a small margin and the Electoral College by a more comfortable one. Even this victory was tainted, however, as a Democratic candidate, Robert F. Kennedy, died by an assassin's hand during the primary race; speculation surely existed over how Nixon might have fared in a second round against a Kennedy.

Nixon set the tenor of his presidential philosophy, which ultimately led to his downfall, as early as July 1970. Approving more in-depth information gathering by governmental agencies such as the FBI and CIA, he quickly changed his mind and rescinded the order.

The first public hint of trouble occurred on June 13, 1971, when the *New York Times* published portions of confidential government documents detailing the Vietnam War. These papers became known as the Pentagon Papers and the gist of the published excerpts showed that the government was not being forthcoming about the escalation of the war in Southeast Asia. Shortly thereafter, the *Washington Post* also published pieces of the report, but then the Department of Justice requested a temporary restraining order, which was granted. The executive branch of the government argued that it must serve as the sole judge of the release of national security information; the press insisted that First Amendment rights must be paramount and that the federal government wished to exercise censorship, rather than protect national security interests. The court ruled in favor of the press and their stand on First Amendment rights, and the newspapers were granted permission to continue to publish this material.

If all had ended at this juncture, Nixon's administration would not have suffered its deep scars but, on September 9, a group of men known as the "plumbers" broke into the office of the psychiatrist of Daniel Ellsberg, the former defense analyst who was discovered to have leaked the Pentagon Papers to the press. These men were dubbed plumbers for their ability to plug information leaks about the Nixon administration and to collect their own data on those seen as enemies of the president's policies. When the psychiatrist office burglary came to light, the charges that the government was pressing against Ellsberg for releasing the documents were dropped. The court, in 1973, was persuaded that the break-in was conducted in order to gather information to discredit Ellsberg.

Nevertheless, if the Pentagon Papers were the sole issue, then a scandal of Watergate's magnitude would not have ensued. The situation, though, continued to escalate—and dramatically—when five men, one of whom used to work for the CIA, were arrested at 2:30 in the morning on June 17, 1972. They were caught in their attempts to burgle the Democratic National Convention Headquarters, which were located in a plush hotel known as the Watergate. It was later discovered that bugging devices had been planted in the Democratic headquarters in May, and, on June 19, the *Washington Post* indicated that a GOP security aide was numbered among the burglars. Meanwhile, the White House denied all connection to—or prior knowledge of—these break-ins.

The situation became even more murky and disturbing. On August 1, a $25,000 check earmarked for the Nixon reelection campaign was discovered to have been deposited into an account of a Watergate burglar; near the end of September, it was uncovered that John Mitchell, former attorney general and the head of Nixon's reelection campaign, used Republican Party funds to conduct investigations into the operations of the Democratic Party. Then, on October 10, 1972, the FBI determined that a thorough political spy campaign had been conducted by the Republicans against the Democrats. Meanwhile, the White House continued to deny prior knowledge about any of these events.

These discoveries did not hurt Nixon's reelection campaign. On November 11, 1972, Richard Nixon won a landslide second term against Democratic candidate George McGovern, the senator from South Dakota. Capturing 60.7 percent of the popular vote, Nixon and his vice president, Spiro Agnew, were awarded 520 out of the 537 electoral votes. The American public had spoken loudly and clearly—and in favor of Richard Nixon.

In retrospect, it is startling to review how quickly all fell apart for his administration. During the first half of 1973, beginning just two and a half months after his landslide victory, members of Nixon's administration either resigned (H. R. Haldeman, John Ehrlichman, and Attorney General Richard Kleindienst), were fired (legal counsel John Dean), or were convicted of conspiracy, burglary, and wiretapping in connection with the Watergate break-in (G. Gordon Liddy and James W. McCord, Jr.).

On May 18, 1973, the investigation began to be televised, with Archibald Cox serving as the prosecutor. Testimony damaged the Nixon presidency fairly early on, as, on June 3, former counsel to the president John Dean testified that he had discussed the Watergate cover-up at least 35 times with the president. Although this didn't conclusively indict the president, Dean's testimony was persuasive. Ten days later, a damaging memo, addressed to former White House aide John Ehrlichman, was found. This memo described the intent to burglarize Daniel Ellsberg's psychiatrist—an action that did occur on September 9, 1971. So, the question narrowed in scope. Although it was still unclear whether or not Nixon himself knew of the Ellsberg break prior to its occurrence, it was confirmed that his close consultants were well aware of the situation, and beforehand.

The plot thickened further in July, when Nixon's former appointments secretary told Congress that Nixon had secretly taped all of his meetings and conversations since 1971. Nixon ordered the taping to stop, but he also refused to turn over already-recorded tapes to investigators.

In October, Nixon became fed up with the Watergate prosecutor, Archibald Cox, firing him and abolishing the office of special prosecutor altogether. The event became known as the Saturday Night Massacre, and both the attorney general and the deputy attorney general resigned in connection with Nixon's actions. Moreover, calls for Nixon's impeachment, previously mere murmurs, heated up.

A Congressional committee then subpoenaed selected tapes and Nixon began reviewing them personally. The most controversial tape, one from June 20, 1972, had more than 18 minutes of conversation erased and many people now believe that Nixon's loyal secretary, Rosemary Woods, deleted portions of the tape that she feared would harm the president. She had demonstrated how that might occur accidentally, but significant doubt exists over that scenario.

After Nixon and his associates reviewed the tapes in question, the White House still refused to turn them over—but on April 30, 1974, it released 1,200 pages of edited transcripts. The House Judiciary Committee was not satisfied with the transcripts, demanding the original recordings, but it wasn't until July that the Supreme Court ruled in favor of Congress. Within three days of receiving undoctored tapes, on July 27, 1974, Congress passed three articles of impeachment against the president for obstruction of justice. On August 8, 1974, Richard Milhous Nixon became the first—and so far, the only—President of the United States to resign from office. By this point, Spiro Agnew had resigned from his office as vice president and so the new vice president, Gerald Ford, immediately assumed the office of president.

It seems extremely unlikely that Nixon's legacy will ever separate from that of Watergate. His foreign policy successes, however, are also noteworthy, most specifically his breakthrough with Communist China and his détente with Soviet Union, and they must be mentioned. Nixon's foreign policy doctrine was summed up as "Peace through Partnership," and he stressed the importance of negotiation with foreign powers.

In February 1972, Richard Nixon became the first U.S. president to visit China. After two decades of a strained and difficult relationship between the two countries, Nixon spent a week discussing a wide variety of political topics of mutual interest with Chairman Mao Tse-tung. Although leaders on both sides did not reveal any specifics of significance about the talks, a breakthrough clearly had happened and a diplomatic coup had

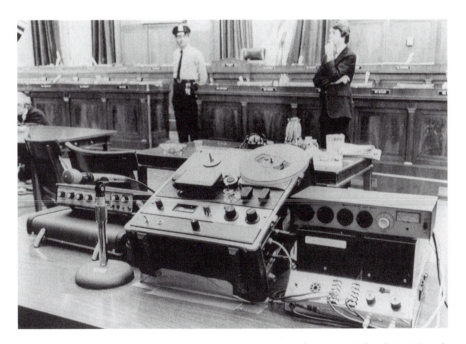

The House Judiciary Committee uses this equipment to listen to Richard M. Nixon's Watergate tapes on May 5, 1974, as it considers possible impeachment charges against the president. Courtesy of Photofest.

been achieved. Moreover, the notion that the United States and China had begun to normalize relationships created the need for the Soviet Union to participate in talks with Nixon, lest two of the superpowers align themselves against the third.

Nixon accomplished this diplomatic feat, in part, by making conciliatory gestures prior to his visit, such as toning down anti-Chinese rhetoric, ending travel restrictions of American citizens to China, and—in what became known as "Ping-Pong Diplomacy"—allowing the American ping-pong team to visit Mainland China.[10] The president also focused more on balance of power issues instead of debating ideologies with the Communist nation.

Three months later, Nixon served as the first president to travel to the Soviet Union, where he met with its leader, Leonid Brezhnev. This nation was rapidly approaching the United States in its number of strategic arms, and Nixon recognized that merely confronting the country and its leaders with military might would only further strain the relationship between the two nations and lessen the chance for long-term peace. Nixon was not seeking friendship from the Soviet Union; rather he wished for more relaxed and open communications that would result in mutual agreements that balanced power.

In May 1972, the two leaders agreed that, in a nuclear age, the two superpowers must find a way to peacefully coexist in the world. They agreed to meet as two equals in their pursuit. They also signed the Strategic Arms Limitation Talks (SALT) treaty, which limited the number of certain types of weapons and the amount of testing allowed. Nixon's philosophy differed significantly from traditional thinking, in that he favored a balance of arms rather than the continuing superiority of the United States. Brezhnev and Nixon met again in 1973 and 1974, but Watergate somewhat hurt the former meeting and served as a significant deterrent to the latter. Nevertheless, although Nixon's political scandals at home overshadowed his détente in the Soviet Union, his diplomatic accomplishments remained significant, changing the direction of future negotiations with other superpower nations.

Gerald Ford

Just as Richard Nixon's name is irreversibly attached to Watergate, Gerald Ford's name will forever be connected with "the Pardon." As the only president not elected to office, much of his presidency consisted of separating his administration from the troubles of Watergate without employing the type of finger-pointing that would damage the future of the Republican Party. Ford's job was not easy, and neither were the ethical choices that he needed to make—with what seemed to be the whole world watching and judging.

On August 8, 1974, Ford's predecessor, Richard Nixon, had resigned from the office of the presidency in a state of shame. Moreover, he faced criminal prosecution for actions taken during the Watergate years—and a trial would occupy much of the nation's time, attention, and financial resources. Furthermore, such a trial would bring forth a plethora of distasteful testimony that would further sully the reputation of the White House.

Only Gerald Ford could prevent such a spectacle, through the use of the presidential pardon. That said, if he pardoned Nixon, especially if granted before any formal indictments were announced, his own reputation and political career would surely be damaged, amid whispers that he and Nixon had forged an under-the-table deal. Polls indicated that nearly 60 percent of American citizens opposed a presidential pardon,[11] which served as a clear indicator of the opposition Ford would face, politically speaking, if he pardoned Richard Nixon.

Whether Ford knew, upon entering his office, that he would pardon Nixon—or if he agonized over the decision while serving as president, as he states and as evidence appears to confirm—on September 8, 1974, Gerald Ford announced that he was giving former president Richard Nixon a full, absolute, and unconditional pardon for any crimes that he may have committed while in office. Nixon did not even need to admit to any wrongdoings for the pardon to take effect. Ford cited the need for national healing, and he favored using the nation's energy for recovery, rather than for revenge.

Presidential press secretary J.F. terHorst resigned in protest over this pardon, while the House Judiciary Committee began an investigation into its circumstances. In an ironic twist, although it is believed that Ford pardoned Nixon, at least in part, to rid his new administration of any further connection with Nixon, this pardon forever melded their identities: the Watergate President and the Watergate Pardon President.

Prior to 1973, Gerald Ford's political career had been characterized by hard work and quiet integrity, free from scandals and controversies. He began his national career in 1949, when he was elected to the House of Representatives. He served in that capacity until 1973, where he also served as the House Minority Leader since 1965.

During the summer of 1973, the current vice president, Spiro Agnew, was being investigated on charges of extortion, bribery, and income tax evasion in connection to his term as Maryland governor. Although Agnew swore that he would not resign over this scandal, and although he insisted that a standing vice president could only be removed from office through impeachment, Spiro Agnew did resign on October 10, 1973. That day, he also pled *nolo contendere* to one count of tax evasion; this plea translates into a claim of not guilty, but subject to conviction. He was fined $10,000 and sentenced to three years of unsupervised probation. In 1974, the state of Maryland disbarred Agnew; a civil court later forced him to reimburse the state for funds accepted as bribes.

It was under these circumstances that Gerald Ford stepped into the office of vice president of the United States. Then, just 10 months later, he became president under even darker circumstances. Not surprisingly, his early months as president were filled with disarray; for continuity's sake, Ford kept much of Nixon's administration, including Alexander Haig and Henry Kissinger. Although this kept the White House running more smoothly, it also added to Ford's difficulty in establishing his own administration, and it prevented him from making a cleaner break from the Nixon one. This reflected badly upon him in some people's eyes. Furthermore, it took Congress four months to confirm a vice president—Nelson Rockefeller—for him and so it was difficult to settle into a routine.

Besides these political difficulties, Ford also faced a dire economic situation when he took office. The oil embargo had ended just five months before and stagflation was about to peak. Moreover, Ford's relationship with Congress, which had previously been quite good, suffered a terrible blow after the pardon—and, in the 1974 elections for the House and the Senate, the American public voted overwhelmingly for the Democratic Party, so much so that House Democrats held more than a two-thirds majority, which rendered the presidential veto as a nearly useless tool if the Democrats chose to make it so.

The Democrats newly voted into Congress in 1974 became known as the "Watergate Babies." Confident in the public's vote of confidence in their party and its policies, they were quite aggressive in their disagreements with Ford, frequently citing their duty of "congressional oversight" when they questioned or challenged the president. Ford's economic plans were not passed without significant alterations by Congress, nor were his proposals to protect energy sources. His foreign policies were criticized and called "too soft on Communism," even though Ford had requested increased spending for defense and had worked on ratifying the longer-term SALT II treaty with the Soviet Union.

Ultimately, Ford paid the price for the overall distrust of the office of the presidency, post-Vietnam and post-Watergate, as he served during a time of reduced executive powers. As the 1976 election neared, Ford radically changed his staff; during what became known as the "Sunday Morning Massacre," he removed Nelson Rockefeller, his more liberal vice president, from the presidential ticket, demoted Henry Kissinger, and removed the Secretary of State from his position. Ford's standing with the Republican Party remained quite tenuous, however, and he barely won its presidential nomination in 1976, almost losing it to Ronald Reagan.

New campaign laws reduced the amount of funds at Ford's disposal; when coupled with his connection with Richard Nixon and Watergate, the poor economy, and his tattered relationships with Congress, Ford's chances of political survival were extremely slim. Moreover, an article in the *Washington Post* pointed out that Ford remained very conscious of the fact that he was not elected into office and therefore not a leader chosen by the people. That fact, the reporter believed, caused a state of passivity in Ford that he could not overcome.[12]

Running against him was Georgia's Democratic governor, Jimmy Carter, who focused much of his campaign message on his outsider status in Washington. People were weary of the corruption associated with the Republican Party, and Carter played on that, as well, frequently reminding voters that he would never lie to them.

Carter, a born-again Christian, gave an interview to *Playboy* shortly before the election, in which he confessed that he looked at other women with lust in his heart. He quoted Jesus Christ calling this behavior "adultery," and Carter admitted that he needed forgiveness. This interview shocked many, and Carter publicly apologized about the *Playboy* article in one of the three preelection debates against Gerald Ford. Some say that this move was a calculated attention-getter.

Perhaps indicating the general malaise that had its grip on America, Carter won by only 56 electoral votes in an election that had the lowest turnout in nearly 30 years. Carter's victory, it should be noted, was the first for a Southerner since before the Civil War.

Ford's legacy, in retrospect, is stronger than what his experiences as president might indicate. Although Ford struggled through his presidential years, his honesty and trustworthiness, it is generally conceded, "helped restore the presidency when it needed some restoring."[13]

Jimmy Carter

His preferred name was "Jimmy," not "James" or "James Earl." He took over his family's peanut farm in Georgia after his father died. After he and his wife made the decision that he would run for the presidency, the first person that he told was his mother, known as "Miss Lillian." (It is said that his mother, upon hearing this plan, replied, "President of what?")

As for Miss Lillian, she recalled eating with her father's black post office employees, something not generally done in the Deep South in the early 1900s. She became a nurse and worked, by choice, in the segregated part of town. She talked about discipline and she talked about love—and, she had a wicked sense of humor. One of her most bandied-about quotes was, "Sometimes when I look at my children I say to myself, 'Lillian, you should have stayed a virgin.'"

The White House would have a child in residence—nine-year-old Amy Cater. Amy was frequently seen carrying a book; her Siamese cat was named Misty Malarky Ying Yang.

Jimmy Carter's brother Billy—named William, but called Billy—endorsed "Billy Beer." The First Lady, Rosalynn, was gracious, smart, and supportive of her husband's decisions. She wasn't submissive, though. Remember that they made the decision together.

After the wearying tension and disheartening years of the Vietnam War, the oil embargo, and the Watergate scandal, and after the partisan bickering and political stalemates of the Gerald Ford administration, it is no wonder that America embraced the Carter family. The American people applauded his promises of honesty, and they welcomed this Washington outsider, who had never held a Congressional slot, to the highest office of the land. Carter practiced the humbleness that he preached, as he and his wife walked the last stretch to his inauguration. He banned the playing of "Hail to the Chief," traded in the presidential limo for something more practical, and was often seen carrying his own luggage. He wore blue jeans in the Oval Office, listened to Bob Dylan music, and quoted Bible verses in his soft Southern drawl, choosing ones that pointed out what he, Carter, needed to do to be a man of God, rather than criticizing others with his Gospel.[14]

Nevertheless, Jimmy Carter could stir up controversy—as he did with his *Playboy* interview—and his administration also became weighted down and beleaguered by economic troubles, struggles with Congress, and an energy crisis. On Carter's first full day as president, he pardoned all "draft dodgers" from the Vietnam War, exempting them from any prosecution or penalties, another presidential attempt to heal the wounds from previous administrations. He pardoned those who did not sign up for the draft and those who fled the country; his pardon, though, did not extend to those who left the service (deserters), those who received less than honorable discharges, and civilian protestors. Peace organizations therefore felt that he did not go far enough in his pardon's scope, while veterans' groups expressed shock and dismay at what they saw as a lack of consequences for illegal acts. The Senate attempted to pass a resolution against this pardon, saying that Carter did not have this authority, but it failed by a narrow margin.

It had been anticipated that Carter would have fewer problems with Congress than Gerald Ford, as the House and Senate were predominately Democratic. This, however, did not happen. The Watergate Babies voted in shortly after Nixon's resignation favored expanded legislative control and reduced executive powers, and they could be strident in this belief. Moreover, although Carter's outside status won him the election, his lack of knowledge about the Capitol and his anti-Washington comments made during the campaign caused him problems now that he was the president. Carter also consistently failed to consult Congressional members before making policy announcements, which automatically reduced the likelihood of their cooperation.

The public listed the troubled economy as their greatest concern during the start of Carter's administration, and for good cause. Unemployment was still at 7 percent, inflation was between 5 and 6 percent, and the deficit was at about $66 billion. Carter thought that the best way to tackle these problems was to create more job opportunities, believing that inflation would solve itself in a high employment nation. He therefore assembled a stimulus package to create jobs and to grant each taxpayer a $50 rebate that would put $11 billion into the economy. This bill, however, did not pass through the Senate.

In 1978, Carter switched his strategy, focusing on fighting inflation rather than creating employment. This inconsistency did not play well with voters or with Congress, and Carter later admitted that he should have listened to his advisors on this issue. Meanwhile, the very real problem of inflation, now exceeding 11 percent, needed to be addressed. Carter recommended voluntary wage and price limits, and he announced that government spending would be cut by more than $24.5 billion to reduce the degree to which the deficit was growing. This angered Congressional Democrats who did not want to cut programs and the bill did not pass. Meanwhile, inflation skyrocketed to 13.3 percent.

Energy concerns also occupied Carter's attention. The United States was importing nearly 50 percent of its oil by the time that Carter took office, which was about 15 percent more than before the Arab Oil Embargo of 1973. Carter attempted to pass an energy bill, but Congress resented its lack of input on the bill and the final result was watered down and ineffective. When Carter gave addresses on the energy problems, people did not seem receptive to his concerns; and yet, when the second oil crisis occurred, the American people questioned why the president did not prevent this from occurring and Carter's political troubles deepened.

On November 4, 1979, Iranian militants stormed the U.S. embassy in Tehran, taking approximately 70 Americans as hostages and keeping 52 of them for 444 days, which extended past the end of Carter's presidency.

Reasons for the hostage-taking were complicated, centering on the Ayatollah Khomeini whipping up militants into a frenzy after Carter allowed the disposed Shah of Iran into the United States for cancer treatments. The hostage crisis commanded attention on television programs and young men feared being drafted into another war in yet another faraway country. Carter tried diplomatic solutions to resolve the crisis and to obtain the release of the hostages, but he was accused of being incompetent and ineffective.

Meanwhile, the Ayatollah swore that he would not release the hostages until the United States turned over the Shah to Iran, along with billions of dollars that the Iranians claim he had appropriated from the Iranian people. When Marines attempted a rescue, three of the helicopters malfunctioned; when one crashed, eight Marines were killed and three more injured. Militant Iranians gleefully showed the remains of the helicopter— and the fact that the rescue attempt was aborted increased the feeling of impotence among Americans. When asked if Carter was to blame for the Iran hostage situation, one expert claimed that the president was given an impossible situation—and then he made the worst of it.[15] It was therefore not a huge surprise when, in 1980, Carter failed in his second bid for the presidency, losing the race to Ronald Reagan. As the transfer of presidential power took place, the hostages were released without harm. Reagan had not done anything in particular to effect this release; the Iranians were simply ready to do so.

Carter's presidency was not without its successes. In September 1978, he brought together the leaders of Israel and Egypt, two countries that had technically been at war since 1948. During the 12-day retreat, held at Camp David, Carter persuaded Muhammad Anwar al-Sadat, President of the Arab Republic of Egypt, and Menachem Begin, Prime Minister of Israel, to sign a shorter-term peace treaty, along with a longer-term peace plan for the Mideast. This historic event is sometimes called the pinnacle of Carter's administration. Other Arab nations became angered at Egypt, though, shunning the nation; in 1981, Sadat was assassinated.

During Carter's presidency, the Soviet Union signed the SALT II treaty, although even that agreement had its darker side. In 1979, the Soviet Union invaded Afghanistan and so the United States never ratified the treaty. Carter—and then Reagan after him—continued to abide by the tenets, though, and agreed to do so as long as the Soviets did likewise.

Carter also oversaw the signing of the Panama Canal Treaty of 1977–1978, wherein he agreed to return the canal to Panama in 2000. Those who opposed this agreement stated that, because the United States built the canal, it should be entitled to keep ownership, but Carter felt that this move would help solidify U.S. relationships with Latin American countries. This did occur for several years, but then General Manuel Antonio Noriega came into power and the cordial relationship deteriorated.

Carter deregulated both the airline and banking industries, and, at the end of his term, he could truthfully state that eight million more jobs existed in 1980 than at the beginning of his term. Carter had also reduced the federal deficit[16] and he removed pricing controls from domestic petroleum, to stimulate production and reduce reliance upon foreign oil.

After Carter left the White House, he and Rosalynn served as spokespeople for Habitat for Humanity, wherein housing is provided for low-income families, and they have also attempted to enact peaceful election processes in third world countries. As a former Carter aide, Jack Watson, put it, when asked about the Carter legacy, "Someone once said, and I agree with them, that he is the only man in American history … who used the United States presidency … as a stepping stone to greatness."[17]

CIVIL RIGHTS AND THE FEMINIST MOVEMENT
Civil Rights

By the time the 1970s debuted, two important pieces of civil rights legislation—the 1964 act and the 1968 act—had already been passed and the initial reactions to each had died down. The Civil Rights Act of 1964 has been called the most comprehensive civil rights legislation in the history of the United States, providing citizens with equal rights to enjoy "accommodations, facilities, and education as well as federally assisted programs and employment." Perhaps better known is Title VII of that act, which prohibits "employment discrimination based on an employee's race, color, religion, sex, or national origin." The Civil Rights Act of 1968 focuses on equal rights in housing, and both acts allow injured parties to sue for damages if someone "illegally infringes with a person's civil rights, conspires to deprive others of their civil rights, or abuses either government authority or public office to accomplish such unlawful acts." Moreover, two pieces of legislation passed in 1965: one made voting registration easier for black Americans and the other affirmed the duty of employers to hire minority employees.

Therefore, with just a few sweeps of the legislative pen, discrimination based upon a wide variety of factors was declared illegal at the federal level. Throughout the rest of the 1960s and during the early part of the 1970s, courts found themselves judging cases, though, of companies that obeyed the letter of the law, but confounded it in spirit. For example, a factory that openly advertised that it did not hire black workers needed to take down the sign. So, they complied. Nothing stopped the factory owners, though, from stating that all new workers needed a recommendation from a current one; assuming that the entire group of factory workers was white—and that heavy peer pressure existed among the workers to keep it that way—how likely would it be that a black man (or even more chancy, a black woman) was hired?

To remedy this type of situation, courts needed to find ways to fight the past exclusionary practices that were currently being used to maintain racial and/or gender imbalance. In 1971, after dealing with many of these instances, the Supreme Court ruled, in *Griggs v. Duke Power Company*, that a company that disproportionately kept a group of workers—in this case, black employees—from inclusion, whether that was the intent or not, was involved in illegal hiring practices and must therefore revise its employment policies.

This ruling significantly changed the scope of discrimination (civil rights) laws. Employers now needed to examine all of their hiring requirements to determine if job qualifications listed were actually necessary for employees to perform their job functions. For example, perhaps a company required all employees to have a high school diploma; even if this rule was not intended to exclude anyone based on racial characteristics, the company now needed to analyze whether or not the cleaning staff, as just one example, needed this diploma to adequately fulfill their job duties. If not, then this requirement was potentially discriminating against the pool of workers who were less likely than other groups to have completed high school. In some instances, the resolutions to these policy reviews were quite clear; in others, what one reasonable person saw as "necessary," another one might not.

Because of the Griggs ruling, huge chunks of human resource policies that were not created to—and were never intended to—discriminate against anyone now needed review and possibly complete revision. Employers needed to determine how each policy affected minorities, how it affected women, and so forth. Moreover, even if one particular policy was innocuous on its own, they also had to consider its cumulative effect when included among the myriad of other company rules and regulations. The task was enormous.

The answer to this problem was affirmative action—which, in turn, created a multitude of new challenges for employers and the courts. The basic idea of affirmative action, though, according to a paper published by the Institute for Philosophy and Public Policy, "was simple: motivate firms to carry on continuous, conscious appraisal of their procedures and rules to detect and eliminate those that excluded minorities and women without appropriate justification."[18] The process, in theory, was also simple. Companies were to broaden their selection base for employee candidates and then predict, out of their pool of potential workers, what the composition of workers should become (racially, genderwise, and so forth). Periodically, the company must check its actual employee demographics with its stated composition goals—and then adjust, as necessary. Even if the actual group of employees on a company's payroll did not match the goals, if a company was hiring in good faith, the courts declared that this was enough.

Anger erupted and controversy ensued, though, with many Americans understanding the ruling to mean that companies needed to match the predicted goals—or, to use a more inflammatory word, to meet a *quota* or be guilty of discrimination. All became much more complicated when courts in fact did order certain companies to hire by precise—rigid—numbers rather than by flexible target goals. AT&T, a company that did create a model affirmative action plan, was hiring men and women in equal numbers—but almost every woman was either an operator or secretary, while men were hired for the overwhelming majority of better-paid, professional jobs. In the instances of Mississippi and Alabama highway patrol employees, the government determined that cultural practices and prejudices were so ingrained in their hiring practices that they must hire one black employee for every white one until a reasonable parity was achieved.

By the mid-1970s, employers faced another onerous problem: reverse discrimination lawsuits filed by white men who claimed that they were not hired for a job strictly because they were male and/or Caucasian, so that the company could reach racial and gender parity. They would claim that they were better qualified for a particular position, but not hired because of affirmative action constraints.

In the latter part of the decade, a man named Bakke filed a similar suit, claiming that he was not accepted into the University of California because it needed to accept more minorities into its institution. In 1978, in the

University of California Regents v. Bakke, the Supreme Court declared that the specific formula that caused the University of California to not accept Bakke, a white man, was unconstitutional; and yet, it also ruled that the university should consider race when making admissions decisions. In 1979, a white worker sued Kaiser Chemical Company because it was hiring one black employee for every white one until 35 percent of its workforce was black. The Supreme Court upheld Kaiser's program and created a law that protected companies that were hiring in a manner to bring about racial and gender parity under an approved affirmative action plan.

The Civil Rights Act of 1964 also empowered the federal government with additional tools to force local school systems to desegregate. In the 1950s, the family of Linda Brown sued the local school district for not allowing their black daughter to attend the all-white elementary school. In 1954, in *Brown v. Board of Education of Topeka, Kansas,* the Supreme Court unanimously over-turned its previous interpretation of law, which allowed for "separate but equal" *(Plessy v. Ferguson, 1896)* schools for people of different races, and it ruled that school districts must desegregate with deliberate speed.

Many school districts in the South did not comply with court orders requiring desegregation. As a result, the 1971 Supreme Court case, *Swann v. Mecklenburg,* ruled that school districts did not need to precisely reflect the racial composition of their city, but that all-white or all-black schools must be shown not to exist because of segregation practices. Furthermore, this ruling stated that busing was a legitimate means to racially integrate school systems. President Nixon spoke out against this interpretation of the law, but forced busing began occurring throughout the country and continued through the 1990s in some locales.

Although many people fought for civil rights during the 1970s, two deserve specific mention. One of the better-known civil rights leaders of the 1970s—the Reverend Jesse Jackson—began his work in the 1960s, fighting for social and political justice and for basic human rights, organizing marches and sit-in protests. In 1963, Jackson led civil rights demonstrations in Greensboro, North Carolina, most notably fighting against segregated lunch counters as a part of Council on Racial Equality (CORE); in 1965, he met Martin Luther King Jr. and began working for his organization, the Southern Christian Leadership Conference (SCLC). In 1966, he launched his first economic boycott, and, on April 4, 1968, Jackson was with King when he was assassinated.

In 1970, Jackson led a march to Illinois' state capital, raising conscious-ness of hunger. As a result, the state increased funding for school lunches. He led a similar march in Chicago, with less favorable results; he then used another tactic to effect change in Chicago, running for mayor. He, however, lost his bid for election.

In 1971, Jackson resigned as the national director of Operations Bread-basket, an SCLC organization committed to finding employment for blacks. Although he achieved much in this organization, his intense—some say aggressive—methods caused others to clash with him, most notably Ralph D. Abernathy. Forming his own organization, People United to Save Humanity (PUSH), in 1971, Jackson continued to work for economic betterment for the blacks of Chicago and throughout the nation, and he kept demanding social and political improvements, as well. He conducted weekly broadcasts on the radio and created awards to honor blacks of achievement. He also created PUSH-Excel, to assist low-income black youth, helping them to stay in school and to then find jobs.

In 1979, Jackson toured the Middle East, visiting leaders in Israel, Lebanon, Egypt, and Syria, and he also met with the leader of the Palestine Liberation Organization, Yassar Arafat. His goal was to further peace between the Israelis and the Palestinians. That same year, he also traveled to South Africa, to speak out against apartheid.

Jackson has always had strong advocates, as well as tough critics. His passion and energy have won him many followers, while his outspoken comments have offended others. His liberal political bent sits easy with a portion of America and is a rallying cry for conservatism in other demographics.

Ralph D. Abernathy also fought for civil rights through most of the 1970s, and he also began his political and social activism several years before. In 1957, he cofounded the SCLC with Martin Luther King Jr. The two men agreed upon the philosophy of peaceful protests for civil rights, creating this phrase for their motto: "Not one hair of one head of one person should be harmed." While serving as the pastor of the Baptist Church in Montgomery, Alabama, Abernathy was extremely vocal about the need for desegregation and for equal rights for blacks. Abernathy and King worked closely together until King's death.

After King's assassination, Abernathy took over the leadership role of SCLC. In 1970, his group formed Politics '70 for Representative Government, a platform for political gains for blacks. In 1971, it worked with the National Welfare Organization and the People's Coalition for Peace and Justice to form the "War Against Repression," which was a series of mass protests that led to the restoration of welfare rights. Over the next few years, it focused on registering new voters, which led to the election of blacks in locales that had never before had black representation. In 1975, it formed "Operation Military" to protect the civil rights of minorities in the armed forces. In 1976, it rallied its energies to support the Humphrey-Hawkins Full Employment program. In 1977, Abernathy resigned from SCLC to run for Georgia's legislature. He did not win.

Feminist Movement

Perhaps the most hotly debated piece of legislation of the 1970s, which required the approval of 38 states to pass, was the Equal Rights Amendment—or the ERA. This proposed amendment was first introduced in 1923, just three years after the passage of the 19th Amendment gave women "suffrage," or the right to vote. The ERA's language was written by Alice Paul, the founder of the National Woman's Party, to amend the Constitution to specifically state that the U.S. government must provide equal rights to both genders.

The language of the amendment is deceptively simple, and, from its dry text, a reader could not possibly discern the degree of passion that it aroused in proponents of the legislation, as well as in its detractors. The ERA reads: "Section 1: Equality of rights under the law shall not be denied or abridged by the United States or by any state on account of sex; Section 2: The Congress shall have the power to enforce, by appropriate legislation, the provisions of this article; Section 3: This amendment shall take place two years after the date of ratification."

Legislators had introduced the ERA in every session of Congress, starting in 1923, with no success. That changed in 1967 when a new organization led by Betty Friedan—the National Organization for Women (NOW)—formed, pledging its dedicated and concerted efforts toward the passage of this amendment. The members kept their word, passionately and vocally demanding to be heard. In February 1970, NOW members disrupted Congress while it was in session, insisting that the full legislative body hear the reading of the ERA. In May, Congress acquiesced—and in June, the legislation passed through the House Judicial Committee, which meant that Congress could now vote on the proposed amendment. The House of Representatives approved the ERA in 1971 and the Senate did the same on March 22, 1972. This approved piece of legislation included a typical phrase in the proposing clause that set a seven-year time span for individual states to ratify this amendment.

Individuals and organizations quickly began aligning themselves either for or against the ERA. During the first year of potential ratification, 22 states ratified the amendment and the AFL-CIO endorsed it; the following year, 8 more states voted for the ERA. Momentum slowed as the target number of 38 states came into view, but 3 more states voted "yes" in 1974, and 1 in 1975, meaning that 34 had voted for the ERA's passage. The year 1976 saw no new "yes" votes, but Indiana joined the majority of states with an affirmative vote in 1977.

Also in 1977, NOW held its first national convention in Houston, Texas. It announced that 450 groups, representing 50 million Americans, had endorsed and were supporting the amendment. NOW used this occasion to publicly request an extension on the time available for ratification; the Constitution places no limits on amendment passage, it argued, and so the seven-year term imposed was artificial and not in keeping with the spirit of the Constitution. It also urged ERA supporters to boycott states that had not yet ratified the amendment, adding that its future conventions would not be held in those states.

The following year, NOW declared a state of emergency for the ERA and organized a march on Washington in which 100,000 supporters participated. In large part because of this march, Congress set a new deadline for ERA ratification: June 30, 1982.

Meanwhile, opponents of the ERA fought to slow down the momentum toward passage. The state of Missouri filed a lawsuit against NOW for its boycott on nonratifying states, claiming that this action violated antitrust laws, while other opponents tried to pass rescission bills in a dozen states in an attempt to withdraw previously granted support of the ERA. All attempts failed. Near the end of the decade, legislators from three states—Arizona, Idaho, and Washington—argued that it was *not* legal to extend the period of time allowed for the amendment's passage and that it *was* legal for a state to reverse its decision and rescind its support for passage of the amendment.

It is possible—and perhaps even likely—that these attempts would have been futile and that the ERA would have passed if not for a well-organized and vocal grassroots effort to prevent the amendment's ratification. Its leader was a social and political conservative named Phyllis Schlafly and her campaign became known as "Stop the ERA." The word STOP, it should be noted, had additional significance in this slogan. Schlafly believed that the ERA would, in fact, reduce the number of rights afforded American women, and so STOP stood for "Stop Taking Our Privileges." She would also state that, if the ERA passed, then women would be drafted to fight in wars, and this was an extremely effective strategy in marshalling support against the amendment. If the ERA was ratified, then the government would begin to fund abortions, Schlafly predicted, and same-sex marriages would become legal. Furthermore, any special privileges that women enjoyed, simply because they were female, would disappear. These arguments were similar to those made pre-1920, when women fought for suffrage—but, this time, they were more effective. The amendment has not been ratified.

Opposition to the ERA often signaled a person's—or an organization's—disapproval of the entire feminist movement, also called the women's liberation movement, or, simply, "women's lib." Defining this movement is difficult as it really was a series of overlapping movements, with one common goal: feminists were fighting for equal rights between men and women, socially, politically, and/or economically. Not all feminists agreed upon the source of inequalities or the remedies desired, but it is fair to say that some definition of equality for women fueled all genres of the feminist movement.

Goals of individual feminists ranged from practical demands that would improve the overall conditions of life for women to more radical philosophical visions. Some wished to abolish specific cultural elements that were embedded within America's patriarchal structure, whereas other women espoused a total separation from men in all aspects of life, including economically, socially, and sexually.

More specifically, some women wanted economic benefits: "equal pay for equal work," paid maternity leaves, more favorable divorce agreements, federally funded child care or the opportunity to work in male-dominated fields—or perhaps to enter an occupation previously denied to women, such as prominent clergy roles in religions where males were exclusively or predominantly ministering. Others wanted control over their reproductive functions, desiring easier access to birth control and/or the legalization of abortion. Still others wanted to change the structure of language, eliminating the use of "man" in words such as fireman, policeman, or mankind, and incorporating the use of gender-neutral terms. Many feminists preferred the marital-status neutral title of Ms., rather than Miss or Mrs., and many jokes of the era employed a punch line that implied that God was female.

What women did not do in documented reality, although the notion is certainly well entrenched in myth and memory, is to burn bras in support of the feminist movement. Many women stopped wearing bras, which would naturally lead to the apparel being thrown away, both as a practical matter and as a symbolic gesture of freedom—and one theory suggests that the tossing away of bras melded with the image of draft cards being burned: thus, the myth of bra burning. Others point out that a prominent feminist allegedly promised a mayor that women would not burn bras at a feminist gathering in his city. Regardless of its origins, bra burning became associated with feminism.

During the 1970s, people frequently debated the "true" differences between the genders. Many scientists, educators, and other professionals championed the notion that gender differences were the result of cultural conditioning rather than genetic factors. Girls, as one example, would be just as successful at math and science, the experts explained, given the same opportunities as boys and the accompanying positive feedback.

Not all feminists of the 1970s were female; there were also a significant number of men who applauded the freedoms and equalities defined by the feminist movement. Moreover, although some detractors of the movement scornfully labeled all of its female adherents as "lesbian," advocates of the feminist movement could be gay or heterosexual or bisexual—with some feminists even disputing the notion of only two genders or three sexual orientations, believing in transgender and transsexual blurring. Some feminists of the 1970s strongly identified with the civil rights movement or the gay rights movement. Meanwhile, some feminists who were also minorities and/or nonheterosexual formed groups separate from white and/or heterosexual women, believing that their aims and challenges were so different that discrete associations were needed to accomplish goals.

Those uncertain about the feminist movement and its philosophies could read a significant volume of material by the time of the 1970s, including: Shulamith Firestone's *The Dialectic of Sex: The Case for Feminist Revolution;* Kate Millett's *Sexual Politics;* and Robin Morgan's *Sisterhood Is Powerful,* as well as Betty Friedan's *The Feminine Mystique.* In 1972, Gloria Steinem and others identifying with feminism began publishing a monthly magazine, *Ms.,* advocating their cause. Toni Morrison's anthology, *The Black Woman,* contained essays of black feminists, some of which debated whether or not theirs was a separate movement from the general feminist one.

The feminist movement, regardless of which side one was on, began to permanently shift the balance of power between men and women—and it caused significant confusion about the roles and identities of both genders in the changing society of the 1970s.

ROE V. WADE

The mere mention of this court case can still provoke extremely emotional reactions, decades after it was decided. At the heart of the case rests the thorny and challenging ethical question of when life begins—at conception or at birth, or perhaps somewhere in between, such as at the "quickening" or perceptibly felt first movement of the fetus. Does a woman have the right to control her body, up to and including the right to abort an unwanted fetus? Or, should the rights of an embryo supersede that right?

During the early part of the 1970s, these questions burst into national prominence as people marched for and against abortion rights, and as they passionately debated the issue and fervently attempted to persuade others to their viewpoints. Those who felt that abortions should be legalized called themselves "pro-choice," whereas those opposing its legalization were "pro-life." Both titles were cleverly chosen; after all, who would want to be dubbed the opposite of either pro-life or pro-choice?

The controversial case that challenged and ultimately overturned abortion laws began simply enough when a single woman in Texas named Norma McCorvey attempted to abort her third child. McCorvey, aged 21, was no longer married, and she did not want give birth to the fetus that she was carrying. At that time, Texas law stated that abortions were legal only when performed because of health issues of the pregnant mother. Although failing in her attempts to abort, McCorvey met two young attorneys—Sarah Weedington and Linda Coffee—who were willing to represent her, and to attempt to change the prevailing antiabortion laws.

The attorneys worried about two points of law. First, in an abortion case, the state would not prosecute the woman aborting the fetus; instead, it would charge the doctor who performed the operation. Therefore, concern existed over McCorvey's "standing to sue." Plus, if McCorvey gave birth or if she passed the time frame in her pregnancy wherein an abortion could be safely performed, the court could rule that the case was now irrelevant. Despite these concerns, on March 3, 1970, McCorvey's attorneys filed a complaint against the Dallas County district attorney, asking the court to declare the Texas abortion law unconstitutional and to order officials to stop enforcing this law. To protect McCorvey's privacy, the case was filed under the name of Jane Roe.

Three judges heard the case on May 22, 1970. As anticipated, the assistant district attorney claimed that McCorvey could not sue because the statutes were enforced against doctors, not against pregnant women who chose to abort. Although that was true, the court allowed the case to continue. The assistant district attorney also asked "Roe" to come forward. She declined, stating that, if identified, she would face discrimination in future employment. Furthermore, the issue of who bears children, she claimed, is private.

Weedington and Coffee then changed the status of the case to a class action lawsuit to argue the rights of all pregnant women who may choose to abort. Shortly thereafter, a doctor joined the lawsuit; two charges of illegally performing abortions were pending against him.

The state defended its law as a protection of the rights of the unborn. In rebuttal, Weedington gave a response that cut to the core of the abortion debate, saying that "[L]ife is an ongoing process. It is almost impossible to define a point at which life begins or perhaps even at which life ends." When the court asked her at what point the state did have a responsibility to the unborn, she admitted that question gave her pause, but added that it was at the time in which a fetus could live outside of its mother.

McCorvey's attorneys attacked the law's constitutionality based upon the "right to privacy" that some judges read into the 9th Amendment. Those judges expressed a belief that any rights not specifically defined as belonging to the government or the people automatically went to the people—and this characterized the right to privacy. The state then argued that, even though women have the right to privacy, the right to life supersedes that. The doctor's attorney further attacked the abortion laws, based on the 14th Amendment and its due process clause, but the court did not agree.

On June 17, 1970, the court overturned the Texas abortion laws, stating that they "must be declared unconstitutional because they deprive single women and married couples of their right, secured by the Ninth Amendment, to choose whether to have children."[19]

The court approved declarative relief, finding the law unconstitutional, but it did not give injunctive relief, which would have ordered the state to stop enforcing the law. Weedington therefore appealed for injunctive relief, while the state asked for the ruling to be overturned. Because of the declarative relief provided, the state could appeal directly to the Supreme

Court, rather than go through the appeals process. The state followed this course, and the trial date was set for December 13, 1971.

In the interim, the court heard another case, *Eisenstadt v. Baird*, in which it ultimately ruled (in March 1972) that unmarried people could legally use birth control. In that case, Supreme Court judges also honed their interpretation of the 9th Amendment in a way that would help Norma McCorvey. "If the right of privacy means anything," the court ruled in the *Eisenstadt v. Baird* case, "it is the right of the *individual,* married or single, to be free from unwarranted governmental intrusion into matters so fundamentally affecting a person as the decision whether to bear or beget a child."

When the Supreme Court heard *Roe v. Wade* in December, Weedington implored them to allow women to make their own decisions about bearing children, free from governmental inference. She presented the Constitution as a document that conferred rights to people at birth, not at conception. The defense disputed this interpretation, which caused the court to ask why, if abortion is murder, women seeking and receiving abortions were not prosecuted. The state admitted to not having answers to all legal nuances.

The Supreme Court did not immediately rule on this case. With only seven justices sitting on the Supreme Court—two had recently retired—it postponed the case until October, when a full court would be in session. On January 22, 1973, the Supreme Court finally ruled on *Roe v. Wade,* stating that one initial purpose of antiabortion laws was to protect women from a dangerous procedure—abortion. That concern no longer applied. It also stated that, whether it applied the 9th Amendment or the 14th to the case, it seemed clear that a woman's reproductive rights were included in the implied right to privacy. Furthermore, the court ruled, it could not find any reference to constitutional rights applying to the unborn. As far as when life started, at conception or at birth, the judges declined to proffer an opinion.

Balancing the rights of a pregnant woman with the right to life of the unborn, the court determined by a vote of 7–2 that first trimester abortions were legal. The state could regulate but not prohibit second-trimester ones and could deny third-trimester abortions altogether. Justices William H. Rehnquist and Byron R. White dissented over the ruling in *Roe v. Wade,* citing a lack of constitutional justification for the decision.

The court also ruled on *Doe v. Bolton,* a Georgia abortion-related case, reducing the state's control over who can receive abortions and in what facility. These two rulings caused abortions to become legal in all 50 states, invalidating laws in 46.

Although these rulings definitively changed laws in favor of reproductive rights, debate did not settle down. People continued to speak out against abortion, and some continued to defend the decision as legally appropriate. Still others felt uncomfortable with the idea of abortion—and perhaps even opposed it—but they agreed with the court's decision to remove governmental interference in women's reproductive rights. Others felt that conditional abortions—ones performed because the baby was the result of a rape or incestuous act—were appropriate, whereas ones based on economic reasons or personal feelings or ambitions were not.

In general, Democrats were more likely to favor the rulings and Republicans to oppose them. The Catholic Church adamantly opposed abortions, as did many evangelical or fundamentalist Protestant ones, whereas mainstream Protestant churches either supported the pro-choice movement or remained deliberately silent and neutral on the issue.

In 1976, Congress adopted the Hyde Amendment to the Medicaid appropriation bill. This amendment prevented federal money from being used to fund abortions, unless the mother's life was in danger.

GENDER ISSUES

On June 27, 1969, New York police raided a popular gay bar in Greenwich Village, called the Stonewall Inn. The raid itself was not unusual, and, typically, police would arrest some of the more flamboyant types as others disappeared into the shadows. The resistance to this particular raid, however, was much more dramatic, and many historians mark this occasion as the official start to the gay liberation movement. Fights and riots broke out in the streets after the raid and these continued for several days—and are now known as the Stonewall Riots. Many rioters threw coins at police officers, mocking the system of "gayola," whereby gay establishments paid off police to remain in operation.[20] If these payments were not made, then charges of public indecency were sure to follow.

Why the Stonewall reaction differed from what transpired in other similar situations is not known, although patrons were frustrated over the multitude of recent raids, and Judy Garland—a favorite of many gays who were film fans—had just died. Furthermore, the summer of the Stonewall Riots was particularly hot, humid, and sticky. Some sources suggest that this caused tempers to become shorter, which possibly contributed to the amount and severity of violent acts committed. Regardless of the underlying reasons, the uprising heated up, with many protestors chanting "Gay Power" as the police attempted to regain control in the streets. Newspapers reported on these uprisings, including when a "chorus line of mocking queens" chanted, "We are the Stonewall girls, we wear our hair in curls, we wear no underwear, we show our pubic hair, we wear our dungarees, above our nelly knees!"[21]

Although the Stonewall raid frustrated its patrons, the riots brought the gay and lesbian cause to national attention, and activists used this momentum to organize. One month after the Stonewall Riots, the Gay Liberation Front (GLF) formed. This radical leftist organization, created in New York, protested the marginalization of homosexuals, but it also supported other causes, such as the end to racial discrimination and the support of third world countries. After this group formed, other GLF organizations started up around the country and the world.

Although the GLF was the most prominent of the groups that formed shortly after the Stonewall Riots, many others did, as well, with their focus being gay and lesbian pride. In December 1969, the Gay Activists Alliance, another major organization fighting for gay rights, formed. It was best known for its "zaps"—or peaceful confrontations with public officials. In 1974, arsonists burned down its headquarters in Greenwich Village, an event that marked the end of the group's prime years. In 1971, the Gay and Lesbian Activists Alliance formed in Washington, D.C., beginning its efforts to garner equal rights for all, regardless of sexual orientation.

On the first anniversary of the Stonewall Riots, 5,000 gay and lesbian advocates marched in commemoration of this series of events. Some of these marchers surely gained the courage to "come out of the closet" over the past year because of the emerging public solidarity of numerous gay and lesbian movements.

Along with the growing number of organized groups and marches, the volume of publications targeted to the gay and lesbian community increased significantly, post-Stonewall. In 1972, Kay Tobin and Randy Wicker published *The Gay Crusaders*, a series of biographies of gay activists. In 1973, Jill Johnston published *Lesbian Nation: The Feminist Solution*, and, in 1974, David Loovis published *Gay Spirit: A Guide to Becoming a Sensuous Homosexual*. Overall, this literature helped many who felt marginalized find a sense of community—and, if it hadn't already occurred—it also helped many to "out" themselves, allowing them to become either partially or fully open about their sexual orientation to friends, family, and perhaps the world at large. This occurred in increasing numbers around the country, whether participants defined themselves as gay, lesbian, bisexual, transgendered, or queer, although those located in larger cities could more easily find accepting communities than those located in rural, isolated areas.

Political advancements also occurred in the years following the riots, with some larger cities creating statues that forbade discrimination based upon sexual orientation. Wisconsin and Massachusetts even included this antidiscrimination language in state-level legislation. In 1975, the Civil Service Commission eliminated the ban on homosexuals for most federal jobs, although the military remained a significant exception. Several states repealed their sodomy laws, gay community centers received federal funding to provide services, and, in 1973, the American Psychiatric Association removed homosexuality as a listed psychiatric disorder.

Gay and lesbian groups began openly meeting on certain college campuses. The University of California, Santa Cruz, for example, held a seminar in December 1971 entitled, "Homosexuality: Exploring an Alternative in Sexual Expression." Several people later recalled being scared away from attending by the large glass windows in the meeting room, which would make their attendance too visible for their comfort level.

Mainstream religious groups had banned gays and lesbians as members of the clergy, pre-1970s. That said, two months before the Stonewall Riots, the United Church of Christ (UCC) publicly declared its opposition to any law that criminalized homosexual acts performed in private between consenting adults. It also stated its position that the U.S. military should not discriminate based upon a person's sexual orientation.

In 1972, the UCC ordained William Johnson, the first openly gay clergy confirmed in a mainstream Protestant congregation. The following year, the UCC stated its openness to clergy of all sexual orientations, and, in 1975, it stated its support of equal rights for all, regardless of orientation. In 1977, UCC confirmed its first openly lesbian pastor, Anne Holmes. The Reformed Judaism community was also more accepting of gay and lesbian rights than many other religious groups but in 1978, the President of the Rabbinical Alliance of America, the Orthodox Abraham B. Hecht, recommended an "all-out campaign" against the legitimacy of gay rights.

Other religious groups struggled with the issues of gay and lesbian integration into the church. In 1975, the National Council of Churches voted to support the rights of gays and lesbians, but not for their inclusion as clergy. That same year, the Presbyterian Church agreed that homosexual behavior was not banned by the Scriptures but did not recognize the Presbyterian Gay Caucus. It also rejected the ordination of gay clergy, without the condition of celibacy. The Episcopalian Church ordained an openly lesbian woman as clergy in 1977; the following year, Episcopalian bishops condemned homosexuality.

Many gays and lesbians who left other denominations formed their own churches, often under the name of the Universal Fellowship of Metropolitan Community Churches; approximately 20,000 people joined this group by the end of the decade. This group, however, was rejected for admission by the National Council of Churches.

Overall, though, as the 1970s decade progressed, gays and lesbians could find increasing numbers of communities, social agencies, and religious congregations that accepted their lifestyles and rights to equality. Their sexual orientation did not necessarily need to remain secret, as it had in the past—although those who lived openly gay lifestyles still faced the risk of discrimination and ridicule. In summation, progress of acceptance was slow, but steady.

In 1977, however, the tide began to turn, as singer, former beauty queen, and current orange juice spokesperson Anita Bryant spearheaded a public campaign to overturn legislation in Miami-Dade County, Florida, that granted civil rights to gays and lesbians. Although hers was not the first such campaign—one was conducted in Colorado in 1974—it was the most publicized. Her crusade, called "Save Our Children," warned of homosexuals molesting children. She also cautioned people that gays and lesbians must convert people to their lifestyle; homosexuals cannot reproduce, she explained, and so they must recruit. She received support from Senator John V. Briggs who commended Bryant for her "national, religious crusade [and] courageous stand to protect American children from exposure to blatant homosexuality."[22] On June 7, 1977, voters repealed the civil rights recently granted to gays and lesbians, by a margin of 69 percent to 31 percent. After this repeal, the gay rights movement seemed to lose much of its momentum.

As the 1970s progressed, more distinctive identities and goals began to split some gay rights movements into ones focusing on gay men and others on lesbian women. Lesbian organizations also formed separately from gay liberation groups, with many lesbians scorning the possibility that a gay man could understand the dual challenges of being both gay and female.

From the very beginning of the decade, lesbian feminists also fought to become the core of the feminist movement. In May 1970, a radical group of 20 women who labeled themselves as "Racialesbians," led by novelist Rita Mae Brown, marched onto a New York stage at the Congress to Unite Women. Uninvited, they wore shirts imprinted with "Lavender Menace" and demanded the opportunity to read their essay, "The Woman-Identified Woman." They insisted that lesbians served as the forefront of the women's liberation movement, as they partnered with other women, rather than with men.

DISCO

Disco as a dance form began primarily as an activity for gay men and then it spread across gender and sexual orientation lines to become a significant part of the pop culture of the 1970s. In discothèques, gay men could more freely express their identities.

Donna Summer has been called the "undisputed queen of disco" for gay audiences, with the highly sexualized song, "Love to Love You, Baby," entertaining disco goers across the country. In 1978, a musical group called the Village People performed a song, "YMCA," which detailed gay encounters in YMCA dormitories. Other hit songs included "Fir Island" (1977), "Macho Man" (1978), "In the Navy" (1979), and "Go West" (1979). One of the band's four singers was openly gay, while the others did not discuss their sexual orientation. Three albums went gold, selling more than 500,000 copies, and four went platinum (selling more than one million copies each).

SEX REASSIGNMENT SURGERY

In 1975, physician and professional tennis player Richard Raskind made the difficult decision to undergo sex reassignment surgery. Although far from the first person to have this operation, his situation brought sex reassignments to the forefront of national news.

As Dr. Raskind, he had married and fathered a child, but he decided that, as a transsexual, he now needed to match his physical structure and appearance with how he identified with himself, psychologically speaking—and that was as a woman. A transsexual differs from a transgender individual, for whom the expression of cross-sexual dress and behavior brings satisfaction. In contrast, a transsexual actually feels himself or herself to be the opposite gender from what physiology would suggest. So, in Raskind's surgery, his physical body, including the function of his genitals, would be changed from that of a man into that of woman; she would need continuing hormonal therapy, as well. In nearly every physical way, Raskind would then be a female, but she could not bear children. The surgery was successful; post-op, she renamed herself Renee Richards.

Perhaps what brought about the biggest controversy was Richards's decision to play professional tennis after her gender transformation. In 1960, Richards had played in the Men's U.S. Open, as Richard Raskind. In 1976, Richards attempted to play in the U.S. Open as a woman, but the United States Tennis Association prohibited her participation. She challenged this ruling, and, in 1977, the New York Supreme Court ruled in her favor. She therefore played against Virginia Wade in 1977, losing in the first round. Some may say that the surgery affected her ability to play, but the same result had occurred in 1960. In 1982, she left professional tennis to concentrate again on her medical profession.

CRIME

During the 1970s, the constitutionality of capital punishment commanded much of the attention of the Supreme Court—and that of the nation. When Gary Gilmore, a convicted murderer, refused to appeal his conviction and sentence, and, in fact, insisted upon receiving the death penalty in an expedient manner, emotions rose higher as the debate over executions reached a fever pitch.

The capital punishment rulings of the Supreme Court during this decade have been described as "flip-flopping." On June 29, 1972, the Supreme Court declared in *Furman v. Georgia* that the death penalty, as currently constructed and applied, served as "cruel and unusual punishment," something forbidden in the 8th Amendment. That case referred to a crime wherein William Henry Furman burgled a private home; upon being discovered by a family member, he attempted to flee, tripped, and accidentally shot and killed someone when his gun discharged during his fall. The Supreme Court, when considering the constitutionality of the death penalty in his appeal, also ruled on two other capital cases that dealt with sentences for rape and murder, respectively. In its ruling, two justices stated that capital punishment was always cruel and unusual, while the majority felt that the circumstances of these particular cases did not warrant the ultimate penalty. In this ruling, the court also focused on the arbitrary manner in which the death penalty was given, with an unfair balance of sentences given to black defendants.

This ruling in effect froze the carrying out of the death penalty in the United States. At that point, 631 men and women in 32 states were awaiting execution, and this court decision potentially affected all of their sentences. More than 50 percent of the states rewrote relevant statutes to address concerns brought up in the Supreme Court decision so that they could thereby regain their authority to carry out death sentences; some new state legislation dealt with the issue of racial prejudice in sentencing by requiring the death penalty for all first-degree murder convictions.

In 1976, the Supreme Court ruled in a manner in the *Gregg v. Georgia* case that may seem contrary to its 1972 decision. A jury had imposed the death penalty on Troy Leon Gregg after he was convicted of armed robbery and murder. The Georgia Supreme Court overturned the death penalty for his armed robbery conviction but upheld it for his murder conviction. Gregg appealed to the Supreme Court, stating that this cruel and unusual punishment violated the 8th and 14th Amendment.

The Supreme Court heard four similar cases with *Gregg v. Georgia,* and it ruled by a vote of 7–2 that, in some extreme criminal cases where the penalty was fairly applied, capital punishment was in fact legal. In Gregg's case, the court found that Georgia's statute "assures the judicious and careful use of the death penalty by requiring a bifurcated proceeding where the trial and sentencing are conducted separately, specific jury findings as to the severity of the crime and the nature of the defendant, and a comparison of each capital sentence's circumstances with other similar cases. Moreover, the Court was not prepared to overrule the Georgia legislature's finding that capital punishment serves as a useful deterrent to future capital crimes and an appropriate means of social retribution against its most serious offenders."[23] The Supreme Court during this decade also began requiring judges and juries to consider the offender as an individual, as well as to reflect upon the mitigating circumstances of the crime before sentencing.

A 1977 Supreme Court ruling *(Coker v. Georgia)* illustrates the difficulty in agreeing upon which mitigating circumstances warranted the death penalty. This case centered on Erlich Anthony Coker who, in 1974, had escaped from the prison where he was serving out numerous sentences for crimes ranging from kidnapping and assault to rape and murder. After fleeing from the prison, he entered a home where he raped a woman and then stole the family car. After being captured and tried for these new crimes, he was given the death penalty, but the Supreme Court found this a "grossly disproportionate and excessive" sentence for a rape of a grown woman that did not result in her death; two justices dissented. Because of the conflicting messages given by the Supreme Court, of which *Coker v. Georgia* qualified, no executions occurred from 1968 until 1976.[24]

In 1977, though, with the path cleared for judicious death penalties by the *Gregg v. Georgia* ruling, the state of Utah executed Gary Gilmore. Accused of murdering a motel owner and a gas station attendant in October 1976, and convicted of killing the former, he was sentenced to die in November 1976; after announcing that he was not going to appeal his sentence, the American Civil Liberties Union (ACLU) and the National Association for the Advancement of Colored People (NAACP) fought to stay his execution, fearful of the precedent that his death would create. For two months, judicial stays were granted against the express wishes of the condemned prisoner; the ACLU fought for a reprieve up until 10 minutes before Gilmore's actual execution on January 17, 1977, shortly after 8 A.M. Given the choice between hanging and the firing squad, Gilmore had preferred the latter. His last words were, "Let's do it."

This execution deeply permeated the culture of the era. On December 11, 1976, about one month prior to Gilmore's death, the cast of *Saturday Night Live* sang "Let's Kill Gary Gilmore for Christmas," set to the tune of *Winter Wonderland.* In 1977, a band called the Advents had a hit song in England called "Gary Gilmore's Eyes," with the lyrics describing an eye donor recipient realizing that he had gotten his new eyesight from the convicted killer. (Gilmore did, in fact, donate his eyes.) On the day of the execution, performance artist Monte Cazazza sent out photos of himself in an electric chair. Author Norman Mailer published a Gilmore documentary, *The Executioner's Song,* in 1979; in 1982, Tommy Lee Jones starred as Gilmore in a television movie, also called *The Executioner's Song.* Jones won an Emmy for his portrayal. Much later, in 1994, Gary's brother Mikal Gilmore wrote *Shot in the Heart,* a memoir about his troubled family; HBO filmed a movie of the same name based on this book in 2001, starring Sam Shepard.

During an era filled with divisive opinions about capital punishment, America saw an increase in both the number of murders and in the people polled who favored the death penalty. In 1960, 9,000 murders were committed; this number nearly doubled to 15,000 in 1970—and then to 20,000, just five years later.[25] The National Association of Evangelicals (NAE)—which represented more than 10 million conservative Christians and 47 denominations—and the Moral Majority were among the religious groups that supported capital punishment sentences. In 1977, Dr. Jay Chapman created the formula for lethal injection executions, first used in Oklahoma; many believed that this method served as a less cruel form of punishment.[26]

Regardless of what people thought or felt about the death penalty during the 1970s, it is clear that the arguably most famous murderers of the era—those involved in the "Charles Manson trials"—benefited from this tumult. On August 8, 1969, Charles Manson had called together his followers, a group that became known as "the Family," and he told them that it was time for "helter-skelter." The following night, Susan Atkins, Patricia Krenwinkel, Linda Kasabian, and Charles "Tex" Watson drove to the home of actress Sharon Tate. Best-known for her recent role in the movie *Valley of the Dolls,* Tate was married to movie producer Roman Polanski and was eight months pregnant with his baby. Polanski was working in London, so coffee heiress Abigail Folger, her boyfriend, and a hairstylist friend of Tate's were spending the night in this somewhat isolated home. When 18-year-old Steven Parent drove up the driveway, Watson shot him to death. Then, Watson, Atkins, and Krenwinkel entered the home while Kasabian kept watch; the trio stabbed the four people inside the home a total of 102 times, saving Tate for last and ignoring her pleas to save her baby's life. Atkins tasted Tate's blood, finding it "warm and sticky," and she used it to scrawl "PIG" on the wall.

The following night, Manson—displeased by the messiness of the killings—accompanied the group who committed the Tate murders on another spree, adding Clem Tuft and Leslie Van Houton to their numbers. That night, Watson, Krenwinkel, and Van Houton murdered Leno and Rosemary LaBianca, stabbing the couple to death and carving "WAR" on Leno's stomach; their blood was used to write "DEATH TO PIGS," and "RISE" on the walls, and, on the refrigerator, they scrawled "Healter Skelter," misspelling the phrase.

After being arrested, the group showed no remorse, only an undying loyalty to Charles Manson. When Susan Atkins, for example, talked of brutally murdering the pregnant Tate, she only displayed emotion when sharing her limitless love for her leader. Meanwhile, Manson continued to shock and horrify America. During the opening court statements, held on July 24, 1970, he showed up with a fresh and bloody "X" carved into his forehead—a symbol, he said, of being "X'd" out of people's lives.

The prosecution needed eyewitness testimony, so prosecutor Vincent Bugliosi promised immunity to Linda Kasabian, who had committed no murders—and she stayed on the witness stand for an incredible 18 days. Atkins had been promised some immunity, as well, and she provided some pretrial testimony; by the time of the actual trial, though, she would not cooperate with authorities. Others to whom Manson had shared specifics about the murders also testified. The defense attempted to immediately rest without having its clients testify, but the three female defendants insisted and the judge ruled that their wish to testify must be honored. After that was completed, Manson also asked to testify, but this occurred without the jury present. (Extradition proceedings prevented Watson from being tried with the others; his trial happened separately, shortly thereafter.)

Cult leader Charles Manson appears in the Santa Monica, California, courtroom with his attorney Irving Kanarek on June 18, 1970, charged with a murder separate from the infamous Tate-LaBianca murders. Courtesy of Photofest.

When the trial resumed on November 30, after Manson's testimony, the attorney of Leslie Van Houton—Ronald Hughes—did not show up to court and was later found murdered; although no one has ever been charged with the killing, many people call this a "Manson retaliation crime." Hughes had been trying to shift the blame off his client, to Manson, while Manson's attorney wanted to place the blame on the absent Watson.

After the trial ended, the prosecutor presented a summary that included a roll call of the dead: "Ladies and gentlemen of the jury, Sharon Tate ... Abigail Folger ... Voytek Frykowski ... Jay Sebring ... Steven Parent ... Leno LaBianca ... Rosemary LaBianca ... are not here with us in this courtroom, but from their graves they cry out for justice."[27]

The jury deliberated for one week; on January 25, 1971, it declared all defendants guilty of murder in the first degree and all were sentenced to death on March 29. The trial of Tex Watson had an identical outcome. When the Supreme Court declared the death penalty as unconstitutional in 1972, however, all sentences were commuted to life sentences in prison.

Although all of those convicted of the Tate-LaBianca murders remained in prison, another high profile case involving "the Family" occurred in the 1970s. After Manson was imprisoned in the summer of 1970, he handed over the control of his organization to a follower by the name of Lynette "Squeaky" Fromme. On September 5, 1975, Fromme attempted to assassinate President Gerald Ford, but her gun failed to operate and the Secret Service intervened. She later claimed that she tried to kill Ford so that Charles Manson could appear as a witness at her trial—and therefore have a venue to share his vision for the world.

Yet another infamous serial killer of the 1970s was David Berkowitz, better known as "Son of Sam." He killed six and wounded several others, starting with the murder of teenager Donna Lauria on July 29, 1976. Her murder did not draw significant attention in the media, but after three murders occurred in the Bronx, police determined that the same .44-caliber gun had been used in all three crimes. Publicity for the crimes increased further when, on April 17, 1977, Berkowitz murdered a young couple and then left behind a letter stating that his vampire father, named Sam, had ordered these killings. Although police did not release this letter to the general public, they allowed a few journalists to see the note, including Jimmy Breslin of the *New York Daily News*; after he dropped a few tantalizing hints in his column about the murders, Berkowitz wrote to him directly on May 30, 1977—and, a week later, the *Daily News* labeled this still-unidentified killer as the "Son of Sam."

On June 26, 1977, another young couple escaped Berkowitz without serious harm. On July 31, he attacked again, killing the female—his sixth victim—and injuring the male. After that shooting, however, a woman spotted someone—Berkowitz, as it turned out—tearing up a parking ticket. Police traced Berkowitz through this ticket; when they tracked him down, Berkowitz simply smiled and said, "I'm Sam." Under questioning, he then claimed that Sam Carr was his neighbor, adding that Sam's black Labrador, Harvey, would communicate requests to kill from Sam to Berkowitz. In reality, someone had attempted to shoot Harvey and it seems at least likely that Berkowitz was the culprit. Berkowitz pled guilty to the six murders and he received a prison sentence of 365 years. In 1979, another inmate attempted to slash his throat; Berkowitz survived, but he now has an eight-inch scar on his neck.

Some people believe that Son of Sam did not act alone. Some suspect that he was acting in concert with the real-life sons of Sam Carr, John and Michael. John Carr strongly resembled a composite drawing from one of the shootings; John himself was shot to death in February 1978. On a board by his body was scrawled SSNYC, which could stand for "Son of Sam, New York City." In October 1979, Michael Carr's vehicle plowed into a streetlight, killing him. His sister Wheat insisted that he was forced off the road.[28]

Another serial killer of the 1960s and 1970s, the Zodiac Killer, was never caught. Stalking those in the Bay Area of California, he sent taunting letters to newspapers, threatening children and mocking police.

One of the most publicized crime cases of the decade, though, did not involve murder. Rather, it began with a kidnapping and ended with armed robbery. Featuring a young woman from a prominent family, it contained all the elements needed to fascinate the American public.

All started on February 4, 1974, when the Symbionese Liberation Army (SLA) kidnapped heiress Patricia Campbell Hearst, aged 19, from an apartment that she shared with her fiancé, Steven Weed. The group first attempted to swap Hearst for imprisoned SLA members; when that failed, it made ransom demands. The Hearst family donated $6 million worth of food to the needy, but that did not result in Patty's release.

On April 15, 1974, photographs appeared wherein Hearst participated in a bank robbery with the SLA; she held an assault rifle. Shortly thereafter, she communicated that her new name was Tania, in honor of Che Guevara's lover, and that she believed in the Marxist goals and philosophies of her kidnappers. Authorities issued an arrest warrant for Hearst, and, in September, she and her captors were arrested.

Hearst claimed brainwashing. In her trial, which began on January 15, 1976, she testified that her kidnappers locked her into a closet, blindfolded, where they physically and sexually abused her. Her lawyers advanced the theory that, because of this abuse, she began relating to her captors, who controlled her life. That strategy failed, though; in March 1976, she

Actress Natasha Richardson reenacts the most famous photographic moment in the Patty Hearst kidnapping saga. She is portraying Hearst, who was using the name Tania, as she helps her kidnappers—the Symbionese Liberation Army—to rob a bank. Courtesy of Photofest.

was convicted and sentenced to prison. President Jimmy Carter pardoned her about three years later, granting her release on February 1, 1979. Two weeks later, on Valentine's Day, Hearst married her former bodyguard, Bernard Shaw.

One of the other prominent criminal acts that captured the attention of America in the 1970s did not happen in the United States, nor did it directly involve its citizens. Instead, it played out in Munich, Germany, in 1972, between a group of Arab militants and the Israeli athletes participating in the Olympics.

On September 5, 1972, with only five days remaining in the Olympics, eight militant Arabs stormed the village, killing two of Israel's athletes and kidnapping nine more. They demanded the release of more than 200 Palestinian prisoners, along with two Germans jailed for terrorism. No agreement was reached; the kidnappers therefore attempted to take the hostages to the airport, where German sharpshooters shot and killed three of the kidnappers. In the fighting and gunfire that ensued, all hostages died. In a memorable—and albeit extremely tragic moment—ABC commentator Jim McKay simply said, "They're all gone."

Olympic competition ceased for 24 hours. After a memorial service attended by more than 80,000 people, the games resumed and were completed. They continued without the participation of Jewish American athlete Mark Spitz, though, who had already won seven gold medals. Fearful of retaliation aimed at Spitz, upon advice, he flew home.

WAR IN SOUTHEAST ASIA

On May 4, 1970, shortly after noon, at Kent State University in Kent, Ohio, a volley of gunfire brought the war home in a bloody and terrifying way; this event still evokes intense emotion at the college campus and beyond whenever the anniversary of the event rolls around again. In 1970, Kent State students were protesting the involvement of the United States in the war in Southeast Asia, more specifically the invasion by American troops into Cambodia. This invasion occurred on April 25; Nixon revealed details about the assault on April 30, stating that, because the headquarters of the enemy, the Viet Cong, were located in Cambodia, this attack was a necessary facet of the war. Students were distressed over this escalation of hostilities; the war had appeared to be winding down in 1969, but the invasion of a second country increased the likelihood of more young men being drafted. One estimate suggested that 150,000 more men would now be needed to finish this war.

In response to this disturbing news, a significant number of Kent State students staged a demonstration on the Commons on May 1, 1970, burying a copy of the Constitution by the Victory Bell to symbolize that this particular war had not been declared. Protests occurred on other campuses around the country, but the one in Kent continued to intensify. Around midnight on May 1, people began tossing rocks and beer bottles downtown, breaking the window of a bank and setting off an alarm. Looting followed, and, by the time the police arrived, they encountered a group of about 100 people, some students, some not; bonfires had been set and it took an hour to disperse the crowd.

On May 2, Kent's mayor, Leroy Satrom, declared a state of emergency and he asked Ohio's governor, James Rhodes, to send in Ohio's National Guard to keep order. Satrom worried about rumors suggesting that further damage would occur to businesses and to the university, and he wanted to be proactive in his protective measures. By the time that the Guard arrived, about 10 P.M., the campus ROTC building, already slated for demolition, was on fire. No one was hurt by the smoke or flames, although a crowd of about 1,000 cheered as the building blazed; some threw rocks at firefighters and police.

The following day, nearly 1,000 Guardsmen were in Kent and Rhodes took a tough stance with the protesters and looters, comparing them to communists, Nazis, and revolutionaries. He announced that he would take whatever steps necessary to place the area under martial law, which would have made the May 4 protests illegal, but he did not follow through on his pledge. That night, the National Guard used tear gas to break up student demonstrations; it's possible that they believed that martial law now existed—or perhaps they were fearful of yet another violent protest.

Finally, on May 4, after four days of increasingly volatile protests, the situation escalated out of control. University officials, believing that Rhodes had in fact declared a state of martial law, distributed 12,000 flyers stating that the war protest rally planned by students was cancelled. Nevertheless, about 2,000 students met, and so the police and the Ohio National Guard once again attempted to disperse the crowd. Their tear gas, though, was ineffective in the wind. Some students tossed rocks at the Guard, along with empty tear gas canisters. At this point, Brigadier General Robert Canterbury ordered the National Guard to load their weapons.

Some Guardsmen attempted to advance on the protesters, with bayonets attached to their guns, but they suddenly found themselves trapped on a football field surrounded on three sides by a fence. After that aggressive strategy failed, they retreated, and, after reaching the top of Blanket Hill, 28 Guardsmen fired 61 to 67 shots into the crowd, a volley that lasted 13 seconds. An officer of the National Guard later said that the men had thought they detected sniper fire, and, believing their lives to be endangered, they discharged their weapons.

These shots killed four students—Allison Krause, Jeffrey Miller, Sandra Scheuer, and William Schroeder—wounding nine others. Krause and Miller had participated in the protests, while Scheuer and Schroeder were simply changing classes; Schroeder was in fact an ROTC member. One member of the National Guard was hurt badly enough during the chaos to need treatment.

Intense anger erupted after the shootings, and, campus authorities, fearful of further escalation by the protestors and potential retaliation by the National Guard, attempted to calm the students and entice them to disperse. One professor in particular, Glenn Frank, pleaded with everyone to leave, and, after 20 minutes, he effectively reasoned with the crowd.

One photo especially captures the sheer horror of the moment, as a 14-year-old female knelt beside the dying Miller; she is clearly in anguish over what had just transpired. The photographer, John Filo, had begun to leave the scene but, when he saw this young teen's reaction to the shootings, he stopped and captured that moment in film. The photo appeared in the May 18, 1970, issue of *Newsweek* with the heading of "Nixon's Home Front."

Vietnam veteran Bob Carpenter, who had returned to the United States and was serving as news director for the student radio channel, was an estimated 85 feet away from the center of the action. "There isn't a day in my life that goes by that I don't wake up without some conscious thought of this," he said. "I was in Vietnam twice before. I didn't have the fear that I had on this campus—helicopters swooping down, tear gas, bullets. It was a scary thing. I get goose bumps talking about it right at this moment."[29]

After the shootings, many colleges and universities—and even high schools and elementary schools—closed, with millions of students protesting the deaths. Meanwhile, Kent State itself remained closed for six weeks; during that time period, about 100,000 people marched in Washington against the war.

This event is now called the "Kent State shootings" or, sometimes, the "Kent State massacre" and it further splintered Americans along political lines. Nixon attempted to mitigate some of the damage by inviting Kent State students to the White House, but that strategy was insufficient.

On May 14, 1970, two students died at Jackson State University and several more were wounded when police and the National Guard attempted to break up a protest that focused on the Vietnam War, the Kent State shootings, and the rumors that civil rights leader Charles Evers had been murdered. This incident, though, did not unleash the passion that had exploded at Kent State University. (In retrospect, the contrast between the two situations serves as an illustration of the ways in which Americans responded to situations wherein the racial composition was more heavily black versus more white.)

Meanwhile, the fury continued over the Kent State riots and killings. On October 16, 25 people—including one faculty member—were indicted on charges connected with the burning of the ROTC building on May 2 or for incidents connected to the May 4 demonstration; those indicted became known as the "Kent 25." The majority of charges were dropped for lack of evidence, although one conviction, one acquittal, and two guilty pleas took place. No charges were filed against any members of the National Guard.

In an attempt to establish ways to prevent such tragedies in the future, in 1971, Kent State University created the Center for Peaceful Change. Eventually renamed the Center for Applied Conflict Management, it is the site of one of the first conflict resolution degree programs in the country. For each of the first five anniversaries of the shootings, college administrators sponsored commemorations; after that, community members and students (the May 4 task force) have organized the annual candlelight vigils and ringing of bells.

Perhaps the most widely recognized artistic response to the tragedy is "Ohio," a song written by Neil Young for Crosby, Stills, Nash, and Young. In this song, he refers to the National Guard as Nixon's "tin soldiers" and many radio stations refused to play this song because of its antiwar and anti-Nixon messages. A number of other songs were written about the occasion, including the Beach Boys' "Student Demonstration Time" (1971) and "Long Distance Runaround" by Yes (1971). A Kent State music professor wrote an opera, "Opera Flies," about his experience during the shootings; this was first performed on May 8, 1971. Documentaries included "Confrontation at Kent State" by Richard Myers (1970) and "Allison," also by Myers (1971); the latter focused on slain student Allison Krause. In 1971, James Michener published *Kent State: What Happened and Why*, and, in 1978, Nixon aide H.R. Haldeman suggested in his book, *The Ends of Power*, that the effects of the Kent State shootings were so significant that these events actually began the descent into Watergate that eventually caused the Nixon administration to collapse.

Families of the deceased filed lawsuits on a state and federal level throughout the 1970s but, for the most part, they were unsuccessful. In January 1979, the State of Ohio provided wounded students and the parents of the deceased with $675,000; the Ohio National Guardsmen involved in the shootings also signed a statement of regret.

Although America's presence in Cambodia in 1970, which led to the Kent State protests and its accompanying tragedies, lasted only 60 days, the United States remained entrenched in the Vietnam War until 1973. During the relatively brief Cambodia invasion, Nixon's position was somewhat vindicated when U.S. troops captured more than 16 million pounds of enemy ammunition, but the antiwar movement remained strong. The Kent State shootings added to the number of voices speaking out against the war, as did the My Lai massacre; although this mass killing actually occurred in 1968, American citizens had just learned of the deaths of more than 300 civilians, including women and children, by the hands of U.S. soldiers in February 1970.

Those opposing the war did not come from specific demographics. Rather, people from a wide variety of political, socioeconomic, and cultural backgrounds disagreed with this war. More specifically, the movement was "attracting members from college campuses, middle-class suburbs, labor unions, and government institutions" as it "gained national prominence in 1965, peaked in 1968, and remained powerful throughout the duration of the conflict."[30] Meanwhile, as protests and political debates over the war occurred in the United States, the fighting continued its deadly progress in Southeast Asia.

In February 1971, the South Vietnamese entered Laos to attack two enemy bases, but more than 9,000 of their soldiers died in an enemy trap; more than two-thirds of the South Vietnamese armored vehicles were destroyed, as well, along with hundreds of American helicopters. By January 1972, fewer than 133,000 American troops remained in the country; by summer, it appeared as though peace talks could come to fruition. Nixon was pursuing détente with both China and the Soviet Union, and he wanted to focus his energies on those initiatives, not on the stagnating war in Southeast Asia. The North Vietnamese feared their predicament if those two superpowers formed good relationships with the United States and so, by October 1972, a ceasefire agreement was crafted. In this agreement, the

Antiwar protests rocked the country during the late 1960s and early 1970s, as many believed that America should not be involved in the Vietnam War and that the compulsory draft system was unethical. Courtesy of Photofest.

United States would leave Vietnam, the prisoners of war (POWs) would be returned, and a political compromise that affected South Vietnam would go into effect.

This agreement fell apart, in large part because South Vietnam's leader, Nguyen Van Thieu, was not consulted or included in the negotiations. Nixon then offered Thieu $4 billion in military equipment and he agreed to reenter the war if North Vietnam did not abide by the peace agreement. Then, for 12 harrowing days, U.S. troops dropped 35,000 tons of bombs on the North Vietnamese in a military effort that became known as the "Christmas Bombing." Twenty five percent of the North Vietnamese oil reserves and 80 percent of its electrical power were destroyed. On January 8, 1973, peace talks resumed, with all parties signing a cease-fire agreement on January 27. By March, all U.S. troops returned home, with the exception of military advisors and Marines protecting American installations. Of the 3,000,000 men who came to serve in Vietnam, 58,000 lost their lives, 150,000 were seriously wounded, and about 1,000 men were still missing in action. The war continued between the South and North Vietnamese for another two years, until Hanoi overpowered its enemy on April 30, 1975, during the "Fall of Saigon."

American veterans did not always receive the best treatment after returning home. A percentage of the people who opposed the conflict transferred their antiwar sentiments, postwar, to those who had fought in Southeast Asia; later studies showed that minority American veterans often struggled even more than what was typical with readjustment issues. Here is one Native American's description of his experiences after returning home: "I was spit on and called a baby-killer in the mainstream culture when I first came home, and no way any college would accept me or any good job would be open to me. I felt too ashamed and enraged to accept the love and gratitude my family and community showed me. I thought I was going crazy, waking up in a sweat trying to choke my wife, seeing signs of Charley around every corner when the weather was hot and steamy."[31] This veteran was also describing posttraumatic stress disorder (PTSD) symptoms, whereby recurring nightmares and unwanted memories of Vietnam flooded his mind, as he struggled to connect emotionally with others in a healthy way. This was not unusual for returning Vietnam veterans and it added significantly to their readjustment issues.

Other veterans suffered deleterious effects from the herbicide Agent Orange that was sprayed in South Vietnam until 1971 by U.S. military forces wishing to strip away jungle cover that would allow the North Vietnamese to hide its troops. Diseases connected to Agent Orange exposure include Hodgkin's disease, multiple myeloma, respiratory cancers, and soft-tissue sarcoma, among others. Moreover, children born to men exposed to Agent Orange were at risk for many significant birth defects.

Meanwhile, other families agonized over the fate of their missing loved ones, veterans who did not return home from the war but were also not reported among the dead. In 1971, Mary Hoff, the wife of an MIA ("missing in action" soldier) created a stark black-and-white flag that symbolized the uncertain fate of the POWs and MIAs and that reminded Americans to remember them and to support efforts for either their safe return or for information about their final disposition. Many Americans also wore bracelets that contained the name of one of these soldiers; the wearer did not necessarily know this soldier personally. In 1970, the National League of Families of American Prisoners and Missing in Southeast Asia formed; this group supported the spouses, children, parents, and other close relatives of POWs, MIAs, and those killed in action without a body being recovered and returned. They sought information and closure about their loved ones.

FAMILY, RELIGION, AND TRADITIONAL VALUES
Family

Clearly, the American family is experiencing unprecedented change. The nuclear family system has been described by some commentators as dead or dying.[32]

The population in the United States had exploded during the postwar Baby Boomer Generation, which in fact encompassed more than one generation, with 76 million babies being born from 1946 to 1964. More than 4 million babies were born during each of the years between 1954 and 1964, with birth numbers approaching that 4-million mark during every year from 1946 to 1953. In comparison, birth rates during the 1970s ranged from 3.1 to 3.7 million annually. Family sizes dropped from 3.58 per household to 3.29, with some experts suggesting that the uncertain economy and higher rates of unemployment caused families to decide to have fewer children. Moreover, the increased availability and acceptance of birth control—and abortion—gave women more freedom in determining the sizes of their families.

Other experts pointed to the surge of women in the workplace and the feminist movement overall, which created in many women different priorities for their lives; careers sometimes delayed—or even replaced—the urge for parenthood. As just one benchmark, in 1971, Bryn Mawr College surveyed the five most recent graduating classes; the surveys indicated a total of 70 children being born to those alumni. In 1975, the college conducted the same survey, finding that only three new babies had been born. It is logical to assume, too, that when women delayed having children, their decreased number of child-bearing years caused many of them to have fewer children overall.

Meanwhile, divorces increased significantly in the 1970s. In 1965, 480,000 divorces were recorded; this number increased to 640,000 in 1969, 773,000 in 1971, and more than 1 million in 1975.[33] Meanwhile, according to information published by the Maryland Population Research Center, more highly educated women in the 1970s expressed the belief that divorces should be even easier to obtain.

The rising divorce rate, in part, surely must be attributed to the "no-fault divorce" laws that began to be passed in the United States. Pioneered by California and effective in that state on January 1, 1970, this law prevented divorcing spouses from having to place blame on one of the parties before a divorce could be effected. Now, a couple could divorce in no-fault states by simply stating "irreconcilable differences." Over the next eight years, all but three states ratified such a law, making no-fault divorces available throughout nearly all of the country.

Moreover, books such as *Open Marriage* (1972) encouraged women who felt that they needed to choose between themselves and their marriages to choose themselves. That year, 84 percent of Americans in their 40s were married; 10 years later, that figure dropped to 67 percent. In a poll taken in 1978 by the Associated Press and NBC, 60 percent of people said that most Americans marrying did not expect their unions to last for life. Meanwhile, movies such as *Kramer vs. Kramer* and *An Unmarried Woman* extolled the courage of women who flourished, postmarriage.[34]

Finally, more churches were finally accepting, albeit sometimes quite reluctantly, the realities of the increasing divorce rate in the United States. In 1973, the Episcopal Church voted to recognize civil divorces; in the past, church members needed to go through another sometimes lengthy process with the church before they could remarry. Even the Catholic Church was relenting, as the number of annulments—which allowed Catholics to re-marry in the church, unlike divorces—increased by 77 percent from 1968 to 1981.[35]

About 1 million children, during each year of the decade, saw their parents divorce. For the first time, many experts began counseling parents that a divorce was better for the children than living in a conflict-filled home. Happier parents, they advised, led to happier children. Relieved of the guilt that divorce could instill, and perhaps believing that they were doing their children a favor, many parents embraced this philosophy.

The 1970s saw a rise in "latchkey kids," children who let themselves into the house or apartment after school, and then spent the rest of the afternoon alone or with other children. Sometimes, children were " latchkey" because both parents worked; sometimes, because of divorce or single parenthood, the custodial parent worked. To remedy this latchkey situation, many working mothers fought for federally subsidized child care, or even free child care, while nonprofit organizations such as YMCAs began running "latchkey kid" programs, or, as they later became known, "after-school programs."

After-school programs, though, did not address the child care needs for preschoolers. In 1974, for example, one in three working women were mothers, with 40 percent of them having preschool-aged children. That totaled 6 million children under the age of six with working mothers, with only 10 percent of these children in a licensed day care program.[36]

Because of this significant need for child care, the 1970 White House Conference on Children recommended as a first priority universally available child care that was family-centered and conveniently located. The committee tempered this priority with a statement calling child care a supplement, rather than a substitute, for care by the children's families.

Congress passed legislation to address this situation, but President Nixon vetoed it in 1971. Arguments against this legislation were that easily available day care would weaken the family structure and cause the "Sovietization" of America's children. (By the 1970s, the Soviet Union, Israel, and Sweden had well-established child care programs.) One must consider the mindset of the average American, especially before the 1972 breakthrough of the Cold War relations between the Soviet Union and the United States, to understand how that word, *Sovietization,* could strike fear in the hearts of parents and perhaps make them question the safety and advisability of day care.

During the 1970s, couples began, in increasing numbers, to live together in intimate relationships without marriage, either as a "trial marriage" or as an arrangement that would not involve marriage. Dubbed POSSLQs by the Census Bureau, or Persons of Opposite Sex Sharing Living Quarters, by 1979, approximately 1 million households fit this designation. Some women lived with a man without the benefit of marriage because this arrangement made them feel less shackled by convention. Some couples wanted to experience how compatible they would be while living together, before making the commitment to marry. Others, who felt disdain for governmental and church rituals and found them meaningless, stated that they did not need a ring and a piece of paper to be committed to their partners.

As in nearly every other cultural and social change, the courts soon became involved in settling a groundbreaking POSSLQ dispute. In 1964, actor Lee Marvin and singer Michelle Triola moved in together and maintained this relationship until 1970. After they split up, Marvin sent Triola support checks, as he had apparently agreed to do. In 1971, though, he married another woman and the checks eventually stopped. Infuriated by Marvin's lack of follow-through on their agreement, Michelle changed her last name to Triola Marvin and she sued him for half of his $3.6 million fortune. Newspapers, tongue-in-cheek, dubbed this a "palimony" suit. Although courts initially rejected her claim, they eventually awarded her $104,000. Countless women across the country applauded this decision; meanwhile, this significantly changed the commitment-free nature of cohabitation. Nevertheless, that year, more than half of Americans polled said that they did not object to cohabitation, a clear indication to the growing acceptance of this lifestyle.

In 1977, the Supreme Court struck down as illegal any laws that discriminated against the children of unwed parents. Perhaps most important, this invalidated laws in some states that did not allow illegitimate children to inherit their share of their father's property unless this designation was expressly stated in the will.

Lest it seem that no one married in the 1970s, it should be noted that many people created personalized wedding services during that decade, to express their unique personalities, spiritual beliefs, and circumstances. Many people shunned traditional church or governmental weddings, writing their own vows. Some women kept their maiden names, and they incorporated that decision into the actual vows. People wore blue jeans to some weddings, and attended others on boats. The variety was endless.

Religion and Traditional Values

Mainstream Christian churches during the early part of the 1970s continued their 1960s initiative to merge nine denominations into one superchurch with 23 million members. This initiative, begun a decade earlier, did not succeed, in large part because of differing points of theology, governance, and procedures in the involved churches. Overall, however, participating churches increased their levels of interchurch collaboration and understanding among denominations.

During the 10 years of this attempted merger, participating denominations had collectively lost 2 million members as they struggled to determine their purpose and position in a world of cultural change. How, for example, would mainstream Protestant churches respond to a growing number of females demanding equal rights, which for many of them included greater leadership roles in their religious and spiritual lives? Would the Episcopalian and Lutheran faiths, for example, decide to ordain women? In 1970, two branches of the Lutheran Church began accepting women as clergy; the struggle for Episcopalian ordination took a more winding route, with decisions and then reversals, but all was resolved affirmatively by 1976.

Mainstream churches struggled with many more issues. How accepting should each church be to gays and lesbians who were open about their sexual orientations? What about the increasing rates of divorce? How should they respond to the issue of abortion?

Most members of the clergy opposed the Vietnam War, and, by extension, many of Richard Nixon's policies. One respected preacher, though, Billy Graham, was close to Nixon, supporting him politically and conducting church services in the White House. Graham began distancing himself from the president in 1973, and later stated his deep dismay over the "dark aspects" of Nixon's personality and administration, but Graham's former relationship with the president hurt his reputation in the eyes of some observers.

Ethical, moral, and cultural questions posed during the 1970s were tough to answer and no church found perfect solutions. Meanwhile, a number of Americans became disillusioned over the responses of mainstream denominations to the controversial issues of the era. It might be expected, then, that those involved in various rights movements would seek out more liberal and accepting churches, which would predict a rise of those denominations during the 1970s; instead the decade witnessed a significant rise in the growth and influence of the conservative Evangelical Christian movement.

Evangelical Christians did not belong to one specific denomination. They did share several characteristics, though, including a more conservative worldview, religiously, culturally, socially, and politically. They also shared a belief in the power of evangelism to spread the news of their faith, and in personal conversion to Christianity and an acceptance of Jesus Christ as their Lord and Savior, which they believed to be the route of salvation. They believed the Bible to be inerrable and everlasting, adamant that its wisdom and guidance should be applied to the questions and challenges of the day.

Perhaps growing numbers of people rejected the rituals of the more mainstream churches during the 1970s because the passion of more evangelical movements appealed to them. In these groups, an intense personal reaction to the church experience was appropriate and this fulfilled a need that came to the forefront during a decade of self-exploration. Furthermore, in an era with rapidly evolving mores and an uncertainty about what changes might occur next—women as priests, perhaps, or the legalization of same-sex unions—the literal reading of Biblical texts surely provided a rock bed of certainty and solidity for many adherents and converts to the Evangelical Christian movement.

The year 1976, *Newsweek* declared, was the "Year of the Evangelical." During that year, the phrase *born again* as a reference to personal conversion to Christianity became well known to Americans as Southern Baptist Jimmy Carter defined himself that way during the presidential campaign.

The rise in television evangelism—or televangelism—greatly increased the ability of preachers to spread the news of the gospel. The advancement of the cable television system had created vast new channels needing content, and so time was sold—and frequently purchased by televangelists. Although some claims of extraordinary viewer numbers must be questioned, 25 million people watched Oral Roberts' Thanksgiving special in 1975; by 1979, his show was broadcast on about 170 stations. By the time the 1970s began, Pat Robertson had created his own network—the Christian Broadcasting Network (CBN)—a strategy followed by Jim and Tammy Faye Bakker with their PTL (Praise the Lord and/or People That Love) Network and Paul Crouch with his Trinity Broadcast Network. Other televangelists of note included Jimmy Swaggart and Robert Schuller.

Funding their shows could be an expensive proposition for televangelists, and so a constant in these programs was the impassioned pleas for viewers to send them money. Amid suspicions that not all televangelists used this donated money appropriately, in 1978, Billy Graham helped create the Evangelical Council for Financial Responsibility, an organization that ministries could choose to join to be open about their financial collecting, spending, and reporting.

The 1970s decade was capped off by Reverend Jerry Falwell's creation of the Moral Majority in 1979. The Moral Majority served as a political and religious force for conservative fundamentalist factions in the country. Platforms included prayers in public schools, as well as the opposition of several causes, including the Equal Rights Amendment, abortion rights, SALT treaties between the United States and the Soviet Union, and rights for gays and lesbians. Falwell pushed for a return to what he defined as America's traditional social values, stating that this was what made the country strong. More liberal policies, which he equated to an increase in sexual immorality, chipped away at this stronghold in his viewpoint.

The Moral Majority also advocated the teaching of creationism—the Biblical explanation of creation, two versions of which are found in Genesis—in schools. In the middle of the decade, courts had heard cases on the appropriateness of including creationism next to theories of evolution and other scientific discoveries in textbooks; they upheld the notion that creationism should not be taught as an alternative scientific explanation of the creation of the world and its creatures.

In 1979, a religious figure traveled to America to advocate for sexual morality: Pope John Paul II. In 1978, Pope John Paul had died after only 34 days as pontiff. His successor, Pope John Paul II, was Polish and the first non-Italian pontiff since 1522. In his visit to the United States, John Paul II expressed fairly liberal views politically and economically, but stressed traditional and conservative positions on sexual issues. He extolled Catholics to reject birth control, abortion, homosexuality, divorce, and nonmarital sex; he also reiterated the positions that women could not become priests and that male priests must remain celibate. Overall, the Pope was well received, as crowds in the hundreds of thousands greeted him. However, a nun who served as the president of the Leadership of Women Religious debated his viewpoint on male-only clergy. Moreover, growing numbers of priests and nuns were leaving their orders as they disagreed with the Church's position on relevant social issues.

In reality, Catholics in the United States were using birth control in increasing numbers despite the pronouncements of the pope. Some of the tension between Catholic theology and Protestant beliefs eased, though, when, in 1970, the restrictions on Catholics marrying outside the faith were lessened, as were the strictures on raising children of these marriages in the Catholic Church.

Cults

Throughout the history of the United States, periods of unrest and social protests—such as those in the 1960s and early 1970s—have been followed by religious revivals and spiritual movements. That pattern repeated itself in the 1970s. By 1975, Americans could choose from more than 800 religious groups; these included Asian religions such as Buddhism and Hinduism, as well as blended faiths such as Jews for Jesus.

Several religions labeled as "cults" also came to national attention during the 1970s, sometimes for tragic reasons. They were labeled cults because of several factors: the group was usually led by one charismatic leader, who was adored by his or her followers; and the participants of the group made this religious organization the central part of their lives, often leaving behind family, friends, college educations, and jobs, donating personal possessions to the group, and living with other followers in a communal setting.

Many outside of these religious groups, including concerned parents, perceived this intense influence as brainwashing; they would sometimes hire "deprogrammers," whose jobs were to track down their "thought-controlled" loved ones. Once found, these cult members would sometimes forcibly be removed from their communal settings, and taken somewhere private where the deprogrammers could dissuade them from following the beliefs of their cult and then persuade them that their family's tenets and wishes were more appropriate. Parents formed support groups to assist their families in deprogramming processes and courts heard numerous cases on the subject.

Religions dubbed as cults during the 1970s included the International Movement for Krishna Consciousness, a theology begun in India; called Hare Krishnas in the United States, this movement began in America in the 1960s and continued through the 1970s. Perhaps the image that still resonates is that of Hare Krishnas dressed in robes, sporting unusual haircuts, and soliciting money from people in airports. The Divine Light Mission, led by a teenager named Maharaj Ji, also had Indian origins.

People flocked to hear the teachings of Transcendental Meditation—or the TM movement. Spearheaded by the Maharishi Mahesh Yogi, approximately 10,000 Americans visited his training centers monthly during the early part of the decade. After being assigned a *mantra*, a word or phrase which a person could repeat and focus upon, a follower could practice the techniques of meditation. Although this movement assisted physicians and psychologists in the study of meditation and its effects on physical, mental, and emotional well-being, the followers of TM also claimed that they could levitate and that their meditation changed the state of world affairs, beliefs not accepted by the mainstream culture.

In 1971, the Reverend Sun Myung Moon from South Korea visited the United States for the third time. During this visit, he and followers from Korea visited college campuses and other centers of youthful activity, recruiting for Moon's Unification Church. Later known for participating in massive weddings, where hundreds of couples were married at the same time, the followers became known by outsiders as "Moonies." By the end of the decade, the Internal Revenue Service had begun an investigation into Moon's wealth.

In 1977, the Federal Bureau of Investigation conducted an investigation into another religion with cultlike features: Scientology. Founded by science fiction writer L. Ron Hubbard in the 1950s, the FBI suspected that, in the 1970s, some members of the church had attempted to infiltrate governmental investigative agencies; some of the arrested were convicted in federal court.

Another cult leader and founder of Children of God, David Berg, changed his name to Moses David in the 1970s, when he began to see himself as the Messiah. Leaving the United States in the middle of the decade, rumors circulated in 1978 that his group promoted sexual intercourse with children as young as 12 years old. Children were also alleged to have been brainwashed; on June 10, 1978, more than 50 members of the sect were arrested in France, with 140 children taken in for questioning. Berg dismissed about 300 people from his group after this scandal; renaming his group the "Family of Love," they began "flirty fishing," offering sex as an opening to their evangelizing process.[37]

The Way International, a religious group operating since the 1940s, was believed to be exercising "thought control" upon its members in the 1970s. They were also said to use "love bombing," an intense show of affection toward someone that they wished to recruit.

The most deadly cult story of the decade, though, is clearly the Peoples Temple and its leader, Jim Jones. Initially Pentecostal, Jones originally affiliated the church that he created, the Peoples Temple, with the mainstream Disciples of Christ. By the mid-1970s, though, his religious beliefs were shifting, as he began to tell his followers that he was God; meanwhile, his politics became increasingly radical along the socialist-Communist spectrum. He therefore moved his followers to Guyana in South America, the "Promised Land," where political beliefs better matched his own. U.S. officials heard disturbing stories about gunrunning and irregular bank transactions by the Peoples Temple; by 1978, Jones was clearly becoming demented, holding "White Nights" wherein his followers would practice the techniques of mass—or "revolutionary"—suicide.

In November 1978, Congressman Leo Ryan of California traveled to Guyana to observe the Peoples Temple for himself. Some followers of

Jones asked to leave with Ryan; they were permitted to do so, but then the plane was attacked on the trip home, and Ryan and all of the former followers were killed. When investigators arrived at the commune to question Jones, they found 914 dead bodies, including that of Jones; most had drunk Kool-aid laced with cyanide, although some were shot. It has been assumed that Jones and his loyal followers shot those who would not drink the poison.

Finally, no overview of the 1970s can be complete without mentioning the New Age followers, who turned away from traditional religions to find individual truth. These seekers, according to Joanne Beckman of Duke University, "might be open to 'trying church,' but are just as willing to sample Eastern religions, New Age spiritualism, or quasi-religious self-help groups of the Recovery Movement. For seekers, spirituality is a means of individual expression, self-discovery, inner healing, and personal growth. Religion is valued according to one's subjective experience. Thus seekers feel free to incorporate elements of different traditions according to their own liking. They shop around, compare, and select religious 'truths' and experiences with what one historian calls their 'à la carte' spirituality."[38] Some New Age followers focused their spiritual energies on angels, while others studied reincarnation, crystals, or chanting.

THE 1970S

2
World of Youth

INTRODUCTION

From antibusing protests to the debates over evolution versus creationism, and from the difficulties inherent in mainstreaming challenged youth to the discussion of sex education—and sexism—in the schools, America's educational facilities became swept up in as many controversies as the rest of the country. The Supreme Court became involved in many judicial disputes, as well, as the civil rights legislation passed in the 1960s became fraught with confusion and differing interpretations in the 1970s.

Meanwhile, the sexual revolution was nothing short of revolutionary, drastically changing the manner in which men and women related. Opportunities for sexual experimentation blossomed for singles and for married couples alike, while a broad spectrum of Americans became more open about sexual orientations and preferences.

The contraceptive pill, cited as perhaps the greatest impetus for change for women in the twentieth century, was improved upon during the 1970s; coupled with the passage of *Roe v. Wade,* the dramatic changes in a woman's potential control over her body were dizzying. All was not that clear-cut, of course, as feminism, *Roe v. Wade,* and birth control were not universally embraced. Moreover, detractors of the sexual revolution pointed to the increasing availability and graphic nature of pornography, rising divorce rates, and alarming numbers of teenage pregnancies as the dark side of this revolution.

The psychedelic movement that began in the 1960s continued through the early part of the 1970s, as drug use continued to rise. As LSD faded as the drug of choice, cocaine debuted as the new glamour drug. Youth experimented with marijuana, sometimes becoming heavy users of the drug, while some Vietnam War soldiers numbed their pain with heroin.

EDUCATIONAL OPPORTUNITIES

Civil rights legislation in the 1960s paved the way for a series of court decisions during the 1970s intended to further desegregate schools in order to provide an equal education for all, regardless of race. Perhaps the most influential was the 1971 decision, *Swann v. Charlotte-Mecklenberg Board of Education,* wherein the Supreme Court ruled that busing was a legal and effective method to accomplish desegregation. This legislation, though, did not solve the problem of desegregation—nor did forced busing.

After the passage of the Civil Rights Act in 1964, some states had set up segregated private schools, which became known as "segregation academies," and then the states provided these schools with free textbooks. Recognizing this as a way to undermine the intent of previous legislation, in *Norwood v. Harrison* (1973), the Supreme Court ruled that states cannot provide free textbooks to segregated private schools.

During the antibusing backlash that occurred after *Swann v. Mecklenberg,* a significant number of white families migrated to suburbs, away from the more racially mixed cities. Some parents resented the imposed busing for racial reasons; others disliked their children being bused away from "neighborhood schools." Controversy then arose over whether youth living in suburbs should be bused to city schools, and visa versa, to effect desegregation. In 1974, in *Milliken v. Bradley,* the Supreme Court determined that remedies between school districts—or intradistrict —are seldom appropriate, and that busing should occur within one particular district, or interdistrict.

In 1974, in Boston, the protests were especially intense, as one district attempted to bus students from Roxbury, the "heart of Boston's black ghetto," into South Boston, which was the "stronghold of opposition to desegregation." When buses arrived, protestors threw rocks, rotten eggs, and tomatoes, and they screamed out racial slurs; they smashed out the windows of a bus, injuring nine students. One woman recalled picking out glass from the hair of crying elementary school students and soothing them about their bruises. As the year progressed, some teachers volunteered to tutor white students at night, as parents planned a boycott of the school system. Fights broke out in the hallways, and, on December 11, 1974, a black student stabbed a white one; in response, an angry mob formed outside of the school and the principal isolated black students for their safety.[1]

In retrospect, it seems that, although racism played a significant role in these riots, some parents were protesting the governmental interference in their children's education. Moreover, this was a tight-knit community that did not welcome outsiders easily; Italian American students also faced difficulties in this region of Boston. Plus, lest it seem as though white parents were antibusing and black parents were in favor of this strategy, the situation was not that clear-cut. In fact, a 1975 survey conducted by the National Opinion Research Center found that 53 percent of black Americans were against busing. Many black parents, just like some of their white counterparts, felt as though they had lost control of their children's education through forced busing.

In 1978, James Coleman—the sociologist perhaps most influential in persuading politicians that racial integration was an important factor in improving the academic opportunities for poor blacks—released a report reviewing the effects of forced busing. In this report, Coleman concluded that his initial recommendations had been completely wrong. Forced busing, he reported, resulted in massive white flight from public schools; furthermore it was the source of significant violence, so much so that it hampered educational standards to the degree that it negated any possible improvement based upon integrated education. From a social and cultural standpoint, he added that it now seemed racist to say that there was something inherently wrong with all or predominately black schools. Other investigators have agreed that busing was more harmful than beneficial and that its attempted implementation by force created inner cities populated increasingly by blacks; this ran contrary to the goal of integrating racially. That same year, David Armor of Rand Corporation conducted his own study, concluding that "white flight" proved counterproductive to the aims of desegregation, and, in fact, in many districts, this phenomenon caused a greater degree of segregation than what existed, prelegislation.[2]

The theme of reverse discrimination also reared up in school-related rulings. Most notably, parents in West Virginia, many of whom were white fundamentalist Christians, wanted more control in the selection of textbooks. Comparing themselves to New Yorkers, wherein parents apparently had some role in this process, they questioned why "Manhattan militant blacks" could have this authority, while it was "abhorrent for militant whites in Appalachia."[3] Similar debates occurred when the Moral Majority and people in sympathy with this organization's goals and beliefs fought to have creationism included in science textbooks. Creationism was also known by other names, including creation science and creationism science—and, later still, as intelligent design.

In 1968, with the ruling of *Epperson v. Arkansas,* the Supreme Court had determined that schools could not forbid the teaching of evolution; so the next tactic used by supporters of creationism was to demand equal time or balanced treatment of what they called two possible explanations for the creation of plant, animal, and human life on Earth: evolution and creationism. Proponents of evolution believed in a gradual creation and evolution of creatures on the earth, starting with simple forms such as one-celled bacteria and advancing to complex ones such as mammals, including man. They believed that life began millions of years ago, whereas adherents of creationism stated that all creatures were formed at one time, by God and in their present state, about 6,000 to 8,000 years ago. In their viewpoint, one life form did not evolve into or descend from another form.

Creationism received a boost in support by the evangelical churches after the Henry Morris Institute for Creation Research was formed in 1970. There, he and Tim LaHaye, now the author of the *Left Behind* series that focuses on passages of Revelation, provided written materials, including results of their research, so that parents and religious leaders could better advocate for the creationism movement. Although the Moral Majority and Morris and LaHaye did not accomplish their goals, they did bring the creationism debate to a national forum.[4] In 1981, Arkansas passed legislation that required balanced treatment, as advocated by these men, but the Supreme Court struck down that law.

Other civil rights issues existed. In 1974, in *Lau v. Nichols,* the Supreme Court determined that the school district in San Francisco violated the Civil Rights Act by not providing nearly 2,000 students of Chinese descent with English instruction. This decision led to the passage of the Equal Educational Opportunities Act of 1974, which declared that "no state shall deny equal educational opportunity on the basis of race, color, sex, or national origin." The state of New York went one step further, requiring that students not proficient in English be taught, at least in part, in their native language.

The following year, Congress passed the Education for All Handicapped Children Act, which meant that schools now needed to create an Individualized Education Program (IEP) for each child with challenges. Moreover, these children needed to be taught in the least restrictive environments possible. (This legislation later became known as the Individuals with Disabilities Act.) Parents of the affected children and the corresponding school districts were to work together to accomplish the goals of the IEPs; the overall goal was to give all students the opportunity for a free and equal education without undue governmental interference. In reality, though, many teachers suddenly found themselves instructing children with significant special needs without enough support and resources in which to provide them with the education that they needed. Thus, "mainstreaming," as it came to be known, was yet another controversial issue in education in the 1970s.

In 1979, the nation's first educational reform plan that included components of student achievement standards and teacher accountability began in New York. That same year, President Jimmy Carter signed into law the Department of Education Organization Act, which provided a cabinet-level department dedicated to education; the Office of Education Research and Improvement (OERI) formed, but it did not receive enough funding to establish itself fully.

During the 1960s and 1970s, school districts added sex education to the curriculum, along with materials dealing with drug and alcohol abuse, environmental concerns, and many other topics previously taught by parents and perhaps churches. Thus, instead of being institutions that taught academic subjects only, the school systems were evolving into places that also taught students about issues of social and cultural concern. Those opposed to sex education in schools, such as Phyllis Schlafly, argued that this curriculum resulted in an increased amount of sexual activity among teens. Others, such as the Christian Crusade, opposed "smut" being taught in schools; perhaps the most radical statement made, though, was by the John Birch Society: that sex education was a "filthy Communist plot." Nevertheless, the subject continued to be taught in public schools.[5]

Although, by the 1970s, parents and educators were well acquainted with the controversies associated with sex education, the term *sexism* was relatively unknown; even some well-educated adults confused the word with sex education. In fact, the concept of sexism was so obscure that, when a groundbreaking book that explored the detrimental effects of sexism in schools was published in 1973, many pornography stores purchased the book for salacious purposes, also misunderstanding the term. Moreover, Harper and Row received a flood of book returns based upon this brand of confusion.[6]

The book in question, titled *Sexism in School and Society* and written by Nancy Frazier and Myra Sadker, explored the gender biases found in textbooks and in school instruction. According to these authors, this bias occurred at all age levels, regardless of geographical, social, or racial factors.[7] They noted differences in the manner in which teachers instructed boys and girls, with boys receiving more active and precise instruction, and girls a more passive approach, with less teaching time and quality given to them. Again, this pattern repeated itself across all racial, ethnic, and socioeconomic backgrounds of students; it appeared to be unintentional on the behalf of the teachers and therefore indicative of the deeply ingrained gender biases in the United States. Taken one step further, it was logical to trace how boys and girls then carried their roles into the workplace and into the world outside of school, with boys engaging in riskier behaviors and girls becoming quieter and more conforming. According to the theories of this book, it was, at least in part, nurture—or the ways in which children were raised—not nature and genetics that caused these behavior patterns in the two genders. Although that notion is not shocking today, it created a stir of controversy when the book was first published.

Based upon its own research, the Council on Interracial Books for Children noted that few books published pre-1973 contained nonsexist language and concepts. This report also stated that the 1970s saw the first flurry of true multicultural children's books.

Other education-related legislation passed in the 1970s included a 1972 act *(Wisconsin v. Yoder)* that officially permitted the Amish to stop educating their children after the eighth grade. Amish believe that attending school past that point endangers their salvation and prevents their youth from participating in their separatist lifestyle.

Yet another piece of legislation, discussed more in depth in chapter seven of this book, was Title IX of the Education Amendments of 1972; the pertinent section of this law declared that "No person in the United States shall, on the basis of sex, be excluded from participation in, or denied the benefits of, or be subjected to discrimination under any educational program or activity receiving federal assistance." Although this language does not specifically mention sports teams and programs, Title IX transformed the funding of athletic programs in educational institutions and it opened up a wide variety of new opportunities for female students.

Finally, although it seems unlikely that many people realized how enormously the computer would change education and the rest of the American society, students began using computers more frequently in classrooms, more often in college and university settings, but also in high schools. Computer science degrees were sought after, as well, although the top five college degrees granted during the 1970s were education, social sciences and history, business, English, and biology.

SEXUAL REVOLUTION

Although the term *sexual revolution* is often associated with the 1960s and 1970s—with some debate about which of these two decades epitomized the revolution—the term was actually created in 1920. Moreover, the phrase was not coined in the United States, but in Germany by the psychoanalyst Wilhelm Reich; he hoped to educate youth about birth control and abortion, and, in general, sexually liberate society. In the 1960s, the advent of the oral contraceptive pill caused the term to be bandied about again; by the 1970s, *sexual revolution* took on different meanings for different demographics.

For gays and lesbians, the term could refer to their newly found freedom as they more openly identified with their sexual orientations, without fear of the former levels of ridicule and reprisal. For young adults wishing to sexually experiment, it might mean having relations with a large number of people, either one at a time or in a group, without having to form a deeply emotional relationship with any particular partner. Some of these adherents attended swinging parties, wherein a person would switch from one sexual partner to another throughout an evening; sometimes more than two people were involved in a particular sexual act. As early as 1971, the *New York Times* ran an article titled "Group Sex: Is It 'Life Art' or a Sign That Something Is Wrong?"[8] The reporter quoted a number of participants and psychologists in this article.

"Wife swapping" suited some established couples who were searching to revitalize their marriage as well as some younger married couples who wished for a more experimental one. In this arrangement, two married couples socialized, but then the men paired up sexually with one another's wives; this lifestyle was highlighted in a 1969 mainstream comedy—*Bob & Carol & Ted & Alice,* staring Natalie Wood, Robert Culp, Elliott Gould, and Dyan Cannon. Some couples formed a foursome, calling it a "group marriage." In these arrangements, jealousy and possessiveness were seen as immature, and those expressing—or even feeling—those emotions were not "keeping up with the times."

In 1973, two professional baseball players, Cleveland Indians Michael Dennis Kekich and New York Yankees Fritz Peterson decided to swap wives and children—and even pets—for a day. For Peterson, this ended up becoming a more permanent swap, as he eventually married Kekich's wife, Susanne. Meanwhile, Kekich and Marilyn Peterson, who also became a couple, soon broke up.

Other couples entered into open marriage arrangements, wherein the man and woman got or remained married—and were usually intimate—but were also free to pursue other sexual relationships. Open marriages could take a variety of formats; some couples told each other about outside relationships, while others did not. Some couples stayed within heterosexual parameters, while others used the open marriage concept to experiment with bisexuality. Although open marriages were certainly not new to the 1970s, the concept rose to public awareness after *Open Marriage* was published by Nena and George O'Neill in 1972; the book, which sold more than 1.5 million copies, focused primarily on more conventional ways in which to enrich communications, but the book did include 20 pages on incorporating sexual activities with other partners into the marriage.

There were other ramifications of the sexual revolution. Some finally felt free to form interracial relationships, while other people enjoyed communal living; some communes permitted—or even encouraged—casual nudity. People also attended workshops wherein participants would play games in the nude, including same sex wrestling, to break through sexual taboos and emotional and psychological hang-ups.

For some women, the sexual revolution allowed them to have premarital sex without fear of pregnancy, because of the highly reliable contraceptive pill; abortion was now available as a potential back-up strategy. Surveys showed that, during the 1970s, two-thirds of women had engaged in sexual intercourse by the age of 19, not much different from the four-fifths figure given for men.[9] Young women could show off their figures in a plethora of revealing halter tops, hot pants, string bikinis, and miniskirts. Bras, although not burned in reality, were optional and their absence served as a symbol of freedom.

For other women, though, who identified themselves as feminists, the sexual revolution was negatively perceived; it objectified women. These feminists despised the portrayal of women in pornography, calling it dehumanizing and warning that as women became increasingly objectified, rates of rape and wife battering would increase, as well. The sexual revolution, in their viewpoint, actually limited the scope of female freedoms.

Regardless of definitions and opinions, one factor that revolutionized sexual options for women during the 1960s and 1970s was the contraceptive pill, the wonder drug that symbolized the new sense of freedom being experienced by females. By 1962, 1.2 million women in the United States were using the pill to prevent pregnancy; by 1965, the figure rose to 5 million, and, by 1973, 10 million American women were using the pill. During the 1960s, though, disturbing reports surfaced about dangerous side effects, including deadly blood clots. Later in the 1960s, reports showed a possible connection between the pill and other diseases, including the increased risk of diabetes and cancer.

In the early part of the 1970s, though, just when some women might have decided that the pill wasn't consequence free, after all, the "minipill" debuted. Unlike the regular oral contraceptive, which contained estrogen and progestin, the minipill contained only the latter hormone and posed far fewer health risks for its users. Although the minipill did not protect women as fully against pregnancy as its fuller-fledged counterpart, it was still a significantly safer birth control method than many options from the past. As the 1970s progressed, researchers continued to experiment with various hormonal combinations for the pill, thereby increasing protection from pregnancy while reducing risk. Therefore, women could feel both safe and in control of their own sexuality.

Moreover, during the 1970s, the freedom to discuss sexuality, to read about sex, and to watch plays and movies about sex became significantly easier—and more acceptable. For example, during the 1960s, mainstream women's magazines discussed cohabitation—the arrangement wherein an intimate couple lives together without the benefit of marriage—in a cautious, even hesitant, manner. According to research conducted by Jennifer Schaefer, *Redbook* published an article in 1968 entitled "Why 'Just Living Together' Won't Work." Six years later, though, the same magazine published this article: "What Lovers Discover about Living Together." Although the basic subject was the same, the tone of the articles changed from somewhat censorious to flirty and fun. Schaefer points out that *Redbook* also published articles such as "How Uninhibited Can a Woman Dare to Be?" and "Look Out! Here Come Naked Men!," two articles that couldn't conceivably have appeared in a mainstream, grocery store aisle publication before the 1970s.[10]

Pornography, not unexpectedly, also flourished during this era, with the hardcore porno business raking in $4 billion annually. "Peep shows" provided men an opportunity to feed coins into machines that caused a curtain to draw back from a window in a private cubicle. From that vantage point, the man in that cubicle could watch a woman—or women—dance seductively; one might allow the viewer to also fondle her breasts. Time would run out quickly, though, and the peep-show observer would need to feed in more coins or prepaid tokens to continue the "show." These establishments were generally located in seedy districts in cities such as New York City, Boston, and San Francisco.

Porn magazines became more mainstreamed in the 1970s, with *Hustler, Penthouse,* and *Playboy* readily available in convenience stores. *Cosmopolitan,* a magazine for the modern and liberated woman, received a huge surge in attention and sales in 1972 when actor Burt Reynolds posed nude for the cover; when he appeared on *The Tonight Show* with Johnny Carson, postposing, the program's ratings reached a record high. Not surprisingly, *Playgirl* debuted in 1973, nipping at the heels of the Reynolds release.

Meanwhile, in 1973, 25 percent of Americans admitted watching an X-rated film over the past year and pornographic movies such as *Deep Throat* and *Behind the Green Door* became quite popular. *Deep Throat* earned an astonishing $25 million and the actors and actresses of both films—including Linda Lovelace, Harry Reems, and Marilyn Chambers—attained celebrity status. Other movies, such as Bernardo Bertolucci's *Last Tango in Paris,* were not pornographic but they pushed the limits of graphic sex inclusion in film. Homemade hippie pornography films also became popular.

Linda Lovelace (Linda Susan Boreman), star of the 1972 porno film, Deep Throat, *appears at the Royal Ascot races in England in 1974, wearing a low-cut outfit that shocked many spectators. Shortly after the 1970s ended, Lovelace began crusading against pornography. Courtesy of Photofest.*

In the late 1960s, a man named Steve Ostrow who was exploring his newly realized bisexuality had opened a New York bathhouse, the Continental Baths. Unlike other bathhouses, which tended to be secretive and even seedy places, this one provided public entertainment from people as well known as Bette Midler, Barry Manilow, and John Davidson. The Continental became a commercial sex club of national renown, or, as Ostrow described it, "a self-enclosed sexual paradise, where women and men could come to eat, drink, sleep and be sexually satisfied."[11] Congressman Bella Abzug and Mayor Abraham Beame even used this venue to give campaign speeches.

Sex manuals were abundant during the 1970s, including *The Joy of Sex* (1972), which sold 3.8 million copies in its first two years. People openly displayed this book on their coffee tables and the illustrations were of "everyday people," including women who didn't shave their armpit hair; the book claimed that deodorant was "banned absolutely."[12] Other manuals were *Everything You Ever Wanted to Know about Sex but Were Afraid to Ask* and *The Sensuous Man,* both of which educated readers on how to improve their sex lives. Meanwhile, novels such as Erica Jong's *Fear of Flying* (1973) portrayed uninhibited sexual relations as the ultimate act of feminism.

William Howell Masters, a gynecologist, and Virginia Eshelman Johnson, a psychologist—and wife of Masters—published groundbreaking material in the 1970s. Pioneer researchers in the field of human sexuality, they had already published *Human Sexual Response* in 1966. In 1970, they published *Human Sexual Inadequacy;* in 1975, *The Pleasure Bond;* and in 1979, *Homosexuality in Perspective.* The first two books are considered classics in the field of human sexuality research. Moreover, they began a sex therapy clinic in St. Louis, Missouri, that served as a model for clinics; they also trained therapists in their techniques, which included a male/female team of professionals. They also created a two-week treatment of sexual dysfunctions, with an 80 percent success rate.

Critics of Masters and Johnson—and of the sexual revolution as a whole—abounded. Those who opposed the overall movement included political, social, and religious conservatives; much of the clergy; and public health officials who decried the rising cases of people with sexually transmitted diseases and the increasing pregnancy rates of teenagers. More than 1 million teenagers became pregnant each year, with 87 percent of them keeping their babies—leading many to talk about "babies having babies."

The sexual revolution was blamed for the increasing divorce rates and the rising numbers of single mothers, and pornography in particular was blamed for the rising rates of crime, juvenile delinquency, and sexual deviance. Although the National Commission on Obscenity and Pornography reported in 1970 that no such correlation between pornography and crime/deviance could be found, President Nixon and others disagreed.

Meanwhile, the fight against pornography caused some feminists, who were also members of Women Against Pornography, to partner with the Moral Majority and other fundamentalist Christians to accomplish their goals, an unusual partnership indeed.

During an attempt to censor *Deep Throat,* one of the most popular porn movies ever, a psychoanalyst testified that its hedonism was paving the way toward fascism in the country. In 1974, Harry Reems was arrested on obscenity charges because of his role in this movie, the first time that an actor was charged under a 100-year-old federal obscenity law. Two years later, he and 11 others were convicted of this charge.

Although objections were widespread and not every group or person had the same concerns, one writer noted: "All critics of the liberalization of sex in the 1970s saw the phenomenon as emptying sexuality of its mystery, joy and intimacy."[13] Few remained neutral on the topic.

TURNING ON AND DROPPING OUT

In 1966, counterculture figure and former Harvard professor Timothy Leary first used the phrase, "Turn on, tune in, drop out" in a speech. In response to this directive, many youth identifying themselves as "hippies" further disassociated themselves from mainstream society. Following Leary's lead, they also used psychedelic drugs such as LSD, which was nicknamed "acid," along with psilocybin mushrooms and peyote to transcend their everyday experiences and to expand their consciousness.

Another 1960s advocate of LSD was author Ken Kesey, who wrote the best-selling novel, *One Flew over the Cuckoo's Nest,* after voluntarily ingesting hallucinogens for a governmental research project. Largely because of Leary's and Kesey's advocacy of LSD and similar substances, the use of psychedelics increased significantly in the 1960s, a trend that continued through the early 1970s; as the decade progressed, though, usage of hallucinogens dropped but did not stop.

The overall psychedelic movement was loosely connected to a subculture comprising people who protested the Vietnam War, embraced the sexual revolution, and rejected and sometimes actively rebelled against the Establishment—which encompassed the government, corporate entities, and overall consumerism. In general, hippies discarded traditional religious practices, favoring Eastern philosophies, including meditation, and they embraced the concepts of peace and love. They sometimes expressed their belief in nonviolent cultural change through "flower power," perhaps giving a flower to police, or, as hippie slang put it, to "the fuzz." Other times, they put flowers in the muzzles of guns to symbolize their philosophy and they wore flowery garb and blossoms in their hair. Often living in a communal or nomadic fashion, the diets of hippies were frequently vegetarian. Music, usually folk or rock, played an important role in their lifestyles. And, although not all hippies and advocates of the psychedelic movement used drugs, many did, either as a mind expansion tool or as a protest against conventional society.

Users of LSD—or, more accurately, lysergic acid diethylamide—referred to their hallucinogenic experiences under the influence of the drug as "trips;" they also called the experience "trippin' out." Because the mood of a user can significantly influence the way in which LSD affects his or her senses and perception of reality, unpleasant or frightening experiences became known as "bad trips" that caused users to "freak out." The drug also creates "pseudo hallucinations" in users, wherein "Colours seem to become more intense, halos or rainbows may appear around objects, and shapes may become fluid in form. Rapidly changing, brightly-coloured geometric patterns and other images may be seen, whether the eyes are open or shut."[14] During pseudo experiences, the user realizes that these unusual perceptions are not real, and he or she recognizes them as symptoms of drug use. Some users also experienced spontaneous and unpredictable "flashbacks," wherein they repeated symptoms that had occurred to them while under the influence of LSD, even though they had not recently ingested the drug—or, in their lingo, they hadn't "dropped acid."

During the 1970s, other youth—including some involved in the hippie/psychedelic movement and others living more mainstreamed lifestyles—smoked marijuana. Combining shredded flowers, stems, seeds, and leaves of *Cannabis sativa*, a member of the hemp family, users generally rolled the marijuana—or "pot" or "weed" as it was commonly known—into a cigarette form. Another option was to put the leaves into a marijuana pipe, or "bong," and smoke the substance that way. Marijuana smoke has a distinct smell, sweet and pungent, and easily recognizable. Burning incense was sometimes used to cover up the odor of the drug. Some people used the more concentrated version of the substance, called hash, which produced a stronger "high."

An entire subculture arose around marijuana use and magazines such as *High Times* served as a communication tool for pot smokers. Created in 1974 by Tom Forçade, the first issue had a print run of 10,000 and sold out almost immediately. Following the example of *Playboy*, Forçade also included centerfolds in his publication, but his were photos of high-quality cannabis plants rather than of beautiful, scantily clad women. According to the editor of *High Times*, Steve Hager, they hired the "cream of the underground press" to produce this magazine, creating a very profitable publication. Advertisers included bong and rolling paper manufacturers; by 1978, circulation figures reached half a million.

Marijuana humor was also popular among many users—and even among some people who did not smoke the drug. George Carlin crafted stand-up comedy routines around the use of marijuana, and, in 1978, comedians and actors Cheech Marin and Tommy Chong (Cheech and Chong) starred in a movie called *Up in Smoke* that focused heavily on marijuana humor. Grossing more than $41 million, this was the 12th highest-grossing film of the year.

A survey taken in 1976 indicated that 1 in every 12 teenagers used pot on a daily basis.[15] During the 1970s, there was significant debate about whether or not marijuana served as a "gateway" drug, meaning that its users were more vulnerable to moving on to more serious, "harder" drugs. Adherents of both viewpoints—that pot was or was not a gateway to other drug use—could cite statistics and quote experts, but the issue was never conclusively resolved. However, it is logical to stipulate that behavioral and psychological factors that led youth to use marijuana could also leave them susceptible to using other recreational drugs that had more serious consequences.

During the 1970s, cocaine became known as a fashionable drug for the wealthier segment of society, including celebrities. Cocaine was seen as glamorous, in part because of its high cost and in part because, during the 1970s, it was generally "sniffed" or snorted through the nose, rather than injected or smoked. Described as a "drug without a downside,"[16] members of the Grateful Dead, a psychedelic rock band, openly wore cocaine spoons around their necks while the drug was being sold to fans.

Actors Tommy Chong and Cheech Marin appear in their marijuana-themed 1978 movie comedy, Up in Smoke. *One scene, where a stray dog eats the men's burrito, was unscripted and Cheech and Chong simply ad-libbed around the food theft. Courtesy of Paramount Pictures/Photofest.*

Popular magazines furthered the notion that cocaine was fairly harm-less when used recreationally. In 1971, *Newsweek* quoted an official from Chicago's Bureau of Narcotics as saying that coke provided a good high without the danger of addiction. *Rolling Stone* called cocaine "America's star-spangled powder," and, in 1974, the *New York Times Magazine* ran an article with the headline "Cocaine: The Champagne of Drugs." *People* labeled Waylon Jennings and Jack Nicholson as part of the "'70s coke gen-eration," and, in 1977, *Newsweek* published an article stating that, "Among hostesses in the smart sets of Los Angeles and New York, a little cocaine, like Dom Perignon and Beluga caviar, is now *de rigueur* at dinners. Some partygivers pass it around along with the canapés on silver trays ... the user experiences a feeling of potency, of confidence, of energy."[17] Even the National Institute on Drug Abuse did not consider the recreational use of cocaine a problem.

Another drug, known as Ecstasy, was used by therapists and New Age advocates by the late 1970s; the drug was believed to increase intimacy. Ecstasy was also used by some gay men involved in the disco scene and this drug also carried about an air of glamour.

Seen as far less romantic was heroin, a drug with more prevalent use among inner-city dwellers and other urban poor. Some users committed illegal acts to obtain the drug, including theft and serving as a middle per-son in the drug's trafficking; therefore, heroin justifiably became associated with the increasing crime rates of the 1970s. Purity of heroin available in the 1970s was low and so injection was the only feasible way to use the drug. Users frequently overdosed on heroin and drug deaths occurred.

Some soldiers used heroin during the Vietnam War, returning home already addicted to the drug. In May 1971, Congressmen Robert Steele and Morgan Murphy released a report detailing their concerns about the "heroin epidemic" among the U.S. military in Vietnam. In September 1971, Operation Golden Flow went into effect, wherein the government tested the urine of servicemen returning to the United States. Results were encourag-ing, though, with only 4.5 percent of them testing positive for heroin.

Even before this heroin scare, as early as 1970, Congress was passing legislation in an attempt to curb illegal drug usage. The Comprehensive Drug Abuse Prevention and Control Act, for example, consolidated previ-ous drug laws and added a "no knock" search policy that strengthened law enforcement's ability to enforce the laws. Penalties for marijuana pos-session, though, were lessened in this legislation.

Eight months later, on June 17, 1971, President Richard Nixon declared a "war on drugs," calling it "public enemy number one" in the country. To counteract this crisis, he formed the Special Action Office for Drug Abuse Prevention (SAODAP); the majority of funding was to go toward treat-ment of those addicted to drugs rather than to law enforcement, a depar-ture from previous approaches.

In 1972, Nixon formed the Office of Drug Abuse Law Enforcement (ODALE) to coordinate task forces from the local level to the federal one in an attempt to cut off drug trade at the grassroots level. Meanwhile, U.S. and French law enforcement officials announced the significant disruption of the "French Connection," a heroin-based drug-trafficking business between "Corsican gangsters and the U.S. Mafia." Shortly thereafter, heroin was difficult to purchase on the East Coast of the United States. In 1973, the Drug Enforcement Administration (DEA) formed, consolidating ODALE and relevant portions of the CIA and customs agencies. Nixon resigned the following year, thus ending his administration's war on drugs; the Ford Administration kept the DEA in effect, but it did not significantly add to or change the direction being taken to combat illegal drug use.

In 1975, the Domestic Council Drug Abuse Task Force requested that the federal government prioritize its war on drugs, focusing on heroin, amphetamines, and mixed barbiturates, calling marijuana a "low-priority drug." In 1976, President Jimmy Carter took this recommendation to the next level, campaigning for the decriminalization of marijuana. Eleven states had already done so, and Carter wanted to eliminate federal penalties for possession of less than one ounce. Not all parents agreed that "pot" was harmless, though, and a group of concerned parents formed Families in Action, the first organization specifically designed to fight teenage drug use and abuse. These parents wrote to the National Institute of Drug Abuse, persuading the group to stop supporting decriminalization.

In 1978, Congress amended the Comprehensive Drug Abuse Prevention and Control Act. Law enforcement could now seize all money and property of value that was being exchanged for controlled substances. This significantly increased the potential for financial loss in connection with purchases of illegal drugs.

The following year, a key member of Colombia's cocaine cartel purchased property on the Bahamian Islands, using that land as a hub on which to refuel when flying to the United States with drug shipments. In July 1979, a deadly shootout occurred among Colombian trackers in Miami, bringing the violence of this cartel to U.S. attention.

PART TWO

POPULAR CULTURE OF THE 1970s

3

Advertising

INTRODUCTION

Shortly before—and after—the 1970s decade began, significant changes took place in the advertising world, in large part because of the increasing concern for consumer protection. Consumer rights issues rose to the forefront largely because of activist lawyer Ralph Nader, who published a significant number of investigative books that questioned the appropriateness, thoroughness, and safety of many contemporary laws, guidelines, and regulations in America; in 1971, Nader founded a group called the NGO Public Citizen that focused even more attention on health and environmental issues.

Changes that affected the advertising world included the 1969 ban on cyclamates—a sugar substitute—used in many diet drinks and food products; this ban occurred in October 1969, which required an immediate reaction by advertising firms. Three out of four American households regularly purchased products containing cyclamates and advertisers moved quickly to assure them that their clients had found healthful and tasty ways to honor the ban; advertisements during the 1970s often contained the phrase "contains no cyclamates."

Similar upheavals took place in the tobacco industry; shortly before the 1970s decade was ushered in, the company producing Pall Mall Golds and Silva Thins was prohibited from stating in ads that their cigarettes were "lower in tar than the best selling filter king"[1] and strictures continued to become more stringent for the tobacco industry during the decade.

Advertising firms also needed to walk a new tightrope, to appeal both to women who still lived the more stereotypical and traditional lifestyle of housewife and stay-at-home mom—and to those who embraced the emerging career possibilities for their gender and who resented advertisements that reflected the woman-as-housewife role as the one that best served society. Advertisers also needed to consider the woman who worked outside the home but still identified her primary role as that of homemaker and/or wife and mother.

Advertising firms at the cusp of the decade therefore needed to consider both evolving legislation and changing societal roles when creating their new ad campaigns. Rather than simply changing how they marketed a particular product, though, many companies altered their strategy in a more radical manner. According to Fred Danzig, the executive editor of *Advertising Age,* increasing numbers of companies began "trying to sell a point of view rather than a product or service. They're explaining why they chop down trees, move oil and do strip mining ... Companies want to explain how they relate to social problems. Mobil, Gulf, IBM, and the paper companies are doing it."[2] As another trend, top corporations were withdrawing their advertising accounts from firms in significant numbers, selecting competing firms to create new and hopefully more intriguing marketing campaigns. Meanwhile, the firms themselves underwent transformations. J. Walter Thompson, the largest advertising agency in the world, changed from a privately held company to a public concern. Meanwhile, Leo Burnett of Chicago bought L.P.E., Ltd, the international agency network of the London Press Exchange, which was the biggest acquisition in the advertising world to date.

These changes surely played a role in the alteration of the advertising world and contributed to the increasing number of creative and innovative marketing ideas of the 1970s. A larger variety of advertisements could also appear, as well, as the transition from 60-second to 30-second commercials was accepted as standard. Finally, advertisers also needed to contend with and consider the emerging presence of cable television. Overall, though, the general public did not object to advertising on television, considering—by a margin of 5–1—that commercials were a reasonable way to fund programs.

SUPERSTARS OF ADVERTISING AND ADVERTISING PHENOMENA

If you were watching the Super Bowl in 1977, perhaps you were rooting for the Oakland Raiders, or maybe you planned to cheer for the Minnesota Vikings. As a third option, perhaps you were simply anticipating what new commercials might appear during breaks.

If so, you wouldn't have been disappointed for, that year, Xerox created what ESPN has named the fourth-best Super Bowl commercial ever, one that—because of its irreverence—serves as "the prelude to every boundary-pushing pitch you see now."[3] In this commercial, Brother Dominic, a humble-looking monk, completes the duplication of an ancient manuscript;

he then learns that 500 more sets are needed. Slipping through a secret passageway, Dominic returns to his modern-day shop that boasts the Xerox 9200, a marvelous machine that can create two copied pages per minute. When he returns to the monastery with his completed task in hand, the head monk proclaims Dominic's work "a miracle!"

When *Advertising Age* named the top 100 advertising campaigns of the entire twentieth century, this commercial was ranked no. 85, and 20 of the advertisements on this list—one out of every five—originated during the 1970s. The number one criteria for making the list was changing the advertising business or pop culture in a significant way. Other benchmarks include propelling the brand to number one in its industry or simply being unforgettable. Although some of the earlier ads on this list appeared in print or on radio, by the 1970s, ads also appeared on television—either solely or as part of a cross-medium advertising campaign. According to analysis provided by *Advertising Age,* "the best advertising is bound eventually to emerge from the biggest categories, and the biggest categories consist of the things people most desire. People do not most desire wheat germ." Award-winning ads from the 1970s bear this out, with the most applauded commercials coming from McDonald's; Miller Lite; Burger King; Budweiser; Coca-Cola; 7-Up; and Blue Nun wine.[4]

Two commercial campaigns in the *Advertising Age* top 10 list originated in the 1970s: McDonald's "You deserve a break today" ads and Miller Lite beer's "Tastes great, less filling." Both slogans are readily recognizable even today; the former campaign gave mothers—many of whom were now trying to juggle parenthood and a career, and facing criticism because of their decision—permission to take their children to fast-food restaurants without feeling guilty.

The Miller Lite ads transformed the entire perception of a product. Prior to this campaign, beers with lower alcohol content were perceived as having less value and/or were products for women and dieters only; now the reduced alcohol and calorie content of this brand was transformed into an asset, and this strategy was later mimicked by other beer companies. In the Miller commercials, retired athletes such as Bubba Smith, Bob Uecker, and Dick Butkus debate whether the taste or the calorie level—the tastes great, less filling argument—was the primary asset of this beverage. These advertisements are credited, to a significant degree, with making Miller Lite the number one light beer in the nation.

Other 1970s advertising campaigns making the century's best 100 list—and the number assigned to them—include:

- Alka-Seltzer, various ads during 1970s, including "Plop, plop, fizz, fizz, oh, what a relief it is," (13)
- American Express, "Do you know me?," 1975 (17)
- Burger King, "Have it your way," 1973 (18)

- Budweiser, "This Bud's for you," 1970s (23)
- Chanel, "Share the fantasy," 1979 (36)
- Keep America Beautiful, "Crying Native American," 1971 (50)
- Coca-Cola, "It's the real thing," 1970 (53)
- Polaroid, "It's so simple," 1977 (56)
- 7-Up, "The Uncola," 1970s (61)
- Sunsweet Prunes, "Today the pits, tomorrow the wrinkles," 1970s (63)
- Life Cereal, "Hey, Mikey," 1972 (64)
- Perdue chicken, "It takes a tough man to make tender chicken," 1971 (65)
- Blue Nun wine, Stiller & Meara campaign, 1970s (74)
- AT&T, "Reach out and touch someone," 1979 (80)
- BMW, "The ultimate driving machine," 1975 (84)
- Xerox, "It's a miracle," 1975 (85)
- Dannon Yogurt, old people in Russia, 1970s (89)
- Jell-O, Bill Cosby with kids, 1975 (92)

Technically, one of these—that of the crying Native American—was a public service announcement (PSA). During these spots, a tear rolled down the cheek of Iron Eyes Cody after he rows his boat through a polluted waterway and then has a box of old food tossed by his feet along a highway; the message of this PSA was that "People start pollution … people can stop it. Keep America Beautiful."

This emphasis on nature and the natural extended beyond the plea for pollution control. Dow Chemical claimed to use nothing that God didn't make—this in spite of the fact that they once manufactured napalm—and both cigarette and alcohol companies shared the "naturalness" of their products with their audiences; one brewer even claimed that his beer was the "sin without the penalty."[5] Makeup ads assured women that their products were "nearly invisible" and "natural," thus sidestepping the issue of whether a truly liberated woman would feel the need to wear makeup.

During the 1970s, John Wayne taped his own PSA wherein he talked about his lung cancer and urged others to see their doctors for a checkup. The National Association of Broadcasters filmed a spot in which a little boy played innocent childhood games while the music of the "Bingo" song ("B … I … N … G … O … and Bingo was his name-o") played in the background; ironically, one of the "innocent" games involved the boy pretending to be shot. The thrust of this PSA was that broadcasters wanted youth to hear appropriate messages on television; bad guys wouldn't be portrayed as heroes and youth would learn that "crime doesn't pay." Yet another PSA played the sound of children reciting the Pledge of Allegiance.

Iron Eyes Cody appears in an antipollution public service announcement on television. In this PSA, he sheds a tear for the earth after gazing at a polluted river. Courtesy of Photofest.

Although the advertisements of the 1970s did not have the message depth of the PSAs, *Advertising Age* calls these ads "important artifacts in our culture. Woe betide future anthropologists and historians who try to trace the American experience without pondering what, exactly, it is that her hairdresser knows for sure … these campaigns have discovered our humanity. They have touched us, understood us, reflected our lives and often enough enriched them."[6] No cigarette ads from the 1970s appeared on the top 100 list; this is to a large degree because commercials hawking cigarettes were banned from television on January 2, 1971, a year after the Federal Trade Commission established strict truth-in-advertising standards for the tobacco industry.

If you're wondering why the television ban didn't begin on January 1, here's the answer. The government made a concession to the tobacco industry and allowed it to advertise on New Year's Day, a big day for football and other programs that were tailor-made for cigarette ads and sales. This ban also applied to radio advertising, so the tobacco industry changed its focus to advertising in magazines, newspapers, billboards, rapid transit advertising venues, and the sponsorship of sporting events. People appearing in cigarette ads now tended to be stylish, attractive women.

The use of women in advertising was a hot topic during this decade, with countless people and organizations weighing in with opinions. In a well-publicized reversal of the expected, a camera panned a pair of feet, calves, and thighs of a pantyhose wearer—which turned out to be those of New York Jets football player and celebrity Joe Namath wearing a pair of Hanes. His punch line? "I don't wear pantyhose, but if Beauty Mist can make my legs look good, imagine what they'll do for yours." Although Namath managed to instill a sense of lighthearted fun into his commercial, more radical feminists expressed feelings of outrage about how women were portrayed in advertisements.

One female writer, who preferred to remain anonymous, bashed the media for supporting sexism by aiming its fashion, cosmetics, and feminine hygiene ads at the men in the audience. According to this woman, advertising in America encouraged men to expect women to "sport all the latest trappings of sexual slavery" and reinforced the notion that a woman must be a sexual object—and must use clothes and makeup to achieve that end.[7] In fact, sales of cosmetics, fragrance, and hair care products suffered during the 1970s.

The Boston Collective also took a stand against the contemporary use of women in advertising, stating that:

Our legs, busts, mouths, fingers, hair, abdomens, and vaginas are used to sell stockings, bras, fashions, cosmetics, hair coloring, a multitude of birth-control products that men would not consider using in any form, powders, sprays, perfumes (again to make us smell "nice" for men because our own smells are not good enough), and such obscene things as deodorant for our vaginas.[8]

Feminist leader Gloria Steinem therefore faced a difficult dilemma when she spearheaded *Ms.* magazine in 1972. Although she wished to share the news of liberated women, she also needed funds from advertisers to publish her magazine. Controversy existed from the beginning; the first issue of *Ms.* sported a large ad of a slender, beautiful, and bikini-clad blonde who advocated the use of Coppertone suntan lotion, and many readers wrote to protest the ad's appearance. Steinem never did stop running beauty ads in her publication; in fact, she sought out sponsorship from Revlon, a major cosmetic corporation.

Revlon itself responded to the trend of feminine liberation by creating a cologne named "Charlie" that was advertised to the "new woman"; ads portrayed a single career woman who was thrilled to be wearing this fragrance. Perhaps Charles of the Ritz even more successfully captured the essence of the times via its perfumes. Creating a scent called "Enjoli," the jingle showed a woman singing, "I can bring home the bacon, fry it up in a pan, and never, ever let him forget he's a man." This seemed to portray the dual roles of women during this transitional decade in a way that other advertisements could not.

More traditional portrayals of women still saturated the media, however; although nearly 50 percent of women held jobs by the mid-1970s, many advertisements still portrayed them, as *Time* magazine put it, as "scattered homebodies, barely able to cope with piles of soiled laundry, dirty sinks and other mundane minutiae."[9] To address these disparities, the National Advertising Review Board (NARB) met in 1975 to create a set of standards to avoid stereotyping women in advertising. Guidelines formed include avoidance of:

- belittling language such as "gal Friday," "lady professor," "weaker sex," or "ball and chain"
- double entendres, especially focusing on sex or female bodies
- unrealistic promises, that is, that a perfume would lead to instant romance[10]

This last guideline addressed the prevalent impression given by advertisements that, "in America, any moral and hardworking citizen could obtain, if not success, at least happiness through materialistic consumption."[11]

While advertisers struggled to change their portrayal of women, another group—the Mexican Americans or "Chicanos"—also fought against stereotypes in advertising. Their efforts were somewhat successful, as they forced Arrid deodorant to stop using a Chicano in an ad in which the message was, "If it works for him, it will work for you," as well as the "Frito Bandito" ads that portrayed "Mexican Americans as indolent, criminal, and filthy."[12]

Black Americans were also protesting their lack of accurate portrayal on television, including its advertisements. A 1978 study conducted by Michigan State University underscored the consequences of inaccurate portrayals on television. According to its research:

- Black children believed that television was "very true to life."
- Forty-six percent of elementary school children believed that blacks on television were representative of blacks in real life.
- Commercials were more believable for black children than white children.
- More than 50 percent of all black children between the ages of 5 and 12 believed that commercials present true and accurate information.[13]

The question, then, is how accurately were black Americans portrayed in advertisements? In research published in 1970 (culled from 1967–1968) only 2 percent of 11,000 advertisements contained black models. The researcher,

Keith Cox, concluded, though, that the portrayal of black Americans had improved; in 1949–1950, media references showed this demographic group in lower-skilled jobs such as maids and cooks, but the 1967–1968 ads did not.[14] In research published in 1972 by David Colfax and Susan Sternberg, that conclusion was refuted; the duo felt that because half of the blacks in the advertisements studied by Cox were musicians displaying their album covers, the shift of the portrayal of black Americans was nowhere near as dramatic as what he reported.[15]

Later in the decade, Dr. George Gerbner reviewed 2,556 television commercials (1977–1979) and discovered that advertisements with white actors are shown 7 out of 10 times; commercials with black actors were aired less than 2 out of 100 times.[16]

Another study compared 1,431 advertisements in *Time, Sports Illustrated, Women's Day, Newsweek, Vogue,* and *Esquire* in the years 1959, 1969, and 1979: 95.9 percent of the advertisements featured white actors; out of the 48 ads with black models, they posed with white actors in 39 of them, leaving only 9 ads with solely black actors. Marilyn Kern-Foxworth, in *Aunt Jemima, Uncle Ben, and Rastus: Blacks in Advertising, Yesterday, Today, and Tomorrow,*[17] concluded that without pressure from civil rights organizations, this representation of blacks would continue in the media. So, although scholars were looking at the role of black actors and models in advertising during the 1970s, significant progress was not made toward a more realistic depiction of this population.

Meanwhile, another group—that of the working class—was also receiving short shrift in advertising. Research conducted by Robert Goldman indicates that the only commercials from the 1970s portraying the working class were truck ads and beer ads, and the most common worksites in ads were auto assembly lines and building construction sites. However, those commercials did present these workers in a positive light as they showed coal miners and construction workers as the core of American society.

During the latter part of the decade, overall, industry tried hard to overcome its image of employing an increasingly disinterested workforce, one that no longer cared about quality. The most known attempt may be Whirlpool's ad containing this message: "Is this country in the autumn of its time? They say that we have lost our pride, and quality no longer is a way of life." Automobile manufacturers perhaps felt this negative perception most keenly, and, in a clever dual marketing move, a Budweiser ad featured a black foreman in a car manufacturing plant. He was competent and he solved problems well, and his peers accepted him and they applauded his accomplishments.

Meanwhile, the oil industry tried a different tactic to improve its image, which suffered because of rising energy prices: it began sponsoring programs on the Public Broadcasting System (PBS) with Mobil's *Masterpiece Theatre* hosted by Alistair Cooke serving as a prime example; the show debuted in January 1971. In 1977, when oil company funding for public television had increased 10 times since the beginning of the decade, cynics began suggesting that PBS really stood for "Petroleum Broadcasting Service." Print ads for *Masterpiece Theatre, Mystery!,* and *Upstairs, Downstairs* appeared in the *New York Times* and the *Washington Post,* thanks to oil industry sponsorship, and Mobil Information Center spots appeared before the news broadcasts, discussing progrowth philosophies of off-shore oil drilling and other proenergy policies that were often protested by environmental groups and frequently restricted by governmental legislation.

Although the oil industry had used print ads to its advantage, newspaper and magazine ads had in fact been declining. Perhaps the high visibility of television during the 1970s—plus internal issues with magazine publishing—was what caused advertisers to turn away from print publications; to recover, the magazine industry began developing an increasing number of special-interest—or niche—publications, a trend that continues today. In these publications, readers interested in very specific information could find what they needed, and advertisers could more effectively target their audiences. As another strategy, magazine companies began advertising on television, usually offering an incentive to purchase their products. Successful cross-pollination among industries therefore occurred; as another example of this, a television commercial for Coca-Cola that featured football player "Mean" Joe Greene in 1979 later served as the basis for an NBC movie.

The Joe Greene commercial focused on his unexpected kindness to a child, and it was during the 1970s that companies appealed to children during the Saturday morning cartoon time; ads for sugary cereals predominated. In fact, by 1976, 43 percent of the commercials on Saturday mornings were for breakfast cereal, followed by candy ads—and then promotions for fast-food restaurants. This was the era of Trix cereal and Sugar Crisp, and toys were often placed in the boxes to entice children to ask for them. In an interesting twist, Quaker Oats selected three freckle-faced boys to feature in its Life Cereal ad; the theme was that, even though the cereal was "good for you," it still tasted good. The two older boys refused to sample the cereal; pushing it in front of their youngest brother, Mikey, they assumed that he'd dislike the taste because he "hates everything." To their surprise, Mikey begins devouring Life Cereal and the older brothers exclaim, "He likes it! Hey, Mikey!" This successful ad continued to run for 15 years.

In 1970, Action for Children's Television attempted to have all commercials eliminated from children's programming; although that initiative was not successful, legislation became effective on January 1, 1973, that reduced ads during children's television programs from 16 minutes per hour to 12. Also banned were the mentioning of specific commercial products in a program and the use of cartoon characters or other recognizable show hosts in ads shown during youth programming. Further restrictions occurred in 1975, when nonprogram material (advertisements) during weekend children's programming was limited to 10 minutes per hour.

THE NEW MARKETS

Although network television clearly featured some of the most memorable—and most likely effective—advertising of the decade, it also faced competition. In 1969, Public Broadcasting Service (PBS or "public television") debuted, and this form of programming depended upon corporate sponsorships and private donations, rather than funds collected from companies wishing to run advertisements during commercial breaks. Viewers therefore had a choice that included watching programming—albeit limited at first—that did not feature slick commercials. One of the initial PBS programs was Jim Henson's *Sesame Street,* an award-winning children's program that aimed to teach preschool children the basic skills needed for kindergarten. Characters included Ernie and Bert, Big Bird, Cookie Monster, Grover, and Oscar the Grouch. In 1975, AT&T began sponsoring PBS news programming; initially called the *Robert McNeil Report,* the show became better known under its revised name of the *McNeil-Lehrer Report.*

From left to right, Matt Robinson, Will Lee, and Diana Sands appear on an episode of Sesame Street *from the early 1970s. Revolutionary elements of the program included the mixing of humans and puppets in skits and the inner-city environment of the set. Courtesy of PBS/Photofest.*

Another competitor to network television was actually invented during the 1940s but was seldom used until the 1970s: Community Antenna Television, or, as it is better known, cable TV. Its original function was to bring programming into communities where poor or nonexistent reception prevented the more standard form of television from airing—and, in fact, the FCC attempted to keep the usage of cable television in rural areas only. As regulations loosened during the 1970s, though, increasing numbers of households subscribed; in 1975, 10 million viewers and 3,506 cable systems existed, but, 10 years later, there were 40 million cable television subscribers—and advertisers needed to be cognizant of the changing markets. The dizzying choice of channels, each boasting its own demographics, presented advertisers with a whole new set of challenges and choices.

Throughout the 1970s, another form of "free-floating billboards,"[18] as Peter Carroll describes the phenomenon, existed. T-shirts proclaimed political statements and religious beliefs, while bands and sports teams sold shirts in mass quantities as a form of promotion. In 1975, Anheuser-Busch gave away shirts with the Budweiser beer logo to college students on spring break in Miami and San Diego, and, "to return to school with a Bud shirt became a supreme status symbol among party animals." Its success paved the way to shirts featuring any number of products—and the shirts were no longer given away for free. People began paying to buy ones that advertised their favorite products.[19]

Meanwhile, an increasing number of cars contained bumper stickers, many of them identifying the driver with a certain political or ideological group; others attempted to turn common sentiments upside down. One such bumper sticker read, "If you don't like cops ... next time you're in trouble, call a hippie!"

4
Architecture

INTRODUCTION

A little dome or fountain here; an arch or fluted column there; maybe
something half hidden, waiting to delight the discoverer—and pretty
soon you're having fun, breaking out of your rut, forgetting to be
boring.[1]

Architecture during the 1970s followed, in general, one of two movements:
international modernism or postmodernism. The first style employed
glass, steel, and concrete as materials in buildings that had regular geometric shapes and open interiors. Using this style, architects designed a
series of buildings, each of which successively became the world's tallest
structure. These included the John Hancock Center in Chicago; the twin
towers of the World Trade Center in New York City; and the Sears Tower,
also in Chicago. In postmodernism, architects attempted to insert the unexpected into buildings in ways that were both whimsical and thought-
provoking. The familiar was turned upside down—figuratively, of course,
but sometimes almost literally, as well. Architects might select shapes and
features symbolically, or they might choose a particular element simply
to be fanciful. The public, overall, was intrigued by postmodern projects,
which ranged from buildings that somewhat resembled those of the international modernism style to ones that incorporated elements of more
ancient architectural styles. Architects from previous decades continued in
their positions of influence during the 1970s. They included—but are certainly not limited to—William L. Pereira, Charles Moore, I. M. Pei, Paolo
Soleri, Philip Johnson, and Frank Gehry.

Economic difficulties during the 1970s, including the dual energy crises, caused many smaller architectural firms—and some larger ones—to
close their doors. Business costs were rising at a time when their potential

clients' budgets were also tightening. To partially address rising heating costs, architectural firms attempted to employ energy-saving solutions such as wind and solar energy options in homes and offices as they analyzed the advantages and disadvantages of passive systems, which use no moving or motorized parts, versus the more traditional active heating systems.

During the 1970s, architects of note were experimenting with offbeat building shapes, using unusual—and sometimes recycled—materials. Meanwhile, as they designed and then oversaw construction of these new buildings, another movement gained momentum in the United States: the preservation of historic buildings.

LEADING FIGURES OF AMERICAN ARCHITECTURE
William L. Pereira

Chicago-born architect William L. Pereira completed more than 400 projects during his long and illustrious career, with perhaps his most famous—the pyramid-shaped Transamerica Building located in San Francisco—being built in 1972. Many residents resisted his notion of the pyramid structure, but Pereira stood by his professional opinion that this shape would allow the presence of more light and air into the surrounding area. This building, according to Pereira and his vision, would be a piece of architectural sculpture. Although not immediately, Pereira's viewpoint came to be the majority one.

Pereira, who worked in California, became well known for his futuristic designs as well as for his ability to envision and plan entire cities. Credited for developing much of Orange County, he designed a number of unique buildings at the University of California at Irvine that featured unusual concrete patterns. When designing the campus buildings, he imagined a place wherein a diverse group of people from a wide variety of socioeconomic backgrounds could live together and mutually respect their environment. Perhaps he achieved this goal even more than anticipated, for not only did humans populate the area, but in 1972, the movie *Conquest of the Planet of the Apes* was filmed at this university, with the campus serving as "Ape City"!

Pereira's respect for the environment apparently resonated with many during the ecologically aware decade of the 1970s. This architect strongly believed that people must respect nature while building their towns and cities, saying that "We are at our poorest when we, as nature's most complex instrument, turn on our environment. But we are at our best when we are nature itself and commence to build in order to supplement nature's own bounty."[2] He added that city planning must also focus significantly on its transportation systems, as well as its educational, technological, and scientific aspects. Leisure activities, Pereira believed, were also vital to a community's well-being. His architectural firm created concepts that became commonplace, including zero lot lines and a combination kitchen and family room located at the rear of houses.

Perhaps it wasn't surprising, after all, that Pereira's buildings served as the set for a Hollywood movie, for he began his architectural career in the 1930s by designing movie sets. Moreover, he won three Oscars, including an Academy Award in 1942 for best special effects in *Reap the Wild Wind*. It wasn't just Pereira's work that appeared in the media, either; his photo served as the cover of *Time* magazine in 1963, with a banner reading, "Vistas for the Future" appearing along the top of the page.

At least one critic used Pereira's movie connections to criticize his architectural designs. *San Francisco Chronicle* critic Allen Temko, who disliked the pyramid design of the Transamerica Building, claimed that Pereira was "Hollywood's idea of an architect." Temko was apparently referencing Pereira's "lifestyle, his statuesque figure, his penchant for Bentleys and Lear Jet travel, his preferential dress in black and white, and the perennial blondes and British that seemed to surround him."[3] His high-profile friends included Walt and Roy Disney; he enjoyed being chauffeured, sailing at a yacht club, being dressed by a manservant, and having his housekeeper serve tea to his guests. He also loved teaching young architects his craft.

Charles Moore

Architect Charles Moore embodied a sense of gleeful fun in the work that he did—and even in his own home. Features that Moore added to the previously nondescript structure that became his home included a wave-topped gate; a boxy wooden tower; a variety of lighting fixtures above jam-packed bookcases that created a sense of columns; a floor that was painted with geometric shapes; a fireplace mantel surrounded by palm trees; and "colors, nooks, sculptures, curios you couldn't begin to put names to, toys and more toys. Steps lead up to a pillow-filled conversation area, from which a window looks out on vine-covered pergolas and a pool. Poke your head up the narrow side stair: There's a tiny loft for guests."[4] Architecture students visited Moore at this home, and friends attended parties there, marveling at his glorious imagination.

Moore designed more than 180 buildings during his career and a Smithsonian writer dubbed him the Frank Lloyd Wright of this era. He mentored aspiring architects, who frequently traveled with him to Mexico, and he encouraged them to incorporate vigorous colors and vivacious details in their work. Moore told them to avoid being boring; wherever Moore went, one student claimed, groups of people followed him in an atmosphere of open doors and friendly chaos.

I. M. Pei

Ieoh Ming (I. M.) Pei, Chinese by birth and educated at the Massachusetts Institute of Technology (MIT) and at Harvard University, is known for his architectural work with stone, concrete, glass, and steel, as well as for his sophistication, large-scale vision, and bold and high-tech geometric designs. He rose to national prominence after Jacqueline Kennedy selected him to design the John F. Kennedy Library in Boston in 1964.

Pei, who designed the Rock and Roll Hall of Fame in Cleveland, Ohio, post-1970s, has been credited with the transformation of the museum concept from a highbrow and exclusive institution to a welcoming and educational type of community center where people can gather to learn about pop culture and overall society. Pei served on many art and cultural boards of directors, including the Metropolitan Museum of Art, and 16 prestigious universities granted him honorary doctorate degrees.

He received many awards during the 1970s, as well, including membership to the American Academy and Institute of Arts and Letters in 1975; only 50 living members are allowed into this academy. In 1978, he became the first architect to serve as this prestigious organization's chancellor. When selected as the Pritzker Architecture Prize Laureate in 1983, Pei was recognized by the jury for his ability to create beautiful architecture by incorporating a skillful—even poetic—use of materials. In his acceptance speech for this award, Pei pointed out that his style was not always appreciated; in the 1940s, he said, he had designed a house for a friend and the bank decided not to mortgage this property because it looked too modern.

Paolo Soleri

Italian-born architect Paolo Soleri, who studied with Frank Lloyd Wright during the 1940s, has been called a "visionary" because he spent a significant portion of his time attempting to address humankind's problems. Focusing on alternate urban planning models, he became deeply concerned about overpopulation in the world and the growth of urban sprawl; he therefore directed his energy to finding architectural solutions to these significant issues—and his overall solution was a concept called an *arcology*. An arcology is, according to Soleri, an ecologically friendly way for people to live in the world, and it is a revolutionary way to consider building design.

Soleri published 30 examples of arcologies in 1970, creating models of high-density structures that could house up to 6 million people, wherein people enjoyed largely self-sufficient lives in the desert. He proposed to use the minimum amount of material possible in his structures, to give people the opportunity to provide service to themselves—but also to their biosphere. In a 2001 interview, Soleri stressed the importance of function in architecture, even if it surpassed aesthetics; he also expressed his philosophy that humans were not meant to live in single-family dwellings.

Philip Johnson

Born in Cleveland, Ohio, Johnson was a Harvard-educated architect whose first job of significance was as the Director of the Department of Architecture at the Museum of Modern Art in New York. Johnson was, already, no stranger to controversy. He didn't inspire consensus. His advocates described his work as brilliant, but his detractors labeled him as uninspired. Prone to stirring up debate about his architectural skills, Johnson worried that his personal life might cause him to lose work. In 1977, he said that he asked *New Yorker* magazine to omit reference to his homosexuality, for fear that AT&T might send its business elsewhere.

In 1978, he won the Gold Medal of the American Institute of Architects, and, in 1979, he served as the first architect selected to receive the Pritzker Architecture Prize; this prize was created to encourage "greater awareness of the way people perceive and interact with their surroundings," and Johnson was selected because of 50 years of imaginative designs of a wide range of public buildings, including libraries and museums, as well as houses and office space. From 1967–1987, he partnered with John Burgee to design these types of buildings. He was well known for helping young architects, and it was said that his table in New York's Grill Room often served as a minisalon of architecture.

HOMES, STORES, AND OFFICES

Architects during the 1960s built primarily in the modernism style, and, as the decade progressed, buildings became even more sleek and contemporary. Near the end of the 1960s, though, builders began to also resurrect more traditional forms of housing, borrowing elements from a variety of eras and cultures for inspiration; this phase is now called *Neo-Eclectic*. These homes could be Neo-French, for example, or Neo-Colonial, Neo-Tudor, Neo-Mediterranean, Neoclassical Revival, or Neo-Victorian. Regardless of genre, the builder or developer would select a few carefully chosen, historically relevant features to add style and character to the homes. Houses such as these were built in suburbs throughout the country, as were apartment buildings. Architects were not significantly involved in designing these developments as builders chose basic building designs and then added appropriate details to create the look that he or she desired.

Early in this Neo-Eclectic phrase, the mansard style of roofing was popular; a mansard is actually a double roof wherein the bottom one— on all four sides of the building—was nearly vertical and the upper one basically horizontal; this created extra attic space. Builders found this roofing style to be a relatively inexpensive way to add flourish to an otherwise conventional structure. These roofs could be embellished in a variety of eye-catching ways, including with the creative use of shingles.

Some experts question whether or not postmodern structures could in fact be called part of a style, because the term *Neo-Eclectic* refers to the revival of an architectural style from the past. In fact, Neoclassical Revival architecture made its third appearance in America in the 1970s. Nevertheless, this is what builders offered their customers during much of the decade, and, overall, clients appreciated these designs, which were a remarkably different style from the sleek and streamlined modernism structures from the previous decade. Perhaps people became interested in postmodernism homes during the 1970s because of the approaching bicentennial celebration of the United States; because of this commemorative event, matters of the past were occupying more of the country's attention than was typical. This resurgence also occurred at a time when many Americans were becoming more interested in the historical preservation movement.

Also popular in the 1970s were Tudor A-frame houses, especially for vacation and beach homes, and for rural getaway retreats. In Tudor A-frames, the side walls of the homes were angled to create a sharp peak at the roof. Second-story rooms were often loftlike in design but more spacious than what it might appear from the outside.

Two specific homes designed during the 1970s deserve special mention: the self-designed Frank Gehry House and the Brant House designed by Robert Venturi. Gehry, a professional architect, would create structures out of scraps of material, including plywood and corrugated metal—and eventually concrete—which resulted in a collagelike appearance in his buildings that some compared to architectural sculpting.

Located in California, the Gehry House has been described as a collusion of parts. After acquiring the structure, Gehry first removed much of its interior, exposing the rafters and studs. He then surrounded the home with metal, including aluminum siding, along with "plywood, glass and chain-link fencing, and … randomly slanted lines and angled protrusions. Although the house retains a certain minimalist sense, the effort here is cluttered expressionistic and the sensibility is freely intended as artistically intuitive, of accident not resolved."[5] Not surprisingly, the architect also designed a line of furniture crafted from corrugated cardboard. In 1979, Gehry used chain-link fencing when constructing the Cabrillo Marine Museum, connecting the structures in the 20,000-square-foot compound.

The Brant House serves as a tribute to pop culture and Art Deco. Built for a young couple in Greenwich, Connecticut, who were wishing to display their modern art, the two shades of green-glazed brick on the exterior serve as another form of artistic expression. Located in a gently wooded area, the environment is serene and peaceful.

Meanwhile, Paolo Soleri and his assistants deserve credit for their ambitious attempts to invent a whole new way of living. In 1970, they envisioned an archetype of a town, to be located just north of Phoenix, Arizona, and to be called Arcosanti.

Soleri believed that a single-story—and a single-usage—building is an enormous waste of resources, creating the need for more transportation, and, therefore, more energy. In Arcosanti, however, stores, homes, and offices would coexist within the same multipurpose buildings, and residents could walk to any building in Arcosanti within 10 minutes. In a town with gentle winters, people could walk year-round—and because the amount of time needed for transportation purposes would be reduced, people could spend more time focusing on the renewal of human relationships and connections.

If and when completed, the city of Arcosanti could house between 5,000 and 7,000 residents; its construction is slow and deliberate, however, as it is funded through the sale of wind bells and tiles, some of which cost several thousand dollars. Labor is volunteer-based and led by Soleri; some workers have already lived on-site for 25 years. Buildings are in the shape of one-fourth of a sphere, and can "absorb the spare winter desert sunlight and reflect its punishing heat during the summer."[6] It is anticipated that Arcosanti would require only 2 percent of the typical amount of land needed for an American town housing 6,000 people.

Two stores built in the 1970s became well known for their architectural ingenuity. First is the Best Products Showroom located in Houston, Texas. Built out of white brick, the bricks in the front of the building appear to be tumbling down, toward the heads of shoppers entering the building. Intended to symbolize the overpackaging of America's consumer society, this concept was described as "de-architecturisation." The other store known for its creative design is the Pacific Design Center, located in West Hollywood, California. Very large—with more than 100 million cubic feet of space—and constructed of blue glass, the store became known as the "Blue Whale."

PUBLIC BUILDINGS

Postmodern architects, remember, figuratively turned the familiar upside down, and I. M. Pei's most famous structure from 1978 almost literally stands upside down. Constructed out of concrete and glass, and serving as the city hall building for Dallas, Texas, it has been described by observers as a right triangle with a point turned down. The ground-level floor of the city hall is, unlike in most buildings, smallest in size; each floor is then larger than the one below, creating a unique, jutting appearance. Upper floors of the building thereby create shade from the hot Texas sun for those waiting by the front door. Pei also created a park—including a fountain—around this structure to create a welcoming atmosphere for this city's central building.

Another building that reflected well upon Pei's architectural abilities is the East Building of the National Gallery of Art in Washington, D.C. John Russell Pope had designed the West Building, which was completed in 1941, in a classical style. Pei and his partners needed to keep the shape and style of the West Building in mind as they created more than 150 drafts of their proposed designs for the East Building. Meanwhile, they faced a significant challenge: the space allotted for their building was shaped like a trapezoid. After they solved this problem and a design was chosen, Pei and his partners constructed an "H-shaped" building; the American Institute of Architects selected this unique 1979 structure as one of the 10 best buildings in the United States.

Some of Charles Moore's most famous buildings were also constructed in the 1970s, including the Piazza d'Italia, located in New Orleans (1976–1979). This glorious mixture of arches and pillars and steps honored the Italian contribution to the city of New Orleans, and observers often find it inspiring. Moore crafted the Burns House in Santa Monica Canyon in 1974; its stucco colors include ochre, orange, and mauve. He built the home on a steep slope; right outside the lower level is a swimming pool and terrace. Another famous building of his design is Kresge College at the University of California at Santa Cruz; built in 1973, the "L-shaped layout rambles through a redwood forest, widening, narrowing, twisting along its central 'street' in his version of the 'Italian hill town'."[7]

One of Phillip Johnson's best-known buildings erected during the 1970s was the Pennzoil Plaza located in Houston, Texas. Described as a "geometrically manipulative, modernist approach" to architecture, this building was "a simple geometric idea, prompted also by not wanting to design a straight-up and unbroken tower," which "affords total visual clarity to the design."[8] In this building, two towers, each 36 stories in height, are located in triangular-shaped plazas. The towers are crafted from bronze glass and dark brown aluminum, a significant contrast to the painted white steel trusses in the roof; the trusses were decorated in a filigree pattern. Johnson also used significant whimsy while designing the AT&T Building—now the Sony Building—in New York City in 1979; using granite panels of pinkish-brown rather than glass, he topped off the building with a shape that reminded some of the top of a Chippendale highboy chest, while still others saw in it a car grille or the top of a grandfather clock.

A public building that used the postmodern technique of recreating ancient archeological styles is the Getty Museum in Los Angeles, California. Modeled after a first-century Roman country house, including columns and quaint gardens, the museum showcased ancient Greek, Roman, and Etruscan art. Two other museums built in the 1970s are the Kimball Art

Museum in Fort Worth, Texas, designed by Louis Kahn, and the National Air and Space Museum in Washington, D.C., designed by Gyo Obata.

The design of the Kimball Art Museum has been called timeless, with its vaultlike structure, and Kahn's perfectionism was compared to that used in creating classic Greek architecture. Funding for Obata's project—the National Air and Space Museum—was delayed because of the Vietnam War, but groundbreaking took place in 1972. Design challenges for this project were daunting: he needed to create a building that would accommodate huge crowds and appropriately display enormous aeronautical equipment. Obata chose to use pink granite as the exterior to match the West Building of the National Gallery of Art, located nearby; he echoed the same basic geometry of that building, as well. Reinforced truss structures were constructed to support the heavy displays and marble blocks were used to create floor display space.

Another public building constructed in the 1970s that was considered among the country's best was the Marin County Civic Building in California. This building was designed by Frank Lloyd Wright in 1958 but not completed until 1972. Nearly a quarter of a mile long, the building consists of a series of arches and was said to resemble a Roman aqueduct.

PRESERVING HISTORY

In 1966, the National Historic Preservation Act (NHPA) codified federal policies to help preserve historic structures in America. According to this act, the federal government would increase its efforts to aid governmental and private agencies, as well as individuals, to accelerate historic preservation programs and activities. Overall, legislation passed during the 1960s began the shift in focus from the preservation of a single home to the creation of historic districts across the nation.

This trend continued when President Gerald Ford signed into law the Housing and Community Development Act of 1974, wherein Community Development Block Grants (CDBGs) were created. Under this system, local communities could decide how their allotted funds should be spent, determining this through a series of public hearings. Frequent CDBG choices included improvements in a community's infrastructure and property rehabilitation loans. Savannah, Georgia, and Charleston, South Carolina, especially benefited from revolving loans given for house rehabilitation. Successful projects of significance include Ghirardelli Square in San Francisco, Quincy Market in Boston, and Pike Place Market in Seattle.

In 1974, Preservation Action, a national lobbying group, formed. Representatives of this group, which included local community activists and preservation experts, historians, and civic and commercial leaders, monitored federal legislation that might affect the historic preservation movement. In 1976, Congress passed the Tax Reform Act, which eliminated the incentive that had existed for people who demolished older buildings. The 1978 Revenue Act furthered the advantages of restoring older buildings by establishing a tax credit for property owners who rehabilitated historic properties. These pieces of legislation, along with the enthusiasm growing for the United States Bicentennial, fueled an interest in many people to creatively adapt older structures for modern living.

Information gathered by annual surveys conducted by the National Trust for Historic Preservation, Mainstreet programs, and tourism organizations in the 1970s spurred local governments to join in this preservation effort. The surveys indicated that cities and towns that focused on historic preservation benefited economically. Locales with historic districts tended to witness increased property values, both residential and commercial, with homes and businesses within the confines of the historical district experiencing the greatest increases. Historic districts, studies determined, created specialized local jobs and encouraged tourism. Furthermore, people are generally more willing to invest in their neighborhood, the studies concluded, perceiving the value in such an investment.

People remodeling homes could, starting in 1973, refer to the *Old House Journal.* This magazine provided information to those wishing to renovate, maintain, and decorate homes that were more than 50 years old, offering practical, step-by-step information for those new to the process.

That said, not everyone was pleased with preservation legislation. In 1978, the Supreme Court heard a case that would determine the legitimate power of historic district designation and its corresponding standards; the case was *Penn Central Transportation Co. v. New York City.* Penn Central wished to erect an office skyscraper above the 1913 Grand Central Terminal that was considered an historical landmark under New York's Landmarks Preservation Law. This proposed skyscraper met all zoning laws, but Penn Central needed permission from the Landmarks Preservation Commission, as well. The commission rejected the request, as it would damage part of the Grand Central Terminal.

When the case made it to the Supreme Court, Penn Central testified that it would lose millions of dollars annually if it could not build this skyscraper, but, with a 6–3 vote, the court ruled for the city of New York and the skyscraper was not built. Those dissenting pointed out the lack of comprehensive labeling of landmarks; was it fair, they questioned, to limit owners of registered landmarks while allowing countless other historic buildings without an official designation to go unprotected? This question was not answered.

5

Fashion

INTRODUCTION

> The 1970s was a period of self-expression, experimentation and soul-searching. From humble working class denims to high style disco garments, fashions mirrored the changing attitudes that contributed to the emergence of a plethora of new provocative and powerful styles … In both politics and fashion, ideas that were once subversive made their way to the forefront and contributed to the abolishment of autocratic rules.[1]

People in the United States had a relaxed attitude about clothing styles during the 1970s. This is the decade of athletic shoes and warm-up suits as fashion statements, of denim as high style. T-shirts were plentiful and jewelry was funky. Even one of the more formal pieces of attire—the leisure suit—was known by a name that implied the casual.

Although French designers continued to provide some influence on American fashion, the 1970s was also the decade wherein the work of U.S. fashion designers appeared on the Parisian stage—albeit for charity fundraising purposes—and the time in which American women declared some independence from the dictates of European designers. As they shed the look of the French designers, though, they incorporated style elements from Africa, Asia, and the Near East, so their independence from foreign influence was in no way complete.

Younger—and some older—Americans embraced more extreme fashions of the decade, wearing the tallest of shoes and the skimpiest of outfits, while rockers introduced outrageous new looks that became known as punk and glam fashions.

AMERICAN INFORMALITY

Nothing says American informality like Nike—both the athletic shoes bearing that trade name and its embroidered "swoosh" symbol that closely resembles a sharply impatient checkmark slashing through the air. Prior to the rise of Nike, the notion of athletic shoe as fashion statement would have seemed absurd. In 1972, though, Portland State University instructor Phil Knight paid advertising student Caroline Davis $35 to design a logo for the lightweight athletic shoes that he was selling out of the trunk of his car—and thus the notion of Nike was born.

Whether the fitness and running boom skyrocketed the sales of Nike shoes—or if shoes such as Nike expedited the exercise trends of the 1970s—the fact is that a simple pair of shoes became strongly connected to a cultural transformation. "Working out" was much more than a fashion statement in the 1970s. Instead, it became a way for people to concentrate on themselves—on their identities as athletes and on their bodies—and what could more appealing than this intense self-focus during the "Me Decade"?

By the spring of 1972, consumers could buy a shoe complete with Nike's swoosh—and Knight raked in $3.2 million in sales that year alone. Each year throughout the decade, sales doubled, and, as more and more Americans wore athletic shoes—even if they weren't necessarily athletes—it became a status symbol to at least appear as someone who exercised.

What precisely, though, did one wear with Nike shoes? In a clever marketing move, the company created a Nike T-shirt that actually debuted before the shoes with the swoosh. Sweatsuits were also fashion statements in the 1970s, worn by people who exercised—and by those who lounged. *Sports Illustrated* in 1972 declared the warm-up suit as one of the hottest fashions around, one worn by people of all ages, genders, and shapes. Warm-up suits came in a wide variety of appealing colors and were generally at least 50 percent polyester, thereby keeping their form better than those made entirely from cotton in the previous decade; people wore them with coordinating headbands. These suits also served as an all-purpose garment; according to writers Jane and Michael Stern, one could "spill Tang down the front and drip a jelly donut on your lap and let the baby spit up on your shoulder" without having to change outfits. It should be pointed out, though, that this observation appeared in their *Encyclopedia of Bad Taste* and should be taken as somewhat tongue-in-cheek.[2]

JEANS

Although people considered denim as acceptable work or leisure wear prior to the 1970s, throughout the first half of the decade, denim became downright fashionable; it was frequently embellished with beads and sequins and decorated with embroidered designs. In 1973, Levi Strauss sponsored a denim art contest, receiving 2,000 entries from 49 states, as well as entries from other countries.

People often personalized the "bell" portion of their bell-bottomed jeans, adding metal eyelets and studs, antiwar graffiti, and iron-on transfers. Once a pair of jeans became too tattered for wear, it was still considered too valuable to simply toss, so people cut off the lower legs to make shorts; squares of denim material were also sewn together to make duffle bags, patchwork skirts, and quilts.

Jeans lost much of their individuality—but garnered even more popularity—when two New York garment makers chose the name "Jordache" for their new line; the designers selected this nonsensical word because it sounded both French and classy. Almost instantly, rhinestones and other embellishments disappeared from fashionable jeans, replaced by a pair of sleek, straight-legged and simple demins with the Jordache symbol placed on the right rear pocket; out went the low-cost pair of pants, and in came "designer jeans" such as those created by Gloria Vanderbilt, Calvin Klein, and Sassoon—with prices as high as $55 per pair.

The popularity of blue jeans in the decade cannot be underestimated. By the end of the decade, it was difficult to find anyone—young or old—who didn't wear blue jeans, and, as more sophisticated design choices became increasingly available, jeans served as a status symbol that didn't require wearers to give up comfort. Meanwhile, the plethora of T-shirt choices—ranging from ones purchased at rock concerts to those making a statement about political, spiritual, or environmental beliefs—made completing outfits a cinch. Tie-dyed shirts were also part of the mix, as were sleeveless tank tops and other halter-style shirts. Footwear choices included clogs and earth shoes.

JEWELRY

Jewelry in the 1970s was often crafted from elements in nature—and was of the type that could be worn with informal clothing. Teenagers often gifted their sweethearts with a silver bracelet—known as an ID bracelet—with their names engraved on the front.

Other popular jewelry trends in the 1970s included puka shells (or beads); silver-and-turquoise "squash blossom" pieces; and spoon rings. The first of these became popular because of celebrity influence from two performers: a teeny-bop singer and actor, and a famous movie star in the midst of her fifth (and most tumultuous) marriage.

Puka beads or shells are doughnut-shaped, light-colored, hard substances found in Hawaii. Manufacturers would string them tightly on a short cord, choosing the length so that the necklace rested above the line of clothing; because people in the 1970s often wore open-collared shirts, these necklaces served as a distinct fashion statement. Some followers of this trend began wearing pukas after teen idol David Cassidy—who played Keith on the television show *The Partridge Family*—wore them. The reaction from Cassidy's fans was immediate and passionate. As one woman reminisced, decades later, "Like teenaged girls across the planet, I ... dreamed of what it would be like to *be* that string of puka beads around David Cassidy's neck!"[3] Yet another woman said the following, also in retrospect: "The poofed-up shag, the puka-shell necklace, the psychedelic pants and the winsome smile ... while my two brothers fantasized about Keith's comely sister Laurie (played by Susan Dey), my sister and I imagined ourselves snuggling up with Keith on the family's groovy, colorful tour bus."[4]

Others fell in love with puka beads after actress Elizabeth Taylor wore a necklace containing these stones in a 1974 movie. Although the total number of shells needed for a necklace cost only about $6, after Taylor's movie premiered, the price climbed to $150.

Another popular—and more exotic—fashion trend in the 1970s was to wear Native American "squash blossom" jewelry, pieces that consisted of hand-crafted silver and turquoise and generally weighed five or six pounds. Perhaps the jewelry item boasted only one chunk of turquoise, or perhaps several stones formed a blossom; in either case, the jewelry was treasured because each one was unique and "the color and veining of the turquoise, along with the intricate tooling of the silver, were like individual fingerprints."[5] Others wore spoon rings in the 1970s, which were fashioned from the top portion of an eating utensil. Varying silverware patterns located on spoons allowed for a wide variety of designs, and a significant number of Americans wore these rings.

LEISURE SUITS

For those who lived through the 1970s decade, the quintessential moment of fashion—or at least the most memorable—may have been the white polyester leisure suit that John Travolta wore in *Saturday Night Fever* (SNF) in 1977. In the most famous still photo from this movie, Travolta is poised beneath the bright lights of the Brooklyn disco, with darkness surrounding him and one hand pointing boldly and confidently toward the sky; that moment, for many, epitomizes the culture of the entire disco era.

This movie both illustrates and contributes to another 1970s fashion curiosity. For the first time in many decades, people paid attention to men's fashion, rather than just women's. As author David Frum puts it, "The 1970s saw the greatest revolution in men's clothing since swallowtail coats and knee breeches passed out of fashion almost two centuries ago. Supertight double-knit crotchhugging pants, ripped-open shirts with a medallion between the pectorals, platform shoes for height, moussed and blow-dried hair—the whole panoply of discowear leapt across the lines of class, race, and sexual orientation to become the evening garb of Mid-western college boys."[6] To further pursue this thought, who remembers what Travolta's dance partner, Karen Lynn Gorney, wore during that famous scene? The outfit—a bright red, knee-length, scoop-shouldered, swirling dress that twirled with Gorney's every move—certainly wasn't subtle, and, had Travolta's outfit not so fully commanded our attention, would have been quite noticeable. Here's a bit of fashion trivia: the colors of Travolta's and Gorney's outfits were supposedly selected to stand out against the duskiness of the disco hall; Travolta allegedly wanted to wear black until he heard and appreciated this rationale.

As the fashion of men began appearing in the spotlight, some women began donning startlingly masculine fashions. After the move *Annie Hall* debuted, also in 1977, some women began wearing tweed jackets, neck-ties, and derby hats. This development echoed Diane Keaton's style in the movie, wherein she donned exaggerated and mismatched male fashions, often oversized. This movie premiered during years of intense feminist debate; it isn't really surprising, then, that some women literally usurped the shirt off men's backs—or that the clothing styles of men and women blurred and crossed over as traditional gender roles themselves shifted and became less distinct.

Apropos of a decade that abolished the autocratic rules of fashion, other women wore soft and romantic dresses, old-fashioned and loosely flow-ing. At least one fashion line—Gunne Sax—provided women with a wide variety of such dreamy choices.

FOREIGN INFLUENCE

The 1970s were a time of individual expression, of clashes, emerging iden-tities, and dichotomies; it isn't surprising, then, that women wore a wide spectrum of clothing styles throughout the decade. Perhaps the skirt length best represents this variety, as some women continued to wear the short miniskirt of the 1960s while others followed the dictates of Parisian fashion and chose to don the midi; still others wore loose flowing skirts—maxis—that draped nearly to the floor, and were often called "granny skirts."

Fashion buyers in America panicked at this broad scope of skirt-length options, having heavily invested in the midi after assuming that American women would—as they had in the past—desire what became fashionable in Europe just six months prior. Younger women especially disliked the midi and they refused to give up their miniskirts for the new style; furthermore, hot pants—a pair of shorts that were skimpier that the mini—gave women an even more daring fashion statement to make, and so the Parisian midi faced significant challenges.

French designers of note during the 1970s included Yves Saint Laurent, Christian Dior, Hubert de Givenchy, Emanuel Ungaro, and Pierre Cardin. All influenced Americans in their fashion choices, especially those seeking a "designer" look. On November 28, 1973, these five designers showed their latest styles at the Palace of Versailles to raise money for the Versailles Restoration Fund. Interestingly enough, several American fashion designers also participated in the fundraiser. These included Anne Klein and her assistant Donna Karan; Stephen Burrows; Henri Bendel; Bill Blass; Oscar de la Renta, who began his career by designing for a Parisian couture house; and Halston.

According to a *New York Times* article that commemorated the event 20 years later, this fundraiser "truly was a clash of cultures, with the opponents unevenly matched. It was widely recognized as a case in which the good guys finished first, for the Americans produced ready-to-wear, which was the wave of the future. The French clothes were custom made, a branch of fashion now fighting to stay alive."[7] Some even suggested, the article purports, that a global style emerged from this event in Versailles and that the American style became, in November 1973, a global fashion force with which to reckon.

That said, although individuals and designers in the United States declared a degree of independence from Parisian haute couture, they did not create a fashion culture free from global influences; rather they incorporated elements from Africa, Asia, and the Far East. During the 1970s, many people searched for their ethnic and cultural roots, which explains why this decade also witnessed a mixture of clothing styles and trends from around the world. From the mid to late part of the decade, loose flowing garments appeared on the fashion scene, including caftans and kimonos, which were available in a wide variety of exotic fabrics.

Asian influences appeared, as well, as women began wearing quilted jackets reminiscent of Tibetan and Chinese styles. Sometimes these jackets were worn over cotton voile dresses imported from India; colors ranged from brilliant pinks to mossy greens and sky blues, often accented with gold. Other times, these jackets were paired with gently pleated patchwork skirts.

Fashion gurus imported macramé bags—and even bikinis—from the Greek Isles, along with shawls from Spain. Light cotton gypsy-style blouses also found favor in the 1970s, as did gypsy dresses. Peasant blouses incorporated sleeves so full that they resemble bell-like *engageantes* from the Victorian era of England. Another British fashion influence appeared when petticoats peeked from underneath peasant-styled skirts. Native American looks were imitated, too, especially lightweight loose shirts and wide dresses.

THE YOUTHFUL LOOK

Platform shoes served as one of the most distinguishing features of 1970s fashions, embraced by teenagers and young adults throughout the country. Soles and heels were cork, wood, plastic, or rubber; by 1975, the sole section needed to be at least 2 inches thick to be considered fashionable, with the heel portion reaching 5 inches in height. Dress shoes, sandals, and even sneakers were modified to the platform style, as were thigh-high lace-up boots. Fans of platform shoes sought out the most original and offbeat designs, which might include floral and fruit embellishments, glitter, painted rainbows, stars and moons—and even goldfish in a clear and detachable sole.

Extremes also existed outside of footwear. The summer of 1974 saw the advent of string bikinis, which were bathing suits that covered only what decency laws insisted that they did. All was string except for the minute triangles that covered women's breasts and another that covered the genitals. String bikinis cost $35–$45, which was somewhat pricey, yet they sold out of them at Bloomingdale's in New York within two weeks of their arrival.

Hot pants—those short shorts that didn't cover much more of one's bottom than a traditional bathing suit—debuted in the United States about the same time as the string bikini. Hot pants were frequently banned as workplace attire, perceived as unprofessional. If one wore hot pants, one needed boots to accompany the look. Boots might be shiny and slick, of textured fabric, covered with rhinestones and beads, or psychedelic in appearance.

Young men often wore their hair at shoulder length, although the trend toward ethnic fashion inspired many of them to sport Afros wherein their tresses would be styled outward until it appeared as though a halo of hair surrounded their faces. Some wore quite extravagant Afros, which led to a 1970s-inspired flashback scene in the *Naked Gun 33 1/3: The Final Insult*. In this film, a character played by O.J. Simpson could not walk though a doorway because of the hugeness of his 'fro.

Women also wore Afros, and, after Bo Derek starred in the movie *10* in 1979, many women copied her look and had their stylists put cornrows— several rows of very tight braids with wide spaces between rows—into their hair. Derek was not the only celebrity to braid her hair with cornrows, but she is the person credited for opening up this style to Caucasian women. In 1972, African American actress Cicely Tyson appeared on television with intricate Nigerian braids—and funk and soul musician Rick James also wore cornrows, pre-Derek. Another extremely popular look for women in the 1970s was the Farrah Fawcett hairdo with asymmetrically feathered hair being styled back using large rollers. Although Fawcett served as the poster child for this hairdo, there were nearly as many variations as there were people wearing the style.

ANTIESTABLISHMENT WEAR

During more sedate or conservative times, fashionwise, finding a look that startled or offended the "establishment" wasn't as much work as it was during the 1970s, when the "swirling psychedelic prints, dotted with geometric shapes, mushrooms and daisies were popular holdovers from the hippie culture" and even *Esquire* magazine thought it appropriate for a man to wear a plaid sports jacket and checkered slacks with a patterned tie to a boardroom meeting.[8] So, those wishing to shock faced a significant challenge.

Girls and women across the country imitated this hairstyle of actress Farrah Fawcett, with its rolled back tresses, while a significant number of males hung up posters of Fawcett in their bedrooms. Courtesy of Photofest.

British rocker David Bowie—and his wife, Angie—were certainly up to that challenge. Almost by accident, in February 1972, the duo gave birth to "The Look of the Seventies, the look that would startle millions of teenagers out of their crushed-velvet flares, headbands and tie-died vest-shirts: the Ziggy Stardust look."[9] The style developed in a couple of stages. First, Bowie's manager, recognizing how David enjoyed incorporating elements of cross-dressing into his attire, suggested that he wear a costume and makeup every time that he left the house. Angie thought David also needed a haircut that stood out from the long straight hair predominating rock culture. Flipping through *Vogue* magazine, they decided upon a short cut on the top of his head and in the back, with two points of hair traveling down the sides of his face. Although David was nervous about dying his hair, Angie persuaded him to color it red. The following day, he panicked and so they added peroxide and a German dye known as "Red Hot Red."

By the time they were finished, Bowie's hair was spiked and as pinky-orange as it was red. "Thus adorned, Bowie's look would reach beyond image, beyond theatre and into a visual expression of youthful defiance … allied to his freakish transsexual costumes—shimmering, skintight catsuits, outsized earrings and knee-length red plastic stack-heeled boots."[10] Suddenly, Bowie was the idol of countless teens and young adults who wanted to be part of the antiestablishment, in his native England—and also in the United States.

Other performers who wore glam fashions include Elton John—whose oversized and glittery pairs of glasses and extreme platform shoes helped define the style; KISS, well known for their outrageous red, black, and white face makeup; and Rod Stewart, a British rocker who appears a bit tame next to his counterparts. Perhaps Tim Curry's performance as the transvestite Dr. Franken Furter in the *Rocky Horror Picture Show* best typifies the excessive nature of the glam fashion movement.

As Bowie was creating Ziggy Stardust, or shortly thereafter, punk was emerging as a musical form and lifestyle. Those who identified with this

Singer David Bowie appears in the persona of "Ziggy Stardust," his rock star alter ego that dressed in a bizarre fashion and served as the apotheosis of glam rock. Courtesy of Photofest.

movement made deliberate attempts to startle—and perhaps even antago-
nize and alienate—others with their wardrobes. Typical outfits included
ripped—or even slashed—clothing pieced together again with oversized
safety pins. Wardrobe items clashed with one another; delicate fishnet
stockings, for example, might be paired with clunky and masculine-
looking combat boots. People incorporated vinyl and other elements of
S&M (sadism and masochism) and bondage fetishes in their wardrobes.
Hair might be dyed a bright and obviously unnatural shade; spiked; or cut
in odd, asymmetrical ways. Accessories ranged from razor blades to lava-
tory chains, and from Nazi armbands to spiked dog collars.

Punk fashion originated in England, and fashion designer Vivienne Westwood and her partner Malcolm McLaren are credited for originating the
style. The couple opened a shop named Sex; a band managed by McLaren,
the Sex Pistols, purchased outfits from them—and followers imitated their
look. Although the punk movement already existed, the Sex Pistols greatly
influenced the wardrobe needed to be part of the punk rock scene.

Observers of the fashion would note how carefully the disparate wardrobe elements were juxtaposed against one another; this antifashion was
clearly not randomly put together from thrift shop items as Bohemian outfits were put together. Punk's movement, though, was not composed of
working class or underprivileged youth; rather nearly one-third of those
playing in punk rock bands were former or current art students, and the
artistic eye of those heading the scene certainly helped explain the precise
nature of the disarray and shock value inherent in the outfits.[11]

The punk look associated with Vivienne Westwood and the Sex Pistols
dominated antiestablishment fashion from about 1975–1978. About a year
after this look began appearing, another somewhat more subtle ensemble
sprang up, perhaps consisting of straight-legged pants and collarless shirts,
or combat fatigues. Adherents might also wear winkle pickers, which were
an elastic leather boot with two-inch heels and pointed toes. Near the end
of the decade, some punk aficionados donned black studded leather jackets and bondage trousers, ironically mimicking a look chosen by more
traditional rock and rollers.

During the 1970s, some who embraced the punk rock culture made
significant changes to their looks, perhaps putting a controversial tattoo
where it could not be hidden or easily erased, or making some other kind
of permanent bodily alternation. These "hardcore" punks also slashed
their hair into dramatic styles that could not grow out quickly. Those more
on the periphery of the movement—perhaps those for whom punk rock
was part of their weekend entertainment, but certainly not a central part
of their identity—may have styled their hair differently and dressed in an
alternate manner at times, but they returned to a more conventional look
when the occasion demanded—or after the weekend ended.

THE 1970S

6

Food and the Environment

INTRODUCTION

Traditionally, women have served as the cooks of the family, the keepers of the hearth and home; during the 1970s, though, they entered the workforce in increasing numbers and so they needed to find ways to balance the management of their hearths and homes with their need and/or desire to also contribute monetarily to their households. This societal change helps explain why an increasing volume of convenience foods and fast foods were introduced and then consumed during this decade. Parents, as well as other Americans, incorporated these quick and easy meals into their lives; benefits included convenience, relatively low cost, and speed of delivery. Although warnings about the high fat content and low nutritional value of the meals had already started to surface, the benefits outweighed those concerns for an increasing number of Americans.

Some of the new foods introduced during the decade became entrenched in the American diet, while others served as mere fads. Realization that the planet was hurting because of the ever-increasing global population fueled the curiosity about the world's diverse foodstuff as Americans explored both European and Asian cuisine and manufacturers created new appliances to aid these cooks in their exploration of ethnic foods. People in the 1970s also an expressed a wish to return to a more natural lifestyle, and this is reflected in the trend of using more "health foods" that were considered "natural."

Congress became more involved in farming, rural living, and agricultural issues, changing its philosophy on how to best help farmers and encouraging the movement toward exporting American crops. Environmental issues rose to the forefront, as well, both on farms and in the country as a whole, and legislators also attempted to address these concerns.

DINING IN STYLE

Rumors had it that Mikey, the freckle-faced kid from the Life cereal commercials who hated everything, met a dastardly fate in the mid-1970s. Mikey, as the story was told, accepted a dare to fill his mouth with Pop Rocks—a fad candy that shattered or "popped" in your mouth—and then he guzzled a Pepsi. Once Mikey did so, pundits declared, his stomach simply exploded. This urban legend, though, was simply not true.

Although the story was fabricated, Pop Rocks were quite real—and also quite popular once introduced in 1974. Pop Rocks consisted of sugar, corn syrup, and flavoring that was cooked to a hard consistency and that contained carbon dioxide gas bubbles trapped inside; as the candy melted, the pressure was released and the candy snapped inside the mouth. Although the explanation is far from glamorous—and actually sounds a bit gross—the Food and Drug Administration (FDA) approved this candy for distribution; moreover, the fizz in a mouthful of Pop Rocks has been compared to only one-tenth of the carbonation ingested from one single sip of a cola beverage.

Other candies, sweets, and goodies debuted in the 1970s, including Orville Redenbacher's Gourmet Popping Corn (1970); canned A&W Root Beer, Jell-O Pudding Treats, and Rolos Candy (1971); Snapple (1972); Honey Maid Cinnamon Grahams (1973); soft frozen yogurt (1974); Famous Amos Chocolate Chip Cookies (1975); Starburst Fruit Chews, Country Time Lemonade, Jelly Belly Jelly Beans, and orange M&Ms (1976); Mrs. Fields Cookies and Twix Cookie Bars (1977); and Ben & Jerry's ice cream and Reese's Pieces (1978).

Other new foods made cooking easier for the women who were focusing more of their attention on the workplace. These foods include Eggo Waffles, Morton's Salt Substitute, and Hamburger Helper (1970); smoked Spam and McCormick's "Roast in a Bag Kit" (1971); Top Ramen, Stove Top Stuffing, Quaker Oats 100% Natural, Celestial Seasonings Herbal Teas, and Tuna Helper (1972); Cup O'Noodles (1973); French Bread Pizzas (1974); Maxwell House A.D.C., for use in automatic drip coffeemakers (1976); and Yoplait Yogurt (1977).

Food-related trends emerged during the 1970s that continued long after the decade ended; one example is the gourmet cooking that promoted the use of regional and organic ingredients, which began on the West Coast. Anything that was perceived as "natural" was considered to be "good," even if the natural ingredients were honey and other sweets. Granola skyrocketed to popularity as one such naturally good food. In 1973, *The Granola Cookbook* appeared on bookshelves, sharing recipes for "granola eggs Benedict, granola quiche Lorraine, granola eggplant Parmesan…and granola fondue."[1] Practically every major cereal company produced some sort of granola breakfast food, as well, and, although granola was perhaps the quintessential "natural" food of the decade, others existed—and magazines such as *Bon Appetit* and *Gourmet* provided readers with a significant number of soybean recipes.

Salad bars began appearing in restaurants, starting in Chicago in 1971. Vegetarian cookbooks continued to emerge while ingredients such as brown rice, whole grain breads, and yogurt appeared in more and more recipes. People bought canning supplies to save money during a time of an energy crisis and a disturbing recession, and 1973 ushered in the Cuisinart food processor, also a help to the frazzled cook. Other appliances purchased by Americans included "Electric woks, crepe pans, fondue sets, hibachis, electric crock pots, microwave ovens, electric juicers, yogurt makers, gelato makers, bread machines, rice steamers, milk shake mixers, pressure cookers, coffee makers, indoor smokeless grills, food dehydrators and vacuum sealers."[2] In the 1970s, we first used the spork—a combination spoon and fork—and we first drank soft drinks out of plastic bottles.

Ingredients in the diet soft drinks changed and/or were challenged, however, throughout the decade. By 1970, the FDA had banned the use of cyclamates used in diet drinks and various food products upon receiving information that the substance caused cancer in lab rats. In 1977, the FDA received pressure to also ban saccharin for similar reasons, but it exercised caution and waited for more studies to be conducted.

Shopping experiences changed when the bar code—a series of lines that identified a grocery product—was standardized in 1970. This was the beginning of an improved inventory system for grocers, and, more immediately, it allowed cashiers to rapidly serve and check out customers. Plastic bags first began appearing in grocery stores, as well, slowly replacing the familiar brown paper sacks. In 1974, the FDA and USDA began their voluntary nutrition labeling program, as well as one that required nutrition labels on foods with added nutrients or those that made claims about nutritional value. So, perhaps the time saved by the bar code standardization was lost as consumers began analyzing and comparing ingredients in products found on the grocery store shelves.

Produce sections in grocery stores offered fewer items when compared to those in the 1990s; approximately 150 fruits and vegetables were available in 1970 as compared to 400 in the 1990s. Furthermore, produce didn't yet command as central a place in American diets. In 1970, per capita consumption was 573 pounds of produce; 27 years later, that had increased to 711 pounds.

Consumers made somewhat different grocery purchases overall. For example, at the beginning of the 1970s, 34 percent of an average household's food budget was spent on snacks and meals eaten away from home; by the end of the decade—perhaps because of the increasing number of working mothers—that figure increased to 39 percent. The main (meat) dish served changed somewhat, as well, as the decade evolved; in 1970, there was a 74 percent chance that red meat—beef, pork, lamb, or veal—would be served; a 19 percent chance that dinner would be chicken or turkey; and a 7 percent chance that fish would be the centerpiece of the meal. Although fish consumption remained constant, by the beginning of the 1980s, red meat accounted for 70 percent of the meats served, with chicken and turkey served 23 percent of the time—a 4 percent change.

These figures do not account for the meals that were strictly vegetarian, because that route was not yet embraced by mainstream cooks. In fact, "Even as late as the 1970s, vegetarianism was associated with the counter culture, a diet adhered to only by flower children and religious fanatics."[3] It should be noted that per capita beef consumption reached an all-time high in 1976 (89 pounds); this is attributed to the liquidation of the nation's beef herd, which allowed for better prices for consumers. The composition of the meat and poultry served was fattier in the 1970s as compared to the 1990s; meat and poultry, for example, had 35 percent fat on average in 1970, which was reduced to 25 percent by 1994. The saturated fat dropped from 37 to 26 percent during that same time span. Pork was 30 percent higher in fat in the 1970s as compared to the 1990s.

Other dietary factors differed from today's menu. Eggs featured more prominently while the composition of dairy products differed from latter decades. More people drank milk in the 1970s—and 81 percent of milk sold was whole, not skim or reduced in fat—but yogurt consumption was only one-sixth of what it was by the 1990s. The average person ate 11 pounds of cheese in 1970; in comparison, per capita cheese consumption in 1997 had risen to 28 pounds. Cooks in the 1970s selected animal fats—rather than their vegetable counterparts—25 percent more often than when compared to the 1990s, and margarine was sold almost exclusively in stick form. As a corollary, the average person ingested 470 milligrams of cholesterol per day per person in 1970, but only 410 milligrams in the 1990s.

Grain consumption differed in comparison, as well. In 1970, the average person consumed 136 pounds of flour in his or her diet; that increased to 200 pounds in the 1990s. Snack foods sales—such as pretzels, popcorn, and crackers—increased 200 percent in that time frame, while ready-to-eat cereal sales increased by 60 percent. Foods such as pizza and lasagna that rely upon a grain base were eaten 115 percent more in 1994 as compared to 1977.

What we drank in the 1970s varies from what we drank in the 1990s. The most dramatic change was our consumption of bottled water—and our perception of that product. Here is a description of Perrier in a 1977 *Time* magazine article: "For more than a century, France's Perrier mineral water has been a familiar presence in Europe's toniest restaurants, glossiest spas and priciest specialty shops. The gaseous drink in the light green bottle—distinctively shaped like an Indian club—has somehow managed to retain an air of exclusivity even though Source Perrier has been for years the world's largest bottler of sparkling water."[4] The impetus of this article was the announcement that Perrier would now be sold in the United States—and the immediate result was that other companies began pushing imitation products.

Long term, this surely helped create the astonishing 908 percent increase in bottled water consumption from 1977 to 1997. During that time frame, other increases occurred, most notably in consumption of soft drinks (61%); fruit juices (42%); and wine (11%). People were not necessarily consuming more liquids, however. To counterbalance those increases, people drank fewer distilled spirits (40%), milk (17%), beer (2%), and tea (1%).

COOKBOOKS AND DIETS

A new version of *The Joy of Cooking* by Irma S. Rombauer was quite popular, while Betty Crocker cookbooks arrived in people's homes every year. More tongue-in-cheek cookbooks mocked the Watergate scandal and popular recipes included Watergate Salad and Watergate Cake. The salad featured pistachio-flavored pudding, crushed pineapple, marshmallows, nuts, and whipped topping, while one Watergate cake recipe involved putting green food coloring into an angel food cake mix and adding nuts. According to one newspaper article, the full name of the cake included icing that was a "cover up."

Other recipes were even more openly mocking of the scandal, and they include:

Nixon's Perfectly Clear Consommé

Ellsberg's Leek Soup

Liddy's Clam-Up Chowder

Magruder's Dandy Ly'in Salad

Sauteed Slippery Eels a la Deanoise

Republican Peeking Duck

Mitchell's Cooked Goose with Stuffing

Cox's In-Peach Chicken

Martha's Sweet and Sour Tongue

Nixon's Hot Crossed Wired Buns with Tapping

GOP Cookie Crumbles

Dr. Robert Atkins first presented his high-protein, low-carbohydrate eating plan in 1972 with the release of *Dr. Atkins' Diet Revolution*. His advice ran contrary to what many medical experts and dieticians advised.

Dr. Herbert Tarnower formulated his own diet in the 1970s, which consisted of following a 7- to 14-day plan; Tarnower stated that a one pound a day weight loss is not unreasonable, given a controlled diet. His plan lists very specific foods in specific proportions to achieve this reduction, using a formula of 43 percent protein, 22.5 percent fat, and 34.5 percent carbohydrates.

ELEGANT EATING

More stylish options existed for those entranced by "Nouvelle Cuisine" or "Cuisine Minceur" trends. Nouvelle Cuisine—or new cuisine—advocated that food presentation was very important, as food should engage all five senses and not just the taste buds. Cooks used herbs and spices, lightening up on their sauces so that the individual flavors were not overpowered. Dishes tended to be simple, but elegant. This cooking style boasts French origins, as does cuisine minceur—or cooking light, low-calorie meals.

According to the International Association of Culinary Professionals, popular foods of the 1970s included homemade breads; Beef Wellington; French foods, most specifically quiche and crepes; fondue; crockpot chili; buffalo chicken wings; pasta primavera; Szechwan cuisine; Bundt cakes; and cheesecakes. Cooks concerned with presentation added garnishes to plates, using scallions, tomatoes, parsley, radishes, and carrots in creative and attractive ways; they often crafted chocolate into forms, as well.

Meanwhile, Sylvia Lovegren in her 2005 cookbook *Fashionable Foods: Seven Decades of Food Fads* discusses the various breads and cakes of the 1970s (zucchini, carrot, apple, lemon, strawberry, and pumpkin); pasta dishes (spaghetti carbonara and fettuccine alfredo); pies; smoothies; and exotic salads. *Waitrose Food Illustrated* offers yet another perspective about what appeared on our plates: "cooking was all about recreating the jet-setting feel of bistro food in your home. Gooey fondues evoked Alpine chalets, while unctuous macaroni à la carbonaras, made with cream, eggs, Parmesan and bacon, conjured up Italian trattorias. Naturally, all were accompanied by vino and candlelight."[5] Meanwhile, while cooking trends such as those listed above gained momentum, so did the quickest and easiest form of feeding one's family: the fast-food restaurant.

FAST-FOOD RESTAURANTS
"You Deserve a Break Today ... at McDonald's"

In 1970, McDonald's reported $587 million in sales from nearly 1,600 restaurants located throughout the United States and in four other countries; that same year, one single franchise, located in Bloomington, Minnesota, racked up $1 million in sales. Just two years later, McDonald's broke the billion-dollar mark; at this point, anyone who bought 100 shares when the restaurant chain first opened in the 1940s now owned 1,836 shares, thanks to five stock splits. By 1975, the company posted revenues of $2.5 billion from its 3,076 restaurants—which were now located in 20 different countries. In 1976, McDonald's boasted the sale of its 20 billionth hamburger. In 1977, more than 1,000 chains reported sales topping $1 million, with 11 of them exceeding $2 million.

Although Ray Kroc, founder of McDonald's, surely must have been pleased by these results, not everyone applauded the trend—including farm activist Jim Hightower, who warned Americans of the dangers of the "McDonaldization of America," and who viewed the "emerging fast food industry as a threat to independent businesses, as a step toward a food economy dominated by giant corporations, and as a homogenizing influence on American life."[6] His efforts, though, did not slow down the "McDonaldization."

In 1972, McDonald's debuted the Egg McMuffin, its ham, egg, and cheese breakfast sandwich. In 1975, Sierra Vista, Arizona, hosted the first drive-through McDonald's restaurant, and, in 1977, the fast-food restaurant began packaging its Happy Meals targeted to its youngest consumers; test-marketed in St. Louis, this product became available nationwide in 1979 as part of McDonald's "Circus Wagon" campaign.

"Have It Your Way ... "

McDonald's wasn't the only fast-food game in town. Overall, Americans spent $6 billion in fast-food items in 1970 alone, which was 28.6 percent of the total "eating out" funds spent. Burger King ranked second in sales and began offering franchises in the 1960s. It claimed to have offered the first fast-food dining-in service; it opened up its first drive-through windows in 1975. Its mascot, the Burger King, first appeared in the 1970s, sporting a magnificently jeweled crown and an ostentatious royal robe. Sometimes, mascots portraying the King performed magic tricks in Burger King parking lots to entertain restaurant patrons. Other marketing characters included the Duke of Doubt; Burger Thing; Sir Shakes-a-Lot; and the Wizard of Fries. This decade also saw the invention of the Kids' Club, wherein youth could receive discount coupons—and a special surprise on their birthdays.

"Quality Is Our Recipe ... "

Dave Thomas opened the first Wendy's Old Fashioned Hamburgers Restaurant in Columbus, Ohio, on November 15, 1969; he named his restaurant after his youngest daughter's nickname. When he opened a second site in Columbus just one year later, he included a pick-up window, the precursor to the drive-through windows of today; the pick-up window even had its own grill, expediting service. Thomas sold his first franchise in 1972 and growth of the restaurant was phenomenal: in September 1976, the public could begin buying stock in Wendy's; by December 1976, 500 Wendy's restaurants existed; by March 1978, there were 1,000 restaurants, and by March 1979, there were 1,500. In November 1979, Wendy's claimed to have become the first national chain restaurant to include a salad bar, and the decade ended with 1,767 restaurants located in the United States (including Puerto Rico), Canada, and Europe.

Other Options

By the time the 1970s rolled around, Kentucky Fried Chicken was already a publicly held corporation, with more than 3,500 locations. On July 8, 1971, Heublein, Inc. purchased KFC Corporation for $285 million. Glen Bell's Taco Bell became a publicly held corporation in 1969; in 1978, the company and its 868 locations were sold to PepsiCo for millions of dollars. Burger Chef peaked shortly before the 1970s began; in the 1960s, though, it was the second most lucrative fast-food restaurant, with only McDonald's being more successful. Burger Chef also stakes a claim to creating the first fun meal for kids, wherein an entire meal was packaged up for the youth. Still other fast-food locales of the 1970s include Hardees and Roy Rogers, and, in 1971, Pizza Hut became the number one pizza chain in the world, both in number and in sales figures. In 1971, the original Starbucks opened up in Seattle, selling the first of its quality coffee. Starbucks, though, did not develop into a chain until well after the decade had ended.

AGRICULTURE AND DEMOGRAPHICS

According to a 2005 study conducted by Anne Effland, Carolyn Dimitri, and Neilson Conklin, 5.7 million farms existed in the United States in 1900 but, by 1970, only 2.9 million farms were still operational; 5.9 million farms existed in 1945 but that number drastically dropped, post–World War II.[7]

Looking at the actual acreage, though, a different picture emerges. In 1900, the 5.7 million farms averaged 146 acres in size for a total estimated acreage of 832 million acres of farmland. In contrast, the 2.9 million farms existing in 1970 averaged 376 acres, for a total farmland acreage of more than 1 billion acres. Therefore, America actually saw an increase of farmland acreage from 1900 to 1970. The authors of this study also compared the number of crops produced per farm; this dropped from 5.1 in 1900 to 2.7 in 1970, suggesting an ever-increasing amount of specialization in farming concerns.

Outside of Amish farms, tractors had replaced animals as farm labor. Furthermore, advancements in farm technology, along with improved plant and animal breeding and more effective fertilizers and pesticides, helped facilitate operations of the larger, more specialized farms of the 1970s. Many farmers and their families sought out nonfarming work to supplement—or even replace—their incomes, as increasing numbers of families left farming altogether. Because of the extremely efficient and effective modern farming technology, farmers often produced more food than they could sell at a fair price; this became a political issue for the U.S. government to address.

During the 1960s, governmental policies had attempted to control overproduction by paying the farmers money *not* to farm certain areas of their property. Presidents John F. Kennedy and Lyndon B. Johnson also explored ways to expand agricultural exporting to increase farming revenue. Although farmers' troubles were far from solved by these measures, during that decade, the farmers—who had previously earned income at a rate of about 50 percent of nonfarmers—increased their revenue to 75 percent of a nonfarmer's income.

Something changed in the 1970s, though, that made Kennedy's and Johnson's farming strategies seem obsolete: many experts predicted that the earth would eventually not produce enough food to feed the world's increasing population and so paying farmers not to till certain portions of their land no longer made sense. Because of this prediction, legislation was passed to increase food production and exports; Congress also increased spending on agricultural programs from slightly more than $5 billion in 1970 to more than $11 billion by the end of the decade. Staffing at the Senate Agriculture Committee rose from 7 in 1970 to 21 in 1975—and 32 by 1980—in response to this perceived need.

Congress took other measures, as well. The Agricultural Act of 1970 set loan rates so that they were near world market price, thus making commercial exports more feasible. The 1972 Rural Development Act allowed the government to back up farm loans granted by commercial lenders, thus expanding the opportunities in rural locales. The Agriculture and Consumer Protection Act of 1973—passed during the same year that farming subsidies created in the 1960s stopped—established target prices and deficiency payments. Target prices were price levels set by the federal government; whenever a farmer could not receive the target price set for his or her particular crop(s), a deficiency payment was made to that farmer. Furthermore, farmers could receive direct disaster payments when production goals were not met for wheat, feed grains, or cotton. In 1973, farm income peaked at $33.3 billion. Outside the United States, many countries—particularly the Soviet Union—suffered from poor harvests and the demand for American grain exports grew dramatically.

The Food and Agriculture Act of 1977 addressed another pitfall that farmers faced; exporting had become an important part of farmer revenue, but demand from foreign countries for their crops had slowed its growth—while the American farmers hadn't slowed down their production rates.

Thus the supply and demand balance favored the buyers. Prices dropped and farmers again needed help from the government. The 1977 act created a more extended storage program, which encouraged farmers to store their grain whenever prices were low and then release the commodities when supply was short.

Overall, the United States benefited from the expanding world markets for its agricultural products during the 1970s. As a further safeguard, the Agricultural Credit Act of 1978 created an emergency credit program to prevent farmers from having to cease operations because of cash flow concerns. Meanwhile, the Agricultural Export Trade Expansion Act of 1978 further strengthened the export efforts; as just one feature of the act, short-term agricultural export credits were now extended to the People's Republic of China.

Congress also bolstered the Rural Development Act of 1972, expanding existing job opportunity programs in rural areas and creating new ones. The government authorized small business loans in rural areas, increased grants for water and waste disposal in these locales, and made available loans for other community resources. Congress also expanded the authority and scope of the Rural Electrification Administration's ability to provide electricity and telephone service to rural areas.

The National Agricultural Research, Extension, and Teaching Policy Act (Title XIV of the Food and Agricultural Act of 1977) created newly competitive grant programs for researchers wishing to improve agricultural conditions, favoring energy and small farm operations as grant recipients; and increased funding opportunities for direct nutrition education for low-income families.

Two new advisory panels formed because of the 1977 act: the Joint Council on Food and Agricultural Sciences and the National Agricultural Research and Extension Users Advisory Board. The former coordinated research and teaching efforts of government and higher education institutions; the latter reviewed research policies and plans.

Appropriate nutrition for American citizens was the focus of other Congressional mandates. The National Food and Human Nutrition Research and Extension Program, part of a 1977 Congressional Act, charged the Department of Agriculture to study nutrition and to develop a corresponding education program.

Meanwhile, the Agricultural and Consumer Protection Act of 1973 expanded the scope of the food stamp program; the Food Stamp Act of 1977 simplified the qualification process while capping the program's potential expenditures. The Food and Agriculture Act of 1977 ensured the provision of food to low-income mothers who were either expecting or lactating, plus to their young children. During the 1970s, funds provided for child nutrition grew from $2.4 billion to $8 billion, while the contribution of the federal government grew from $750 million to more than $4.7 billion.

POLLUTION

> City after city, state after state, had essentially failed in their efforts to protect their air and their water, the land, the health of their citizens. By 1970, our city skylines were so polluted that in many places it was all but impossible to see from one city skyscraper to another ... We had rivers that were fouled with raw sewage and toxic chemicals. One actually caught on fire.[8]

The date was June 22, 1969; the place was the Cuyahoga River located in Cleveland, Ohio; and the speaker was former EPA Administrator Carol Browner. The fact that a river could catch on fire was seen as a sure sign that pollution was rampant, and it seemed to indicate that local and state regulations did not suffice to prevent further polluting. The burning of the Cuyahoga served as partial impetus, then, for the passage of the Federal Water Pollution Control Act of 1972, its initial three-year budget of $24.6 billion, and its Clean Lakes Program; the fact that rivers stopped burning was used as a symbol of the success of the act—and of other similar acts of Congress.

Jonathan H. Adler disputes this view, stating that traditional recountings overemphasize this moment when reviewing the history of America's pollution, its crisis—and then turning—point, and the remedies needed to improve the environment. To quote Adler, "The conventional narratives, of a river abandoned by its local community, of water pollution at its zenith, of conventional legal doctrines impotent in the face of environmental harms, and a beneficent federal government rushing in to save the day, is misleading in many respects."[9] Points raised by Adler include the fact that the Cuyahoga—or, rather, the oil and debris floating on its surface—had caught on fire numerous times before, and this had occurred at other waterways, so this event was not unique; furthermore, cleanup efforts began well before the federal government intervened, so credit for the revival of the river's health cannot be easily attributed.

Regardless of which interpretation you choose to accept, Cleveland faced a difficult challenge when attempting to clean up the Cuyahoga. Because the river flowed into Lake Erie, pollution from other locales could still affect its waters. Potential pollutants included sewage, pesticides, and contamination from heavy metals. To add to the challenges of Great Lakes pollution control, two countries shared the boundaries of these lakes: the United States and Canada. In 1972, though, the same year that the federal government passed its water pollution control act, the United States and Canada signed the Great Lakes Water Quality Agreement, wherein the two countries agreed to maintain the integrity of the lakes based on mutually agreed upon pollution control levels. The two governments renewed their commitment to this pledge in 1978.

Indeed, once Americans realized in the early 1970s that it was in fact possible to "run out of" clean air and water, concerns about pollution, the loss of open space, and the decimation of wildlife took over. Those concerns led to the kind of passionate opposition that proved capable of fueling a new generation of reform politics.[10]

Awareness of environmental issues rose to the forefront in the 1960s, with the National Environmental Policy Act (NEPA) serving as baseline legislation for the onslaught of environmental laws passed by Congress in the 1970s. NEPA began requiring all federal agencies to consider environmental factors in their decision making, including the future impact of their policies on the environment and potential alternative policies.

To continue to address overall environmental concerns, the federal government created the Environment Protection Agency (EPA) in 1970, after President Richard Nixon merged the environmental functions of the Department of Health, Education, and Welfare; the Department of the Interior; the Council on Environmental Quality; and several other lesser organizations. "The 1970s," Nixon said, "absolutely must be the years when America pays its debt to the past by reclaiming the purity of its air, its waters, and our living environment. It is literally now or never."[11] Since that time, the EPA has served as the primary agency responsible for establishing federal environment policy. Effective in 1976, the EPA needed to approve the use of all new industrial and commercial chemicals; this process included premarket testing, and all chemicals manufactured in the country would now be registered with the EPA.

Other actions taken by the EPA and/or Congress in the 1970s include:

- 1970 Clean Air Act regulated auto emissions and set clean air standards
- 1971 Lead-based paint restricted in cribs and on toys
- 1972 DDT, a cancer-causing pesticide, banned, and a review of all pesticides instituted; the Marine Mammal Protection Act passed
- 1973 Lead-based gasoline begins to be phased out
- 1974 Safe Drinking Water Act allows regulation of drinking water
- 1975 Tailpipe emission standards set; catalytic converter invented to address issue; Toxic Substances Control Act phasing out production and sale of PCBs, substances linked to cancer
- 1976 Resource Conservation and Recovery Act regulates disposal of hazardous materials and Toxic Substances Control Act seeks to minimize damage from hazards
- 1977 The Surface Mining and Reclamation Act required companies that stripped land for coal to restore the land to original contours
- 1978 Scrubber technique cleans air emitted from coal-based power plants

Congress enacted the Land and Water Resources Conservation Act of 1977 (RCA) to address farmland erosion; the Soil Conservation Service therefore began monitoring soil and water. The Forest and Rangeland Renewable Resources Planning Act of 1974 created a plan whereby the Secretary of Agriculture assessed the forests every 10 years. The Eastern Wilderness Act of 1975 added more than 200,000 acres of wild land to the eastern national forests and other bills added more than 350,000 acres of wilderness to protection status under the National Wilderness Preservation System. Acts passed in 1976 and 1978 strengthened the legislative mandates to protect and manage these lands.

Although these ecological measures received praise from those concerned about the environment, spokespeople for industry sought to stem the tide of regulations that added a significant financial burden to their companies, and they "began to portray environmentalists as hysterical radicals who wanted to bring the nation to its knees."[12] The best-known clash between environmentalists and industry involved the snail darter versus the Tennessee Valley Authority (TVA). During the early 1970s, the TVA spent $116 million constructing a dam on the Little Tennessee River; construction stopped in 1977, however, when environmentalists cited the 1973 Endangered Species Act and noted that the snail darter's habitat was being destroyed in the quest to build the dam. The Supreme Court sided with the environmentalists, but, in 1979, President Jimmy Carter signed legislation that allowed the dam project to continue.

ENDANGERED SPECIES ACT

In 1973, Congress passed the Endangered Species Act, which considerably strengthened similar legislation from the 1960s. Lists of threatened or endangered species were created and all federal agencies were now required to consider the conservation of these species in all actions undertaken; moreover, these agencies could no longer authorize, fund, or carry out any action that might jeopardize a listed species—or its habitat. The bald eagle came to represent the endangered species of the world, in large part because it also symbolized the American culture, its people, and its sense of freedom.

EARTH DAY DEBATE

According to some sources, the founder of Earth Day was John McConnell who, on October 3, 1969, submitted a proposal to the San Francisco Board of Supervisors, requesting that a special date and time be set aside to honor the earth; the mayor issued the proclamation, as did officials in a few other cities in California. This resolution, which referred to humans as "Earthians," created a day to celebrate global unity, to share concerns about the planet's future, and to remind people of their responsibilities toward the earth. The resolution suggested that people plant trees and flowers, clean rivers and wooded areas, and observe an hour of quiet reflection.

McConnell and his committee celebrated Earth Day on March 21, the vernal equinox—or, as it is more commonly known—the first day of spring. On April 22 of that year, the Environment Teach-In honored its own Earth Day and this event garnered national attention. In 1971, Senator Gaylord Nelson proposed an annual Earth Week, to be honored the third week of April.

According to proponents of McConnell as Earth Day founder, the Environment Teach-In hadn't turned in a proposal using the term *Earth Day* until January 1970, a couple of months after their proposal was already submitted to San Francisco officials. Those who purport that Gaylord Nelson actually founded Earth Day—and this includes former President Bill Clinton who awarded Nelson the Presidential Medal of Freedom as the "Father of Earth Day"—state that Nelson had announced at a Seattle conference in September 1969 that there would be grassroot environmental commemorations across the country in the spring of 1970.

According to the Environmental Protection Agency, 20 million Americans participated in Earth Day activities on April 22, 1970, and these included 10 million school-aged children picking up trash in their neighborhoods and local nature spots. Congress adjourned for the day, while 10,000 people celebrated by the Washington Monument. Although many applauded the commitment of participants, one author says that day took on a tone of "saccharine sentimentality."[13]

Earth Day projects tended to focus on very specific tasks that an individual or small group of people could accomplish, such as weeding a public park and cleaning up the surrounding litter, rather than large undertakings requiring government action. The attitude, according to author Pagan Kennedy, was that the "earth wasn't beyond repair. It was sort of like a basement rec room filled with partying teenagers who throw cigarette butts on the floor, nick the wood paneling, and crank the volume up to ten. The solution, of course, was to scream down the stairs, 'You kids clean up—and turn off that stereo.'"[14] Noise pollution, as this description suggests, was considered a real danger during the 1970s, and risks included the clanging or whirring sounds of home appliances; one source even suggested that loud noises could impair sexual performance.

Environmental activist Denis Hayes chastised Americans for their limited understanding of how the United States consumed the earth's resources, stating that American citizens used half of the world's goods, while only being 6 percent of its population.

LOVE CANAL, NEW YORK

If you get there before I do / Tell 'em I'm a comin' too / To see the things so wondrous true / At Love's new Model City.[15]

That turn-of-the-century advertising jingle promoted the development of Love Canal, but all was not so wondrous nearly 70 years later.

In a 36-city-block area of Niagara Falls, New York—known as the Love Canal—doctors and residents alike noted high rates of birth defects, miscarriages, chromosomal deformities, and cancer. Investigations revealed unusually high rates of toxins in the soil, and it was discovered that several houses and one school were built above nearly 20,000 tons of toxic chemical wastes that had been stored underground in the 1940s and 1950s in a manner now deemed illegal and dangerous. Chemicals leaked into the soil above, rising to the surface. In 1978, the government evacuated families from the area and President Jimmy Carter declared the Love Canal a national emergency.

Ironically, Love Canal was initially conceived of as a "dream community," envisioned by William T. Love in the late nineteenth century. He intended to dig a short canal by the Niagara River so that water could power his proposed city and so shipping concerns could bring commerce to his town. Workers started to dig the canal, but financial issues plus an evolving understanding of how to transmit electricity halted his plans. The partial ditch turned into a dump site in the 1920s, and companies began storing industrial waste in the area. In 1927, an aerial photo showed a gash in the earth that was 60 feet wide and 3,000 feet in length, and the landfill situation continued without proper regulation and management.

Of course, this was in an era when conservation meant leaving the wild bears alone, nutrition meant "fruit, cereal, milk, bread, and butter," and pollution was a term that only communists, oddballs, or crazy people ever used.[16]

In 1953, the Hooker Chemical Company covered up the site with earth and sold it to the city for $1. Deed transfer papers listed both a "warning" about chemical wastes and a statement absolving Hooker from assuming any liability, posttransfer. As time passed, however, new homeowners were not cautioned about potential dangers from the chemicals—or even given the information that the homes and school rested above a former chemical landfill. One hundred homes and one school building were initially constructed over the chemical dump, transforming William T. Love's vision of a dream city into one fraught with nightmares. By 1978, 800 single-dwelling homes and 240 low-income apartments existed in Love Canal.

Heavy rainfall triggered the climatic disaster. As a *New York Times* reporter who visited the site shared, "Corroding waste-disposal drums could be seen breaking up through the grounds of backyards. Trees and gardens were turning black and dying. One entire swimming pool had been popped up from its foundation, afloat now on a small sea of chemicals. Puddles of noxious substances were pointed out to me by the residents. Some of these puddles were in their yards, some were in their basements, others yet were on the school grounds. Everywhere the air had a faint, choking smell. Children returned from play with burns on their hands and faces."[17] Because of the extent of the disaster, the Love Canal tragedy played an important role in American environmental legislation, as it was the first man-made disaster to receive the federal emergency designation.

The chemical company paid more than $20 million to the families and city officials of Niagara Falls; in 1994, the company settled with the state of New York for $98 million, and, in 1995, they agreed to pay the federal government $129 million for cleanup. Nevertheless, as a 1978 report given to the New York Legislature stated, the devastating effects of Love Canal, in terms of human suffering and environmental damage, can never be genuinely measured. Even more dire was the fact that unsafe chemical storage was not an isolated event; in 1979, 17,000 drums of leaking chemicals were discovered in a Kentucky town.

THREE MILE ISLAND NUCLEAR SCARE

Many Americans favored finding ways to supplement or replace the use of fossil fuel as energy, and this sentiment increased during the Arab oil embargo of 1973. Some believed that nuclear energy might suit this purpose, while others feared the danger of radioactive energy. *The China Syndrome* (1979), starring Jane Fonda, only increased this fear and caused many to believe that a nuclear meltdown would destroy the earth.

At 4:00 A.M. on March 28, 1979, the Three Mile Island nuclear power plant was in danger of becoming the site of a real-life radioactive disaster. Located by Middletown, Pennsylvania, the plant experienced failure in the nonnuclear portion of its site when the feed water pumps stopped working; the steam generators could no longer remove heat from the building, and the turbine and the reactor automatically shut down in response.

This increased pressure in the nuclear part of the building, and a relief valve that should have decreased this pressure did not operate appropriately and the core element overheated. Instruments measuring coolants in the core provided confusing information, and so, when alarms flashed, staff did not respond in a way that improved the situation or reduced the risk of a radioactive disaster. Approximately half of the core melted during the beginning stages of this accident, and the building was evacuated except for key personnel by 11:00 A.M. By evening, the core appeared to have cooled and stabilized.

Governmental agencies did not anticipate this near disaster and the small amounts of radiation measured outside the reactor caused significant concern. Furthermore, on the morning of Friday, March 30, new worries arose as radiation was released from the auxiliary part of the building that was intended to provide relief to the main nuclear part. As a safety measure, the most vulnerable population, including pregnant woman and young children who lived within five miles of the Three Mile Island nuclear plant, were asked to evacuate the area. Throughout Saturday,

March 31, experts discussed the large hydrogen bubble located in the container holding the reactor core; if this bubble exploded, the situation could become quite dangerous. By April 1, it was determined that, because of a lack of oxygen in the pressure vessel, the bubble could not burn or burst; plus the experts had already succeeded in reducing the size and scope of the bubble.

According to government reporting, a combination of human error and design deficiencies caused the accident. Fortunately, the worst-case scenario—melting nuclear fuel causing a breach in the walls of the building and releasing extremely hazardous radiation—did not occur. No deaths resulted, nor did any injuries; but it did bring about, according to the U.S. Nuclear Regulatory Commission, significant changes in emergency response planning and training.

Postcrisis, governmental agencies and other independent bodies studied the level of released radiation and determined that the average person was exposed to approximately 1 millirem of radiation, which is about one-sixth of the amount given off by a full set of chest x-rays. Nevertheless, human, animal, and plant life continued to be closely monitored. Some experts claim that Three Mile Island came within 30 to 45 seconds of a complete meltdown and more than 100,000 people rallied in Washington, D.C., to protest nuclear power as energy. And, although 9 new nuclear power plants opened in 1979, 11 others—that were planned but not yet started—were not built.

GREENPEACE

This proenvironmental group formed in the 1970s to protest the nuclear testing done by the United States in the Pacific Ocean. The members hired a boat and attempted to travel to the testing site; bad weather thwarted their trip, but also gave them national attention. The group also focused attention on the well-being of whales, which were being hunted in significant numbers. In 1975, members of Greenpeace stationed a boat between whales and those hunting them from Japan and the Soviet Union—and, although they seldom stopped the hunting, their bloody documentaries encouraged the "Save the Whale" movement. This group did something similar for baby seals the following year. When they discovered that hunters clubbed these animals to death, Greenpeace members sprayed a harmless dye on these animals that rendered their fur useless for resale.

DESTROYING THE OZONE

Propellants used in deodorant and hair spray, among other items, harmed the environment by slowly destroying the ozone layer that surrounded the earth. Because the ozone layer prevents harmful ultraviolet rays from reaching the surface of our planet, experts predicted a rise in skin cancer and cataracts as the ozone deteriorated. Environmentalists therefore proposed a ban on fluorocarbon gases used in the propellants; although this was met with opposition from industry, by the time that the FDA banned the substance in 1979, most companies had already found more acceptable alternatives.

THE 1970s

7
Leisure Activities

INTRODUCTION

> The 1970s were a giant cauldron of fads, fancies and fetishes … trendy
> times.[1]

Certain fads of the 1970s—such as Mood Rings and Pet Rocks—instantly
captured the attention of Americans; other trends, including the Little People Originals—eventually renamed Cabbage Patch Kids—were
invented in the 1970s but didn't receive widespread acclaim until the
following decade. Still other trends, such as the ubiquitous smiley face,
were conceptualized in an earlier time, but became hallmarks during this
decade.

Some fads had practical value, including the toe socks; these were knee-
high in length with bright stripes and glittery threads in their design, and
they kept the base of the body warm, including the spots between the toes.
Other fads, such as the clackers, were more curious—and not quite as cozy
and safe. Clackers were basically two pool ball–sized marbles connected
by a string. In the middle of the string was a ring; users slipped a finger
into the ring and then began swinging the balls together, "clacking" them
and then attempting to maneuver trick moves with the toy. Unfortunately,
the glass versions shattered, causing injuries; subsequent plastic versions
never caught on.

Starting in the 1970s, experts predicted a growing amount of leisure
time in industrialized nations; in fact, the inverse proved to be true in
the United States, post-1970s. As two benchmarks: in 1973, the average
adult reported that he or she spent 41 hours per week in work-related
activities, which included time spent at jobs, in schools, and doing house-
work—while approximately 26 hours per week were spent relaxing, in-
dulging in hobbies, and socializing. By 1975, the average work time was

43 hours weekly, and leisure time accounted for 24 hours; in 2003, the work time averaged 49 hours per week and leisure time had dropped to 19 hours. Here is how much of that 1970s leisure time—and discretionary income—was spent.

FADS

Mood Rings

If the 1970s truly were the "Me Decade"—as journalist Tom Wolfe declared in 1976—then no fashion, no fad, no piece of jewelry could better represent these years than the "Impulse Stones"—or, as they were better known, the "Mood Rings." Created in 1975 by Josh Reynolds—a direct descendent of one of England's greatest portrait painters, Sir Joshua Reynolds—mood rings were basic bands of metal that were connected to a large oval-shaped piece of glass that either contained thermotropic liquid crystals or were coated on the back with the substance. These crystals changed color based upon the body heat of the wearer, causing the "jewel" of the ring to also change hue—and, by consulting a chart provided with the purchase of the ring, the person wearing the jewelry could determine his or her mood.

For those questioning why a person would need outside verification of his or her own state of mind, Reynolds explained that a mood ring "makes you more self-aware. You see it change and say, 'Gee, I wonder what's affecting me.'"[2] Reynolds, who has described himself as a "self-schooled behavioral scientist," didn't initially intend to invent a mood ring; he originally meant to use the liquid crystals—which are similar to what was being used in certain types of thermometers and aeronautical instruments—as a tool in his "sensitivity and body control training business." The crystals were, according to Reynolds, "an authentic instrument for bio-feedback … to give a person more information about his body than he would normally take in … for people who wish to monitor themselves."[3] This philosophy touched a chord in many during the 1970s.

These rings apparently helped satisfy, for many consumers, the urge to explore the self, which dovetailed with the introspective frame of mind of those involved in gestalt therapy or Esalen—or one of the decade's many other popular self-awareness techniques or philosophies. This is not surprising as Reynolds himself, pre–mood ring, went through a "'monk-like' journey, a hermit's voyage through group analysis, primal therapy, transcendental meditation, e.s.t." after he quit his job to "search for the new enlightenment" of life. When he returned to work, he began to teach businessmen "rejuvenation techniques, ways in which we could all cut back, mellow out, check hypertension and learn to become aware of stresses and moods."[4] The ultimate result was the creation and marketing of the mood ring.

According to literature provided with the rings, the following colors corresponded, more or less, with the following moods:

Dark blue: Happy, romantic, or passionate

Blue: Calm or relaxed

Blue-green: Somewhat relaxed

Green: Normal or average

Amber: A little nervous or anxious

Gray: Very nervous or anxious

Black: Stressed, tense, or feeling harried

Even if a ring-wearer did not feel that the results garnered by mood rings were scientific, the rings at least served as conversation starters on the subject of feelings and emotions.

People could purchase basic (plastic look-alike) mood rings for as little as $2, while those set in sterling silver cost $45; if willing to invest in a genuine gold setting, you would expect to pay $250. By December 1975, more than $15 million of rings had been sold. After the first flush of success caused the initial stock of mood rings to sell out in New York, innovators—or, more accurately, imitators of this concept—created other products to sell, including more masculine-looking rings, a "mood watcher" that both kept time and monitored moods, mood pendants, and nail polish containing liquid crystals. Mood shirts were sold and manufacturers also attempted to sell handbags with stones in the straps and belts complete with mood buckles.

The veracity of mood rings was debated on the editorial pages of the *Los Angeles Times,* prompted by a letter written by Evelyn McKeever—who suggested that, if mood rings really worked, then those in store windows were actually reflecting the mood of the velvet cloth upon which they rested. Another letter writer wrote to support McKeever, stating that, when he wore two mood rings, one turned blue and the other green, perhaps reflecting the money-hungry state of mind, the writer suggested, of people selling the rings. At least one person wrote in to defend the rings, saying that professionals used a similar principle to treat headaches and hypertension. Meanwhile, celebrity enthusiasm for the product didn't hurt sales. Star-quality owners of mood rings included Sophia Loren, Barbra Streisand, Paul Newman, and Muhammad Ali—who even wrote a poem about the object.

Crystals used in mood-detecting devices usually maintained their effectiveness for one or two years; it wasn't surprising, then, that the shelf-life of this fad also lasted about that long. By 1977, these rings were no longer a hot commodity.

Pet Rocks

The "Pet Rock" concept has come to represent the ultimate exception in marketing; rather than satisfying an obvious need or filling an important niche, the Pet Rock seemed to create its own demand—and then filled it en masse. All began in April 1975 when Gary Dahl, an advertising professional from California, socialized with friends after work. Conversation turned to the high maintenance required by traditional pets such as cats, dogs, and birds, and Dahl informed his pals that pets made too much of a mess; they misbehaved; and they cost too much money. As a tongue-in-cheek alternative, he suggested owning a rock.

His friends found humor in Dahl's off-the-cuff joshing, and so he decided to further pursue the concept by writing a training manual that shared how to have a good relationship with your pet rock and that explained how to make your pebble sit, stay, roll over, play dead, and be housetrained. (It was quickly determined by Dahl that "Come!" was far too complicated a command for a rock.) After creating his manual, Dahl bought a supply of round gray pebbles—Rosarita beach stones—from a building store in San Jose, California, for one penny each. He packed each individual rock in a gift box that looked like a pet carrying case—complete with air holes—and then he began marketing the stone, gift box, and pet rock manual at a gift show in San Francisco in August 1975; he followed up that event with a show held in New York. For publicity, he sent out a quirky press release of himself surrounded by Pet Rocks.

Almost immediately, Neiman-Marcus bought 500 rocks, and *Newsweek* published a story about the concept. By the end of October, Dahl shipped out about 10,000 rocks daily. He appeared on the *Tonight Show* twice, and, by Christmas, Dahl had sold two and a half tons of rocks; his product had appeared in editorials and articles in three-fourths of all daily newspapers across the country. Within a few months, Dahl had sold more than 1 million Pet Rocks at $3.95 each, making him a nearly instant millionaire.

Copycat products inundated the market; ironically, although Dahl never used the word "genuine" or "original" in his marketing, imitators did. Some copycat versions boasted painted-on facial features and some boxes contained a cluster of rocks that represented a pet rock family. Others, hoping to cash in on the fad in another way, offered obedience lessons for pet rocks or burial at sea services for rocks that had perished. (How one could detect its demise is another matter entirely.) The demand for this product, though, evaporated almost as quickly as it began, and imitators did not get the return on investment that they anticipated. Dahl himself, after an extremely successful Christmas selling season, attempted to repackage the allure of the rocks as a quality Valentine's Day gift, but he also had to face up to the fact that the frenzied fad had faded. It is said that he donated large quantities of pet rocks to charities before moving on to another career: that of a motivational speaker who advised people on how to make cash—quick.

In retrospect, how can one explain this frantic fad? No fad before—or since—has been quite as inexplicable. Ken Hakuta, author of *How to Create*

Your Own Fad and Make a Million Dollars and the inventor of the Wacky Wall Walker, suggested that Pet Rocks "gave people a few moments of absolutely meaningless pleasure in a troubled world—no small accomplishment." Hakuta further observed that, if more fads existed, "there would probably be a lot fewer psychiatrists."[5] It's hard to debate Hakuta's logic, but here are two additional factors. First, what a perfect pet for the Me Decade! This creature required no commitment from its owner—other than to feel good about his or her life, however briefly. Next, perhaps women who were entering the workforce for the first time, and who were juggling career and family without the support systems that later developed, found humor in a pet that didn't require one moment of their precious time.

Streaking … "Boogie-Dad … Boogie-Dad … "

People who lived through the 1970s automatically associate this nonsense word with another fad of the decade: streaking—or darting through a public place while nude, usually for the shock value and/or for the entertainment or provocation of an audience. That word association occurs because of a Ray Stevens song, "The Streak," which began playing on radio stations in 1974 and frequently used "boogie-dad" in its humorous chorus. A significant portion of streakers were college students running naked across some portion of their campus; had Stevens's song not become a huge hit, perhaps the effects of this trend would have been more contained. But, a number one song it became—and awareness of streaking hit the national landscape. The thrust of the lyrics was the singer's attempts to prevent his wife—Ethel—from seeing the full frontal view of a male streaker. His cautions of "don't look" apparently fell on deaf ears, though, as at the end of the song, the narrator is demanding that Ethel get her own clothes back on …

Some streakers ran the nude gauntlet without being arrested, while many others simply tried to run as far as they could without being stopped; some arrested were charged with indecent exposure and at least one town created specific laws against streaking.

One infamous streaker is Robert Opal, who raced across the stage of the 46th Academy Awards in 1974 at the peak of the streaking fad. He flashed a peace sign at the cameras that were broadcasting nationally; NBC quickly cut away to avoid a frontal nudity shot. Host David Niven is well remembered for his response: "The only laugh that man will ever get in his life," he quipped, "is by stripping … and showing his shortcomings."

Some did not find streaking funny, including an unnamed doctor who pronounced the following: "Streaking is a recent dramatic example of the thumb-to-nose hurray-for-me-and-to-hell-with-everybody-else syndrome in modern society. It is the latest attempt to erode and destroy convention, decency, and decorum and is primarily an act of teenage and young adult defiance rather than an isolated, innocuous student prank. Its precursors are long unkempt hair, dirty jeans, dirty feet, hippyism, 'ups,' 'downs,' LSD, heroin, and so-called total female liberation."[6] Others, including Ronni Lee Scheier, a recent college graduate in 1974, saw the trend as a way for young adults to blow off steam and release frustrations in a world that was difficult to understand and nearly impossible to master. In a section in the *Chicago Tribune*, "Perspective," readers were invited to express their opinions and to speak out on topics that mattered. Scheier therefore wrote the following: "So, as budding spring freshens the air, why not conspire with Dionysus, that joyful escapist, to cast aside all that confines, dance upon our frustrations, and dwell on nothing more scandalous than the impudence of our own nakedness under the sun!"[7] It seems unlikely that Scheier would successfully persuade the doctor of her viewpoint—or vice versa—but these two comments juxtaposed above clearly show the wide range of emotions provoked by the relatively short trend of streaking.

GAMES, TOYS, AND HOBBIES
Rubik's Cube

Erno Rubik of Hungary invented this puzzle in the mid-1970s and it became one of the most popular games in America by the end of the decade. Rubik worked at the Department of Interior Design at the Academy of Applied Arts and Crafts in Budapest; he was determined to discover a way to enlighten his students about the nature of 3D objects—and the ultimate result was the Rubik's Cube. Perhaps the fact that his father worked as an engineer and his mother as a poet gave him both the technical and expressive backgrounds to create such an object; perhaps the fact that Rubik first studied sculpture before working at the interior design academy also helped expand his ways of thinking and imagining.

Regardless of why and how Rubik was able to create his cube, he definitely invented an object that has fascinated people around the globe. An article in *American Scientist* explains the complexity of the Rubik's Cube as "the most mathematically sophisticated toy ever produced, requiring and popularizing a branch of mathematics rarely seen in earlier mathematical toys, namely the theory of groups."[8] Rubik patented his invention, but imitations soon appeared on the market. Most versions of this toy consisted of a three-inch-by-three-inch-by-three-inch plastic cube-shaped toy with nine multicolored subcubes, internally hinged, on each of its six sides. The cube contains six different colors of subcubes. At the beginning of the challenge, all subcubes on a particular side are the same color; after scrambling the cube so that subcubes are intermingled in hue, the person solving the Rubik's Cube must restore the object to its original configuration. Competitions continue to this day to determine who can solve the puzzle the fastest.

Rubik talked about his product in a lyrical fashion, sharing how he took satisfaction in watching the colors randomly mix together—and then return to the appropriate order again. Tackling this challenge, though, isn't simple or straightforward. According to the UCLA School of Engineering and Applied Science, more than 43 quintillion possible configurations exist. Interestingly enough, the solution to this puzzle—one invented during a decade filled with a search for meaning—has been dubbed "God's algorithm."

Other Popular Toys and Games

The 1970s saw the invention of a wide range of innovative toys, including the Star Wars action figures in 1977. Based upon the popular movie of the same name, these action figures were slightly less than four inches in length, much smaller than the Barbie dolls and GI Joes from previous generations. Because they were smaller, they were less expensive and children could more feasibly collect the entire set. Not surprisingly, the main characters of the movie (including Darth Vader, Luke Skywalker, and Han Solo) had their own action figures, but so did the background aliens—many of whom didn't even have names until one was needed on the toy's packaging. More boys than girls were interested in Star Wars merchandise in the 1970s, a trend that changed in subsequent decades. That didn't stop entrepreneurs from using the main female character from Star Wars—Princess Leia played by Carrie Fisher—in their merchandising efforts.

The year after the Star Wars action figures premiered, Milton Bradley Company invented a game—SIMON—that contained electronic lights and sounds that enhanced the typical board game; it introduced the game at New York discotheques, including at the ultrachic Studio 54. The black, plastic, circular-shaped toy named SIMON was divided into four sections. One section contained a red light that could flash on and off in random patterns; another section was blue, the third yellow, and the fourth green. The player had to correctly repeat the ever-increasing complexity of the pattern—or lose the game.

It's important not to underestimate the effect that SIMON—which was an electronic version of the old childhood game, Simon Says—had on society. According to the *Chicago Tribune*, "'SIMON' shows how far toymakers have come in learning to combine psychological principles with electronic innovation to produce gadgets that can motivate and stroke human beings."[9] People threw SIMON parties, and, early in the morning, extremely dedicated players would show up at FAO Schwartz before work to play. *People, Money, Esquire, GQ,* and *Newsweek* published articles about the game and SIMON was also featured on the *Today Show*. The game sold out during the 1978 Christmas season and remained popular. Perhaps for the first time, a game intended for children became a pop culture phenomenon for adults—and for the country as a whole.

Television Console Games

The inventor of SIMON also created a revolutionary new concept in 1972: TV console games. On January 27, 1972, Magnavox introduced the first-ever home video game system: the Odyssey. Invented by Ralph Baer, an employee of a defense contractor, the original notion was to create a "television gaming apparatus" that would help develop the reflexes of those serving in the military. Baer shared his invention with Magnavox in 1970, and he signed a licensing agreement with them. The original Odyssey cost $100 and it allowed users to play games that used basic black-and-white graphics as its game board. During the first three years, 200,000 units sold; perhaps more would have been purchased, but Magnavox implied in its advertising that the Odyssey would only work on its brand of television; this was not true, but the company hoped to fuel television sales.

A man named Nolan Bushnell saw an early version of the Odyssey's tennis game, and he invented his own game—PONG—for rival Atari. People first played this coin-operated game on machines in bars and arcades, and then Atari partnered with Sears and Roebuck to create a television-based version of the game. This system also cost $100—and, during the 1975 Christmas season, more than $40 million of Atari game systems sold.

After Atari's success, Coleco released Telstar and Magnavox created Odyssey 100, each of which found some sales. In August 1976, Fairchild Camera released the first-ever programmable home video game system; programmable meant that the games themselves were contained on devices separate from the actual hardware of the game system, which gave users more flexibility in the games that they wanted to play. The Fairchild system cost $169 and individual games, contained on cartridges similar to eight-track tapes, cost $20 each. Users were disappointed with the graphics and limited game choices, though, and they felt the same about RCA's Studio III system.

In October 1977, Atari released a $199 programmable video game system that sold more than 25 million units. Many consider this unit the beginning of "true" home video games; these included Space Invaders, Asteroids, and Pac-Man.

Computer User as Hobbyist

When the decade debuted, teens and adults interested in electronics were building games, radios, and other light-controlled devices, much as they had been for the past two decades. Early in the 1970s, though, they could begin purchasing integrated circuit boards at a reasonable price,

Members of a Space Invaders Club enjoy the television console game by Atari. Rows of aliens would move from the top of the screen toward the bottom, and, if one successfully reached the bottom without being "shot" by the player, the game ended as a loss. Courtesy of Photofest.

greatly extending the options available for their experimentation. During this era, then, hobbyists created increasingly more sophisticated devices—at younger and younger ages.

When Intel began selling the 8080 microprocessor in the mid-1970s, people first attempted to build their own computers; MITS, Inc. sold kits for $395 each. The January 1975 issue of *Popular Electronics* featured this do-it-yourself project—which snagged the attention of Paul Allen and Bill Gates. Those two young entrepreneurs moved into the building where these computer kits were being sold, establishing their original software company of Micro-Soft. Throughout the decade, electronics hobbyists could find increasing numbers of books and magazines describing computer building projects; although the notion of computer kits was short-lived, the product itself was still in its toddler stages.

Citizens Band Radio

The Citizens Band (CB) radio existed since 1947, but its usage did not become popular until the mid-1970s when long-distance truckers used CB radios to communicate information to one another—about traffic conditions, detours, or "speed traps" set up by police officers—and to chase away the loneliness during long hauls. CB radios consisted of a microphone, speaker system, and control box; they were relatively easy to set up and to use, and they served as a precursor to cellular phones. Moreover, by the 1970s, the cost of technology had become more affordable, which fostered even wider usage.

CBs gained popularity, with more than 11.3 million units sold in 1976 alone.[10] Reasons for CB popularity potentially include:

- Truckers—and other users—bonded with others while still maintaining a sense of anonymity; users frequently selected colorful nicknames—or "handles"—for themselves, much like people chose e-mail addresses later in the century.

- Users created special slang that helped solidify their subculture: "Smokey" indicated a police officer; "bubble gum machine" referred to a police car; "wrapper" meant an unidentified/undercover one; "negatory" was a lively way to say "no"; and "10–4" signified that a user was signing off.

- Explicit or vulgar language was forbidden; although this rule was generally respected, CB owners used this forum to vent their frustrations over the rising gasoline prices, the oil boycotts, political scandals, and the Vietnam War.

- Movies such as *Smokey and the Bandit,* starring Burt Reynolds, Sally Field, and Jackie Gleason, and songs such as "Convoy," wherein a CB user dubbed "Rubber Duck" organizes a powerful bumper-to-bumper conglomeration of vehicles, shared "trucker culture" with society at large.

These movies and songs showed CB users in a positive light, as the characters involved tended to be rugged individuals who often fought against the status quo, sometimes humorously.

Dungeons and Dragons

In 1971, Gary Gygax and Jeff Perren invented a fantasy game called Chainmail that involved the use of medieval warfare miniatures; within a couple of years, this game evolved into the Dungeons and Dragons game (D&D) that also incorporated significant role playing. On the one hand, D&D was deceptively simple and straightforward. Game boards and playing pieces were optional, and there were no traditional winners or losers in this noncompetitive activity; rather, "You survive and you learn from your mistakes and you have a good adventure."[11] On the other hand, D&D was a "frightfully complex, infinitely open-ended game that can be played with calculators and computers or with nothing but pencils, paper and a strange array of multisided dice"[12] and successful players needed to possess strong imagination and intellect.

Burt Reynolds and Sally Field star in the 1977 hit Smokey and the Bandit, *a movie that featured the use of CB radios as Reynolds attempted to illegally smuggle Coors beer into Georgia. Some call this the ultimate truckers' movie. Courtesy of Universal Pictures/Photofest.*

In D&D, the central player of the game, the Dungeon Master (DM), created an imaginary world peopled with characters that are evil and good, weak and strong, and he developed a fantasy landscape complete with castles and dungeons, monsters and treasures. The DM must know all agreed-upon rules and he monitors the actions of the players. Players further develop their assigned medieval characters as they attempt to escape from the make-believe dungeon; obstacles stand in their way, of course, ranging from goblins to physical obstructions.

Games could last for hours, days, weeks, months—or even years. Devotees of the game—who were often either teenagers or college students—might spend hundreds of dollars to purchase the countless manuals and accessories that furthered their ability to play the game. By the end of the decade, creator Gary Gygax estimated that one quarter of a million Americans engaged in D&D play, while other estimates ranged up to 300,000; merchants stocking D&D items reported a 40 percent increase in sales near the end of the decade, and the men who produced the game earned $2 million in 1979 alone.

Controversy, however, surrounded D&D. Some parents applauded their children's participation, calling the game challenging and an effective way to work out psychological issues using imaginative solutions to unexpected problems. Psychiatrist Jerry Wiener points out that, in D&D, children who feel powerless can feel otherwise because of the "great ingenuity and stimulation" of the game.[13] Other parents worried, though, about signs of depression in their children after their character died in the game. At least one participant, a 16-year-old who was attending Michigan State University, became so involved in the game that he disappeared for nearly a month while allegedly engaging in a live version of the game using eight miles of steam tunnels located beneath the campus as the dungeon. After he was found, his parents stated that his involvement in D&D was not a direct cause of his disappearance; they gave no alternate explanation.

Although it is seldom possible to determine, with certainty, why a specific activity appeals to a certain generation, some experts pointed out that, during a decade of disillusionment such as the 1970s, an escape from reality is certainly understandable.

Genealogy and the Search for Ethnic/Cultural Identity

By the mid-1970s, the *Los Angeles Times* estimated that half a million Americans pursued genealogy as a hobby, often belonging to one or more of the 700 genealogical clubs and societies in the country; at that time, genealogy ranked as the country's third most popular hobby. According to the *Chicago Tribune,* the intense interest in genealogy and the search for ethnic, cultural, and familial history could be attributed to three factors: a yearning for family ties in an increasingly mobile society; the greater amount of leisure time afforded post–World War II; and the Bicentennial. As the 200th birthday of the United States loomed, people began gathering together "rambling recollections of family elders, old tattered family Bibles, and musty Civil War-era photos"[14] to piece together their own family history, which had either occurred in the United States for several generations or more recently led them to the country.

According to Harold Hazelton of the New York Genealogical and Biographical Society, "People who always vaguely thought they had an ancestor who was a close associate of George Washington or some other figure of the Revolution are feeling themselves challenged to find out whether it's true or not."[15] In response, libraries, schools, and YMCAs offered genealogy classes, while publishers began printing books and magazines on the subject. Alex Haley's *Roots* served as the most easily recognizable of these printed materials as he traced his genealogy back seven generations to the continent of Africa and to his ancestor, Kunta Kinte. The book, which became a television miniseries, helped fuel an interest in genealogy, particularly among African Americans.

Roots, though, was not the first foray into the subject in the 1970s. Richard Gambino's *Blood of My Blood* shared his Italian heritage, while Irving Howe's *World of Our Fathers* explored the first-generation Jewish American experience in New York City. In *Journey to Aratat,* Michael J. Arlen shows how he traced his roots to Armenia.

In 1974, Congress approved the Ethnic Heritage Studies Program, providing nearly $6 million to allow citizens the opportunity to research their roots, and for Americans of all ethnic backgrounds to learn about that of others; this act helped create ethnic studies programs at universities around the country. For Chinese Americans, the resumption of diplomatic discussions between their two countries allowed them the opportunity to finally visit the homes of their ancestors. Furthermore, the Church of Jesus Christ of Latter-Day Saints (Mormons) continued to add to its genealogy collection during this decade; the members' belief that they could "perform proxy 'temple work' for ancestors so that the dead could receive the benefits of the Mormon religion in the afterlife"[16] fueled much of their enthusiasm for the project. By the mid-1970s, Mormon structures housed more than 130,000 volumes of family genealogies along with more than 1 million rolls of microfilm containing census records, birth and death certificates, probate documents, and countless other minutiae from around the world.

One other factor existed in this feverish search for roots. In previous generations, it was largely assumed that adopted children would remain ignorant of their birth family and its history. That assumption was challenged in the 1970s, with adoption agencies reporting increasing amounts of requests for biological family information.

SPORTS

Women and Sports

Pre-1972, educational institutions were not required to provide equal program activities to its students based upon gender. On June 23, 1972, however, this changed when President Richard Nixon signed into legislation Title IX of the Educational Amendments of 1972. This law prohibited discrimination based upon gender in any educational program that received any federal funding whatsoever. Its exact wording is as follows: "No person in the United States shall, on the basis of sex, be excluded from participation in, or denied the benefits of, or be subjected to discrimination under any educational program or activity receiving federal assistance." Although little controversy arose when the act first passed, heated debate soon began. Prompted by concerns stated by the National Collegiate Athletic Association (NCAA), a significant portion of American citizens soon expressed the viewpoint that male sports programs would suffer if funds were diverted to either begin or strengthen athletic programs for females.

In 1974, a senator proposed the "Tower Amendment" that would exclude any revenue-producing sports from being included in this act; the amendment was rejected but the debate didn't die. On July 21, 1975, President Gerald Ford signed into legislation language that specifically prohibited gender discrimination in athletics, giving educational institutions three years in which to fully comply. Legislators continued to introduce amendments that would limit the scope of Title IX, with this debate continuing for decades past its introduction. Nevertheless, Title IX significantly changed the landscape of women's sports. Comparing athletic participation of females who were under the age of 10 before the passage of the legislation (born in 1963 and later) with those who were born before 1963 shows an increase of 19 percent in participation.

Tennis player Billie Jean King served as a symbol of female athletic ability during the tumultuous early days of Title IX. Shortly after its passage, she was challenged by Bobby Riggs to a televised match that became known as the "Battle of the Sexes."

Riggs became a world-class tennis player in 1939, when he was just 16. Although his tennis career basically ended in the 1950s, he returned to the spotlight early in 1973 when he challenged—and beat—tennis player Margaret Court; he then announced that women could never beat men in the athletic arena and demanded a match with the "women's lib leader," Billie Jean King, who was 29 years old to his 55. Riggs had already won 20 Wimbledon titles, whereas she had won the Associated Press's Woman Athlete of the Year award in 1967 and 1973; moreover, *Sports Illustrated* chose her as the Sportswoman of the Year in 1972. King, who resented the fact that male tennis players were paid so much more than female champions, accepted this challenge eagerly. Prematch, Riggs would wear T-shirts asking for "Men's Liberation," and, during interviews, he would proclaim that if he was going to symbolize a male chauvinist pig, he would ensure that he was the biggest male chauvinist pig ever.

On September 20, 1973, the Riggs-King match appeared on prime time television with approximately 50 million people watching the match. Riggs arrived in a carriage pulled by women while University of Houston football players carried King onto the court. Billie Jean King subsequently beat Bobby Riggs in three straight sets (6–4; 6–3; and 6–3), with Riggs crediting King's speed and overall excellence for the results.

King was not the only successful female tennis player of the decade. Chris Evert served as another powerhouse; in 1970, when she was just 15 years old, Evert beat the world champion, Margaret Court, in a tournament. One year later, Evert reached the semifinals of the U.S. Open, the youngest tennis player to ever accomplish this feat. Keeping amateur status until 1973, Evert had earned $1 million in tennis by 1976—again the first tennis player to reach this benchmark. In 1978, she won the U.S. title for the fourth time, the first tennis player to accomplish this since the 1930s.

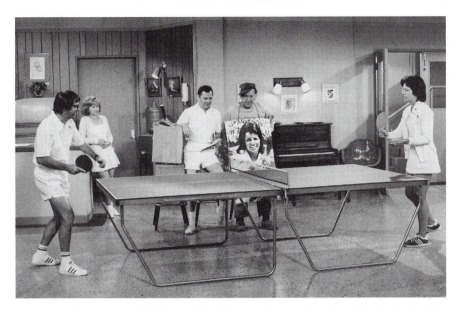

In 1973, Bobby Riggs and Billie Jean King, the tennis stars who played in the Battle of the Sexes match, guest star on the popular sitcom The Odd Couple *with Sandra Giles, Tony Randall, and Jack Klugman. The title of the episode, "The Pig Who Came to Dinner," played off the male chauvinist pig image of Bobby Riggs. Courtesy of ABC/Photofest.*

Although Evert received press coverage because of these wins, her romance with tennis star Jimmy Connors also kept her in the eye of the public. On July 25, 1972, when news of this romance was just becoming known, the *Cleveland Plain Dealer* noted that Chris was late to a team practice. She was tardy because of time spent with Connors, and the article's opening line read, "Love may make the world go 'round, but it sure raises havoc with tennis practice."[17] Passionate as the romance became, Evert's tennis playing serves as her true legacy.

Olympics, 1972: "Games of Peace and Joy"

Mention the 1972 Olympics held in Munich, Germany, and three memories come to mind—the first one, tragic. This was the Olympics wherein eight terrorists killed two Israeli athletes and took nine more as hostages; all were killed by the following day. Included among the dead was 26-year-old David Berger, a dual-citizenship American who had returned to Israel. Another American, Mark Spitz, was also Jewish, and he left Germany after the act of terrorism. His Olympic performance before the tragedy served as the second memorable aspect of the 1972 games. Spitz had already won four individual gold medals in swimming and he participated in three gold medal relay events; all set world records and countless Americans took tremendous pride in his accomplishments.

The final event, extremely controversial when it occurred, still causes debate. After the U.S. basketball team lost the gold medal game against the Soviet Union—the first basketball game ever lost in the Olympics by Americans—the U.S. team refused to accept the silver medal. The players did so because they felt that they had lost unfairly; they were winning the game until officials granted the Soviet team three chances to convert an inbound pass, and, on the third attempt, the Soviets succeeded in their attempts, winning the game with a score of 51–50. Olympic competition was intense between the United States and the Soviet Union during the Cold War era under the best of circumstances, and this controversy added significant fuel to the fire. To this day, people discuss this game.

Olympics, 1976

Perhaps the most spectacular performances of the 1976 Olympics (held in Montreal, Canada) were given by 14-year-old Romanian gymnast Nadia Comaneci, who scored seven perfect 10s and won three gold medals. Nevertheless, four American athletes established themselves as world-class athletes, as well; these include decathlon runner Bruce Jenner and three boxers: "Sugar" Ray Leonard, Michael Spinks, and his brother, Leon Spinks.

Jenner set a world record by scoring 8,634 points in the decathlon, caus-ing some to label him the "World's Greatest Athlete." He received the Sullivan Award, given to the greatest amateur athlete of the year, in 1976, and his photo appeared on Wheaties boxes.

Leonard won a gold medal in the Olympics and he went on to win the 1979 welterweight championship. He was later named "Fighter of the Decade" in the 1980s. Michael Spinks turned pro the year after he won his gold medal in the 1976 Olympics, using a punch known as the "Spinks Jinx"; he is now considered among the four best light heavyweight boxers in American history. Meanwhile, Leon Spinks, postgold, briefly took away Muhammad Ali's heavyweight boxing title.

Boxing

Heavyweight boxing was dominated by three superstars in the 1970s: Muhammad Ali, Joe Frazier, and George Foreman, and it witnessed the rise of another star, Larry Holmes. One of the sport's greatest matches, "the Fight of the Century," took place on March 8, 1971, between Ali—who was born Cassius Marcellus Clay, but who often went by the moni-ker, "the Greatest"—and Frazier, who was the reigning heavyweight champion. Ali, who called himself the "People's Champion," claimed that

Frazier couldn't truly be champ unless he had beaten Ali—which is just what Frazier did in the 15th round of their match-up at Madison Square Garden; the decision was unanimous.

In January 1973, George Foreman, who was known for his sheer brute strength, challenged Frazier for the title in what served as the first boxing match aired by HBO. Broadcaster Howard Cosell's comments during the culmination of this fight, when Foreman clinched the heavyweight title, still serve as one of the sport's most memorable phrases. Repeated in an emphatic, staccato tone, Cosell simply said, "Down goes Frazier … Down goes Frazier … Down goes Frazier … "

In 1974, Ali, who could "float like a butterfly, sting like a bee," captured the heavyweight crown from Foreman. This fight took place in the Congo and was known as the "Rumble in the Jungle." Ali used his "Rope-a-Dope" strategy, wherein he rested against the ropes of the ring, allowing Foreman to attack him, hoping that he would wear himself out in the process—which Foreman obviously did.

On October 1, 1975, Ali and Frazier boxed against each other one more time, with 28,000 people in the arena and an estimated 700 million

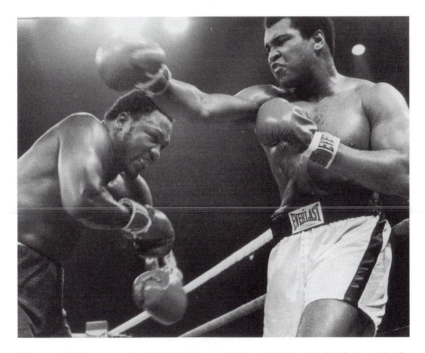

Heavyweight boxers and rivals Muhammad Ali and Joe Frazier battle it out in the seventh round of the Thrilla in Manila fight held on October 1, 1975. Ali won the match on a technical knockout in the 14th round. Courtesy of Photofest.

television viewers. Ali, well known for his pithy sayings, promised that the fight would be a "killa and a thrilla and a chilla when he got the gorilla in Manila." Ali won the fight.

Baseball

Powerhouse teams of the 1970s include the 1970 Baltimore Orioles, Cincinnati's "Big Red Machine" in 1975, and the Oakland As during the early part of the decade. In 1970, the Orioles put up a 108–54 record, winning its division by 15 games. The team beat Minnesota in three straight games to win the American League Championship—and then captured the World Series title against the Cincinnati Reds in just five games. The following year, the Orioles' roster included four pitchers who won at least 20 games.

In 1975, the Reds exactly duplicated the 1970 Orioles' win-loss record. Its star-studded lineup included Pete Rose, nicknamed "Charlie Hustle" for his boundless enthusiasm and "can-do" attitude, and Johnny Bench, arguably the sport's greatest catcher. During the 1970s, a Cincinnati player won the Most Valuable Player award six times, and Bench won two of them. Joe Morgan's MVP season in 1975 helped lead the team into the World Series, where it beat the Boston Red Sox in seven games.

The As boasted stars such as pitcher Rollie Fingers and outfielder Reggie Jackson, and it won the World Series in 1972, 1973, and 1974. Jackson, after being traded to the New York Yankees, hit four consecutive home runs against the Dodgers during the fifth and sixth games of the 1977 World Series; Jackson's nickname was "Mr. October."

Controversy also occurred in baseball during the 1970s. On January 16, 1970, player Curt Flood filed a lawsuit protesting a trade deal that he did not wish to fulfill. He requested free agency and the ability to make his own choices, and he compared baseball's system wherein owners decided which players played on which team to the system of pre–Civil War slavery. The Supreme Court did not buy that argument or the antitrust one, ruling in favor of organized baseball.

Shortly before the 1972 season was to begin, on April 1, players went on strike, demanding more health benefits and a better pension plan. The season was delayed by nine days, with 86 canceled games, before owners satisfied the players' demands. Although that season was played to its conclusion, spring training was delayed in 1973 until March 1, as players and owners attempted to hash out more contractual details. One feature newly granted to the players and their union, salary arbitration, radically changed the power balance between team owners and players, as players could now request arbitration after two years of major league play; owners were bound by the decisions.

Tennis

Billie Jean King and Chris Evert featured prominently in women's tennis; men's tennis included Arthur Ashe, who was already an established star after winning both the U.S. Open and U.S. Amateur championships in 1968. In 1975, he beat reigning champion Jimmy Connors, who was a full decade younger than Ashe, at Wimbledon. That year, Ashe ranked number one in the United States and fourth in the world; in 1976, he ranked number two in the United States.

John McEnroe sprung into prominence later in the decade, perhaps as well known for his aggressive, tantrumlike behavior on the court as for his stellar play. Nicknamed "Superbrat," he qualified for Wimbledon play in 1977 at the age of 18, the youngest to do so. He reached the semifinals where he lost to Connors, who was ranked number one in the world during every year from 1974–1978. McEnroe won his first U.S. Open in 1979.

Football

The Pittsburgh Steelers and its "Steel Curtain" defense served as the powerhouse National Football League team in the 1970s, making the playoffs eight times and winning Super Bowl titles in 1974, 1975, 1978, and 1979; nine of its players ended up in the Football Hall of Fame. Led by quarterback Terry Bradshaw and NFL Defensive Player of the Year in 1972 and 1974, "Mean" Joe Greene, other outstanding players included Franco Harris, Lynn Swann, John Stallworth, Mel Blount, Jack Lambert, Jack Ham, and Mike Webster. In 1974, the team selected four Hall of Famers in one year (Webster, Swann, Stallworth, and Lambert). Coach Chuck Noll led all four Super Bowl teams, the only NFL coach to win four of these titles.

"Mommy, why does Daddy cuss the TV and call it Howard?" Football fans began to watch games broadcast live on a weekday when "Monday Night Football" first aired on September 21, 1970. Initial commentators included Keith Jackson, Howard Cosell, and Don Meredith; after the first season, Jackson was replaced by Frank Gifford. Alex Karras and Fran Tarkenton also served as commentators during the 1970s, as did Fred Williamson for the 1974 season.

Basketball

Spectacular teams from the decade include the 1969–1970 New York Knicks, which boasted players such as Willis Reed, Walt Frazier, Dick Barnett, Dave DeBusschere, Bill Bradley, and Cazzie Russell. The team's winning percentage of .732 fueled its effort to make the NBA Championship Series for the first time in Knickerbocker history; two inspirational baskets, made by injured team captain Willis Reed during the decisive game of the championship, sealed its first league victory.

Another team of significance was the 1971–1972 Los Angeles Lakers, with Gail Goodrich, Jerry West, Wilt Chamberlain, Jim McMillian, and Happy Hairston capturing the first Laker championship with an .841 winning percentage; the team won 33 consecutive games that season, breaking the NBA record for consecutive wins.

The 1974–1975 season ended with one of the sport's most exciting championship playoffs, as the Boston Celtics played against the Milwaukee Bucks and its star player, Kareem Abdul-Jabbar. Going all the way to seven games, Boston won the series.

The end of the decade served as the beginning of the Boston Celtics rivalry—led by Larry Bird, Kevin McHale, and Robert Parish—against the Los Angeles Lakers, with multitalented rookie Earvin "Magic" Johnson and veteran player Abdul-Jabbar, with his amazing sky-hook shot.

Another player of note, Julius Erving—or "Dr. J."—who eventually scored more than 30,000 career points, began his professional career during the 1970s. He incorporated mid-air twists and turns and slam dunk shots into his play, a style sometimes called "show time."

THE 1970s

8
Literature

INTRODUCTION

Literary novels published during the 1970s tackled challenging issues, including those associated with the feminist and civil rights movements, political disillusionment, violence, and changing family roles. Characters became alienated from their spiritual roots and disconnected from their place within the family unit and in society as a whole.

Short stories frequently focused on characters with no discernable motives for their actions, people who performed tasks and lived life without any sense of meaning or purpose. According to critic Carol Iannone, these minimalist stories served as the "'deconstruction' of literature's pretensions to meaning and range, of its claim to speak a higher and subtler language than that available in popular culture of everyday life."[1] *New York* magazine was a prime publishing spot for these types of stories.

Readers of popular novels were faced with a dazzling array of choices, which were available in a wide variety of genres. Romance novels, mystery novels, political and spy thrillers, and horror novels were included in the mix.

The push toward new journalism, a genre of nonfiction that incorporated elements of fiction to tell its story, continued through the first half of the decade, both as a practice and as a source of great debate.

Writers of both fiction and nonfiction received conflicting messages about the definition of obscenity and its legal strictures. In 1970, the Commission on Obscenity and Pornography issued a 700-page report in which the majority of participants agreed that the government should not interfere with the rights of adults to read, obtain, or view explicitly sexual materials involving other adults. The committee did not reach consensus, however, and 250 pages of the report contained dissenting opinions. President Nixon called the report "morally bankrupt" while Vice President Agnew proclaimed that, "As long as Richard Nixon is President, Main Street is not going to turn into Smut Alley."[2] The Senate voted 60–5 to reject the report, and the debate over what was obscene continued, with inconsistent rulings continuing to be made in the court system.

Poets continued to pursue many of the same experimental avenues as they did during the 1960s, with surrealism a key area of exploration; they used surrealism as a "tool to shatter older conventions and revitalize their approach to language."[3] Magazine publishers began targeting more and more niche audiences; underground and alternative newspapers and magazines would set themselves up and then fold throughout the decade.

From a business standpoint, publishing was evolving, and, for the first time, the marketing function surpassed the editorial function in book publishing houses. Meanwhile, savvy professionals in the publishing world were not optimistic about the direction their business was taking. Near the end of the decade, a publishing survey revealed a sense of pessimism about the industry, one felt so keenly that some experts asked to not be quoted. In general, they saw four major problems: the drying up of middle-range books, conglomerate takeovers, problems of distribution, and giant deals in which the majority of dollars went to a select group of writers.

FICTION

Literary Fiction

Joyce Carol Oates is a prolific and award-winning author who, during the 1970s, published seven novels, along with a number of novellas, short story collections, dramas, and poetry anthologies. Oates bases her work in contemporary times and critics have noted a group of themes clustered within her body of writing. These include violence and its effects on people; the combination of strength and frailty in the human spirit, especially in women; and the rapidly evolving twentieth century. Her detractors have claimed that she limited herself by focusing on those themes; her defenders point out that, within this assemblage, she has created works of significant complexity.

Oates's characters attempt to find a niche within a world without security, and they struggle to meet that challenge. These characters, on the whole, are ordinary people who endure the random violence of modern-day life and for whom these acts of violence are not climactic moments; rather, they are commonplace events that are absorbed without significant importance placed on them. Perhaps these themes and characters appealed to readers of the 1970s because they mirrored the challenges inherent in their own lives and reflected their own insecurities about what the future might bring. Although Oates was not identified as a feminist writer, her focus on women who persevere resonated with many readers.

She penned an essay about another major literary figure of the 1970s: John Updike. In her fiction, Oates told stories about the collision between violence and love; in her essay, she wrote that Updike's genius is "best excited by the lyric possibilities of tragic events that, failing to justify themselves as tragedy, turn unaccountably into comedies. Perhaps it is out of a general sense of doom, of American expansion and decay."[4] Updike's Rabbit series bears out that observation. In 1960, Updike published *Rabbit, Run.* His main character, Harry Angstrom, is a former basketball player who struggles with middle-class married life; early in his marriage, he has an affair that indirectly causes the death of his infant daughter. In 1971, Updike released the sequel to this novel, setting *Rabbit Redux* in 1969 and using two historical events, Apollo 11 and the Vietnam War, as a backdrop.

In the sequel, Angstrom learns of his wife's affair while watching the Apollo launch on a television located in a bar; he envisions the rocket going into a great emptiness, a metaphor for his own sense of loss. Although critics have called the passive Harry a "nonentity," author Charles Berryman discounts the idea that a storyteller as strong as Updike would create such a bland character; instead he proposes a much more intriguing scenario. "If the moon is traditionally associated with love and madness," he writes, "it may be that Updike's protagonist learns more about both of these subjects than either Armstrong or Aldrin with their footprints in the moon dust."[5] In a plot twist that does justice to Oates's comment about Updike's tragedies turning comic, two people enter Harry's life and home: 18-year-old Jill, who is fleeing her rich parents' home in search of sex, drugs, and radical politics; and Skeeter, a fundamentalist who imagines himself as a black Jesus. Throughout the book, Angstrom attempts to find his place in the world and within his relationships while Updike uses the themes of space and war to illustrate Angstrom's emotional upheavals.

Another series of Updike's novels focuses on a character named Henry Bech; critics assert that this series contains semiautobiographical material. Another author—Kurt Vonnegut Jr.—was also established in the 1960s. In his 1970s works, Vonnegut began openly to use his public persona— represented as a character named Kilgore Trout—as the narrator in his novels. This practice began with *Breakfast of Champions* in 1973; in this novel, a Midwest car dealer believes that Trout's novels are not fictional at all, but in fact are real. According to the *New York Times,* Vonnegut "wheels out all the latest fashionable complaints about America—her racism, her gift for destroying language, her technological greed and selfishness—and makes them seem fresh, funny, outrageous, hateful, and lovable, all at the same time."[6] Most critics point out a sometimes overwhelming sense of pessimism in Vonnegut's world perspective as he writes about contemporary society and its pervasive sense of emptiness. His bitter sense of humor, though, serves to counterbalance that darkness. In 1979, Vonnegut wrote *Jailbird*, wherein he delves into the values that middle-class Midwesterners hold dear and see as ideal. This novel also received praise.

Toni Morrison also emerged as a major writer of the 1970s, publishing her first three novels. The first, *The Bluest Eye*, shares the story of Pecola Breelove who prays for blue eyes, believing that her horrible life will improve when her eyes change hue. The second book, *Sula*, explores the intense relationship between two black women who are bound together by a terrible secret. The third novel, *Song of Solomon*, won the National Book Critics Award; in this book, a character named Milkman searches for a hidden treasure of gold. Although he never finds those riches, he does discover important family traditions.

Morrison sets her first novel in her hometown of Lorain, Ohio, and she incorporates some of the colloquialisms that she recalled from her childhood. "My first published phrase," she said, "was 'Quiet as it's kept.' Now, if you were a black woman in Northeast Ohio in the 1940s, you'd know that a huge lie was going to be told. Terrible, over the back fence gossip about some relationship they probably invented."[7] Morrison's critics have suggested that writers should transcend divisions; they aver that she should write about whites as well as blacks, but critic Hilary Mantel ridicules that notion: "Morrison has shown through her distinguished career," she writes, "that there are other eyes to look through and other mouths through which to speak, and that these visions and discourses are in no way 'alternative'; if you are black, and a woman, they are simple, central and natural."[8] Fans support Mantel's viewpoint, praising Morrison for allowing them to hear the authentic voices of an urban minority population.

Another novel, this one focusing on a former slave, also captured the attention of American readers: *The Autobiography of Miss Jane Pittman* by Ernest J. Gaines. He writes the story from the perspective of Pittman when she was already 110 years old, reminiscing about her life and memories.

Saul Bellow had already received numerous awards before the 1970s began. In 1970, he won the National Book Award for *Mr. Sammler's Planet* and he was the first writer to win this prize three times; in 1975, he won the Pulitzer Prize for *Humboldt's Gift*, and, in 1976, he won the Nobel Prize for literature. At Bellow's funeral in 2005, author Philip Roth suggested that Bellow was one of the two most important writers of the twentieth century, listing William Faulkner as the other. He was commended for bringing a sense of the "immigrant's hustle, the bookworm's brains and the high-minded notions of the born romantic"[9] to American letters.

Other 1970s writers of note include Gore Vidal (*Two Sisters, Burr, Myron, 1876*, and *Kalki*) and Joseph Heller, whose 1960s' war satire, *Catch 22*, appeared in theaters in 1970. In 1974, he published *Something Happened*, and, in 1979, he published *Good as Gold*.

Philip Roth, whose 1969 novel *Portnoy's Complaint* brought him recognition, published several novels in the 1970s, including *Our Gang: Starring Tricky and His Friends* (1971), *The Breast* (1972), *The Great American Novel* (1973), *My Life as a Man* (1974), *The Professor of Desire* (1977), and *The Ghost Writer* (1979).

Tom Robbins wrote *Another Roadside Attraction* and *Even Cowgirls Get the Blues* during this decade. His style, according to one reviewer, can be defined by those who read his work, and she continues with, "Die-hard Tom Robbins fans … trade his novels on chicken buses crawling through Third World countries. They want to climb inside the books, light up a joint and join the fun."[10] His books have also been described as totally bizarre while still being completely coherent.

In 1975, William Gaddis published *Penguin,* a novel in which he turns expectations upside down, refusing to follow any traditional form of narrative. He presents his story almost entirely through dialogue as the characters frequently interrupt one another.

Finally, it seems appropriate to complete this listing of award-nominated and award-winning authors by discussing one who refused to accept a prize. In 1973, Thomas Pynchon published *Gravity's Rainbow,* which won the National Book Award for fiction in 1974. Also selected for the Pulitzer Prize, the advisory board overruled this choice, calling the book "unreadable," "turgid," "overwritten," and "obscene." The following year, this book received the Dean Howells Medal of the American Academy of Arts and Letters; after stating that this award was a great honor, Pynchon declined to accept, saying that any further imposition on the part of the Academy would make him look rude. Pynchon stopped publishing for several years after that refusal, and his whereabouts were not well known.

Popular Fiction

Readers interested in less intellectual material could enjoy fast-paced fiction, ranging from romance to horror, from pulp fiction to political thrillers, with plenty of choices available on bookshelves. Although literary critics often scorned these books, preferring more "serious" fiction, mainstream readers devoured these novels and were eager for the publication of the next book written by their favorite authors.

Barbara Cartland and Phyllis A. Whitney served as two key romance writers of the decade. Cartland, a British writer with a wide American readership, was known as the "Queen of Romance"; she published more than 700 novels, many of them during the 1970s, a period during which she wrote dozens of books annually. She specialized in historical romances with chaste females; her books included such titles as *The Innocent Heiress, The Penniless Peer,* and *The Devil in Love.*

Whitney also was a prolific writer; an American who spent her childhood in Japan, China, and the Philippines with her missionary parents, she set her novels in a wide variety of exotic locales. She frequently wove supernatural elements into her tales, and her 1970s releases came with titles such as *The Vanishing Scarecrow, Mystery of the Scowling Boy,* and *The Glass Flame.*

Rosemary Rogers, who was to become known as the "Queen of Historical Romances" began her career in the 1970s. She published books such as *Wicked Loving Lies,* a story with a pirate theme, and *Wildest Heart,* set on the New Mexico frontier.

During this decade, Harlequin Enterprises, a publishing house, began to focus almost solely on romance novels. It sold its mass market paperbacks on what were called "job racks" at grocery stores, in beauty salons, and at other locales frequented by housewives that were not previously regarded as likely places to buy books. This turned out to be a highly successful marketing strategy that was imitated by other category fiction producers. To attract the attention of shoppers otherwise distracted by sales at the butcher counter and the freshness of the produce section, Harlequin began paying special attention to cover design and dedicated funds to make its covers more eye-catching; this strategy worked well and was soon imitated by other category houses, particularly by those producing westerns, crime fiction, and horror fiction.

Mystery novels also abounded during the 1970s. According to author Leon Lad Panek, the publication of Robert B. Parker's *The Godwulf Manuscript* "signaled the beginning of the hard-boiled renaissance, and no one can say that Parker was anything but adroit at recognizing and employing many of the elements of the classic story."[11] Panek also includes James Crumley in his list of upcoming "hard-boiled writers"; Crumley published two mystery novels during the decade: *The Wrong Case* (1975) and *The Last Good Kiss* (1978).

Tony Hillerman began publishing his Joe Leaphorn and Jim Chee series in 1970, beginning with *The Blessing Way;* Hillerman uses this series to explore the challenges that can occur when modern-day culture clashes with the traditional beliefs of more ancient ones. Other novels from the Leaphorn and Chee series include *The Fly on the Wall* (1971), *Dance Hall of the Dead* (1973), and *Listening Woman* (1978).

Several other mystery writers published a first novel during the 1970s. In 1974, the British author Robert Barnard, who also enjoyed an American audience, published *Death of an Old Goat.* In 1975, Elizabeth Peters published *The Crocodile on the Sandbank,* an historical novel featuring the strong-willed Amelia Peabody. Marcia Muller began her Sharon McCone mystery series in 1977 with *Edwin of the Iron Shoes,* and, in 1979, Anne Perry began her Thomas Pitt series with *The Cater Street Hangman.*

The horror field was dominated by Stephen King, an author who revived the genre in the 1970s. It's possible to compare the underlying psychological themes in King's work to those of the disaster movie, something that was also popular in the decade. In such films, all hope seems lost, but the hero finds a way to salvage the situation; in King's novels, his characters face life-threatening situations and need to rely upon their own inner resources to solve their horrifying crises. King frequently centered his novels on a child in danger; the number of baby boomers with young children was significant during this era, and they would particularly feel the terror of these plot twists.

King's first novel, *Carrie*, debuted in 1974 and featured a taunted teenager who uses telekinetic powers to exact revenge. The film version appeared in 1976, as did his second novel, *Salem's Lot*, wherein small-town residents find themselves transformed into bloodthirsty vampires. In 1977, he penned *The Shining*; the movie based on this novel was directed by Stanley Kubrick, and was memorable for numerous disturbing scenes of a family isolated in a resort hotel high in a snowbound mountain pass and threatened by a father who is going progressively psychotic.

Dean Koontz wrote dozens of suspense novels during the decade, including several under the pen names of K. R. Dwyer, Brian Coffey, Deanna Dwyer, Anthony North, John Hill, and David Axton. As Koontz established his reputation as a writer, these novels were reissued under his own name.

Another writer, Mary Higgins Clark, a New York housewife-turned-novelist, wrote suspense novels such as *Where Are the Children* (1975) and *A Stranger Is Watching* (1978). Known as the "Queen of Suspense," Higgins Clark played on the commonality among fears of her readers. In *Where Are the Children*, a woman needs to start life over after the macabre deaths of her two children. She remarries and has two more children; one day, though, when she looks out the window to check on the children from her new marriage, all she sees is a red mitten. Her nightmare begins again. In Higgins Clark's second novel, a man is about to be executed for a murder he didn't commit; the family of the victim, who believes that their nightmare will be eased after the death sentence is carried out, is wrong. Their nightmare will also occur anew.

Peter Benchley's *Jaws* is perhaps better remembered in movie form, but the book was also highly successful, selling more than 20 million copies and spending more than 40 weeks on the *New York Times* best-seller list.

Glitz and glamour pulsed through the "trash fiction" novels of Harold Robbins and Judith Krantz, among others. Money, sex, and power served as dominant themes. *Scruples*, for example, Krantz's best-selling novel from 1978, was set in the world of high fashion, of champagne and designer clothing.

In a twist that evoked the darker side of personal relationships, Judith Rossner's *Looking for Mr. Goodbar* delved into realities created by the sexual revolution from the perspective of a single parent. She based this book on a real woman who, although brought up in a strict Catholic environment, decides to find sexual partners in New York bars. Although she decides to stop this practice, she makes that determination too late.

Harold Robbins, whose sensational 1961 novel, *The Carpetbaggers*, was loosely based on the life of eccentric billionaire Howard Hughes, continued his career throughout the 1970s. A 1979 novel, *Memories of Another Day*, tells the story of a fictional union leader with close connections to the real life Jimmy Hoffa—a labor boss who disappeared under mysterious circumstances just a few years before. Another novel, *The Betsy* (1971), was made into a movie starring Laurence Olivier, Robert Duvall, and Tommy Lee Jones.

Political espionage novels and spy thrillers found a ready audience in the 1970s, perhaps because, after the Watergate scandal, people were disillusioned by their own leaders and governments. By the time Robert Ludlum published his first book, *The Scarlatti Inheritance*, in 1971, he already had an extensive playwriting career behind him. His novel features Nazis working hand-in-hand with international financiers; his next thriller, *The Osterman Weekend* (1973), focuses on a news executive recruited by the CIA to break up a Soviet spy ring. Ludlam published about one novel per year during the 1970s, and he continued his writing successes after the decade ended.

Leon Uris, perhaps best known for his "Exodus Trilogy," already had numerous novels to his credit before the decade began. In *Trinity* (1976), Urig uses his experiences garnered while living in Dublin, Ireland, to write an epic about Northern Irish farmers from the 1840s until 1916. Central characters include Catholics and Protestants caught up in economic and religious struggles.

One of the most successful examples of historical fiction based on a broadly factual construct was *Roots* by Alex Haley. Writing about his ancestors in Africa and their forced journey to America as slaves, Haley saw his book form the basis of television's first true miniseries.

The American Bicentennial revived an interest in American history, and James Michener, venerated author of the widely popular *The Source* and *Hawaii* in earlier decades, came out with *Chesapeake*, a novel that focuses on several generations of a family living in Maryland from 1583 to the present. His next book, *Centennial*, was set in Colorado in the 1870s and was later filmed as a miniseries. John Jakes also created a series of historical novels that captured the attention of America's readers.

During the 1970s, Larry McMurtry published two western novels: *Moving On* (1970) and *All My Friends Are Going to Be Strangers* (1972). He also received an Academy Award for the screenplay he penned in 1971 for the filming of his 1966 novel, *The Last Picture Show*. Overall, fewer people read western novels during the 1970s than in previous decades. One of the few prolific writers in this genre was Louis L'Amour, a man who saw himself as a simple storyteller. His work has been translated into dozens of languages and his books served as the basis for 30 movies.

Feminist novels became a significant focus of publishing during the 1970s. According to author Lisa Maria Hogeland, these "consciousness-raising novels both reflected and furthered the Women's Liberation Movement's analyses of sexuality, gender, race, and political responsibility and that through their narrative structure the novels actually engaged in consciousness-raising with their readers."[12] These authors include Joan Didion, Erica Jong, Marilyn French, Alison Lurie, Marge Piercy, Joanna Russ, and Alix Kate Shulman. Jong and Didion were known for their literary fiction, while the others published more commercial books.

Other novels that captured the attention of the American public include *Jonathan Livingston Seagull*, Richard Bach's parable about an outcast seagull; its spiritual tone was especially appealing in the 1970s. Erich Segal's *Love Story* shared the relationship between a collegiate athlete and his dying girlfriend. The initial print run was 4,350,000; Ryan O'Neal and Ali McGraw starred in the subsequent movie. As yet another example of a novel turned into a movie, William Peter Blatty's *The Exorcist* climbed to the top of the *New York Times* best-seller list. In it, a priest exorcises demons from a young female patient, played by Linda Blair in the film.

CREATIVE NONFICTION

Let's talk about Me ... Let's find the Real Me ... Let's get rid of all the hypocrisies and impediments and false modesties that obscure the Real Me ... Ah! At the apex of my soul is a spark of the Divine ...[13]

Tom Wolfe pens this satirical mantra in his essay, "The Me Decade and the Third Great Awakening," which was published in his 1976 book, *Mauve Gloves & Madmen, Clutter & Vine*. This essay begins with a woman confessing to the other 249 people in her EST group that she suffers terribly from hemorrhoids. If she could eliminate what she describes as the peanut in her tail, she would be rid of the most negative and repressive thing in her life. Wolfe also shows this woman in another persona, that of the most sexually attractive female in her office, one who can get whatever she wants through her magnetism and alluring appearance. Hemorrhoids, though, are holding her back from living a fulfilled life, so the tanned and coifed group leader encourages her to let out her rage and release the pain. By the end of this cathartic experience, the woman is prone on the carpet, moaning and shrieking as the others join in the keening, centered on his or her own personal pain. Each person at the EST seminar focuses on *Me*, and, through Wolfe's skillful portrayals, we absorb his point about the focus of the 1970s without having to read through dull statistics and quotes from the experts, staples of the "old journalism."

If this essay were written in the twenty-first century, we would consider it an example of "creative nonfiction." In 1976, it was labeled as
"new journalism," a recently defined genre for which Tom Wolfe has received significant credit. New forms and genres of writing rarely, if ever,
spring up overnight with the efforts of one single writer, of course, and
new journalism is no exception. Some have even traced the genesis of this
creative form of nonfiction back to Mark Twain. Nevertheless, it is generally accepted that Tom Wolfe officially ushered in the era of new journalism in 1965 with his book, *The Kandy-Kolored Tangerine-Flake Streamline
Baby*—although it wasn't until 1973 that he published an anthology with
the title *The New Journalism,* thereby making that phrase even more familiar
to writers, editors, and savvy readers.

New journalism put a fresh twist on traditional nonfiction writing by
incorporating elements of fiction writing: using dialogue in a conversa-
tional style; listing everyday, mundane details in the setting; developing
characters through the use of third-person point of view and unique narrative voices; and crafting scenes rather than simply sharing information in a
more linear manner. Some believe that new journalism rose to prominence
during the 1960s and 1970s because a strictly factual recounting could not
possibly impart the nuances of—and passions attached to—the Vietnam
War, civil rights, women's lib, and gay rights, among other events and
causes. Journalists increasingly began focusing on emotional truth as much
as—or perhaps even more than—imparting information in their essays
and articles.

Published pieces of new journalism—whether book-length or a magazine essay—fall along a continuum. Some contain significant features of
this genre and the writer doesn't deviate from the format; in other instances, the influence of new journalism can be detected in the writing,
but the resulting publication is not a pure example of the genre.

Clay Felker, who edited *New York* and *Esquire* magazines, suggested
that the immediacy of television created a need for magazine journalists to
bring a fresh style to their writing in order to compete. Perhaps this sort of
pressure—to transform solid, well-written articles into something more—
is what caused some adherents of new journalism to stretch the boundaries
of what qualified as nonfiction. As just one example, Gail Sheehy later said
that the prostitute featured in her article, "Redpants and Sugarman," that
appeared in *New York* in 1971 was not an actual woman; rather she was a
composite.

Unfortunately for readers, not everyone had the ability to walk new
journalism's "high wire acts"—as William Zinsser has described this style
of writing—which led to plenty of bad writing. Those who did have the
ability and panache to pull off this approach include Tom Wolfe; Truman
Capote, whose book, *In Cold Blood* (1966), was an early example of this genre;
Norman Mailer; Gay Talese; Hunter S. Thompson; and Joan Didion.

Wolfe published *The Painted Word* in 1975, an inside look at America's art world. In 1979, he published *The Right Stuff*, investigating why astronauts put themselves at risk during space exploration. He focuses on the first seven men chosen by NASA, the "Mercury Seven," as well as Chuck Yeager, who broke the sound barrier, but was never selected by NASA to serve as an astronaut.

Mailer wrote several books during the 1970s, including *The Prisoner of Sex* (1971), wherein he suggests that gender determines how a person interprets reality. He received criticism from feminists for this viewpoint. His 1975 book, *The Fight*, details the boxing match between Muhammad Ali and George Foreman. He also published two biographies during the decade: one on Marilyn Monroe and one on convicted murderer Gary Gilmore and his refusal to appeal his death sentence. Mailer received his second Pulitzer Prize for the latter book, titled *The Executioner's Song*.

In 1971, Talese published *Honor Thy Father*, an in-depth look at the New York Bonanno crime family. Known for his willingness to investigate so-called unreportable stories, such as the inside story of the Mafia, Talese was admired by his readers for his in-depth research, and, whenever a topic captured his attention, he returned to it again and again, finding new angles to explore.

Hunter S. Thompson became well known for taking new journalism a step further—into gonzo journalism. Some say that a *Boston Globe* reporter dubbed Thompson with that designation, "gonzo" being an Irish term for the last person standing after an all-night drinking marathon, but another explanation for the term exists. A friend was said to tell Thompson that his writing was "totally gonzo," which may be a bastardization of the Spanish term, *gonzagas*, loosely translated as "fooled you." Regardless of which explanation is accurate, Thompson immersed himself in the stories that he told, lacing his sense of humor—which has been described as both manic and drug-induced—throughout the adventurous telling of his stories. Two books published by Thompson during the 1970s were *Fear and Loathing: On the Campaign Trail '72* (1974), in which he "intersperses behind-the-scenes reporting, hyperbolic political commentary, and humorous fantasy"[14] and *The Great Shark Hunt* (1977).

Editor Clay Felker did not believe that Thompson fit into the new journalism category, stating that he did not stick to the truth and that he made things up to suit his purposes. "Hunter Thompson," he adds, "was kind of an out-of-control buffoon in many ways, who managed to capture a crazy moment in American history."[15] *Rolling Stones* editor Jann Wenner disagreed with that assessment, saying that Thompson's jokes and fantasies could easily be distinguished from what he intended as reporting.

Although many of new journalism's stars were men, this was not an exclusively male club. Joan Didion also published a significant amount of material, including the nonfiction book *The White Album* in 1979. She suggests that her nonthreatening and physically petite appearance helped her gather material. Writer Carolyn Wells Kraus quotes Didion expressing her personal philosophy of writing, that as "nonfiction writers, we interpret what we see, select the most workable of the multiple choices"[16] and therefore present the world through authorial lenses. Kraus and Didion point out the risk of autobiographical intrusion into new journalism-style essays and books; although all writers—whether novelists, poets, or journalists—must make critical selections of what to include and what to leave out of their work, new journalism puts the writers in an especially vulnerable position.

Maya Angelou, although not identified with the creative nonfiction/new journalism movement, became well known for the story of her often-terrifying childhood. She published *I Know Why The Caged Bird Sings* on the cusp of the 1970s; although reviews were mixed for this book, some critics have compared her work to that of Frederick Douglass's autobiography as they both have shared their experiences as an African American facing racism.

True crime novels found a ready market in the 1970s with Vince Bugliosi's and Curt Gentry's *Helter Skelter* a prime example. The two write of Bugliosi's experiences when he prosecutes Charles Manson for the murder of Sharon Tate; the title comes from a Beatles' song that Manson liked to hear. In *The Onion Field,* Los Angeles police officer Joseph Wambaugh describes the murder of a police officer, along with how it affected his partner who survived—and its impact on the men who committed the crime.

Other books tackling serious subjects include *Bury My Heart at Wounded Knee* by Dee Brown, and *All the President's Men* and *The Final Days,* both by *Washington Post* reporters Bob Woodward and Carl Bernstein. The first book discusses how white settlements have affected Native Americans and the second two reveal behind-the-scenes details of the Watergate scandal and Richard Nixon's presidency.

Several other popular best-selling nonfiction books focused on ways to feel better, ranging from *Everything You Always Wanted to Know about Sex (But Were Afraid to Ask)* by Dr. David Reuben, *The Joy of Sex: A Cordon Bleu Guide to Lovemaking* by Alex Comfort, and *Your Erroneous Zones* by Wayne Dyer. Although the first two titles are fairly self-explanatory, the third may need clarification. This book attempted to simplify concepts of psychology so that people could find ways to live happier lives. Yet another book, *The Complete Book of Running* by James Fixx, encouraged people to become healthier and feel better through a particular form of exercise.

POETRY

Joseph Parisi, former editor of *Poetry* magazine, lists the poetry trends of the 1970s as "surrealistic, Deep Image, confessional, and protest poetry."[17]

Poets ascribing to the surrealist movement believed that, by tapping into their subconscious or unconscious mind, they could create poetry that was more authentic. Practitioners of the surrealist movement include Romanian poet Andrei Codrescu, who immigrated to the United States in the 1960s to escape the Communist government in his homeland. During the 1970s, he published two poetry collections: *A Serious Morning* and *The History of the Growth of Heaven*. Surrealist Russell Edson received the Guggenheim Fellowship in 1974 and published four collections during the 1970s.

Robert Bly's work is connected with Deep Image poetry, although he himself did not like or use that label, stating that he finds all objects to be deep. Bly believed that poets should delve deeply into themselves for their poetry and he has criticized poetry that focuses on the external. He also criticized poets who followed "false surrealism," defined as "light verse surrealism," in which poems appear to be images dredged up from the poet's subconscious, but are not. Bly feels that false surrealism occurs because "the rational mind of Western man is so terrified of losing control and allowing itself to sink into depth that it makes up images imitating the unconscious."[18] During the 1970s, Bly began using Jungian archetypes in his poetry, and his work expressed his desire for psychic wholeness.

Confessional poetry—or the "I" poetry—seems especially appropriate for the Me Generation, although it had its roots in the earlier poetry of Anne Sexton, Allen Ginsberg, and Sylvia Plath, among others. Confessional poets shared raw and private feelings about topics that were previously taboo: death, sex, depression, and the like.

According to critic David Yezzi, what makes a poem confessional is not only its subject matter—for example, "family, sex, alcoholism, madness—or the emphasis on self, but also the directness with which such things are handled."[19] Robert Lowell, who suffered from manic-depression and spent stints in mental hospitals, has been called the father of confessional poetry. He published three collections in 1973: *History, In for Lizzie and Harriet,* and *The Dolphin,* the last of which garnered him a Pulitzer Prize—plus plenty of criticism for the incorporation of excerpts of his wife's letters in the book; at the time, Lowell was leaving his second wife, Harriet, to marry writer Caroline Blackwood. Lowell published one final collection of poetry, *Day by Day,* in 1977. At the time, he was leaving Caroline to return to Harriet—but he died of heart failure before reconciliation could be effected. Lowell received a posthumous National Book Critics Circle Award for his last collection of poetry.

Protest poetry, more commonly associated with the 1960s, continued during the 1970s. This form focuses on challenging bodies of authority or "the establishment," which often translates into the government; poets may use shocking language or ideas to startle readers into awareness of the cause being championed.

Adrienne Rich can be placed into this category of poets. Her poetry reflects both feminist and lesbian themes as she critiques traditional female roles. Rich believed that, as a poet, it was her duty to speak out for those who could not. During the 1970s, she published poetry collections with these titles: *The Will to Change* (1971), *Diving into the Wreck* (1973), *Twenty-One Love Poems* (1976), and *The Dream of a Common Language* (1978). *Diving into the Wreck* received a National Book Award.

In 1971, a new form of poetry emerged, known as L-A-N-G-U-A-G-E poetry. It first appeared in a magazine called *This.* Seven years later, the magazine was renamed L-A-N-G-U-A-G-E; experimental poet Charles Bernstein served as co-founder. Poets of this ilk attempted to draw attention to how language was used, and "how ideas are represented and formulated to transmit ideas, thoughts, and meaning" as they "fractured the language in an attempt to wage their own rebellious assault against the social and political structure inherent in the Imperial force of the English language."[20] Bernadette Mayer employed this philosophy in her poetry; she suggested that those new to L-A-N-G-U-A-G-E poetry try these exercises: read an index as a poem; write a poem strictly using prepositional phrases; and attempt to write in an unsettled state of mind. Bruce Andrews also served as a key figure of this poetic movement.

Before the 1970s, there are no records of any American Sign Language (ASL) poets, although perhaps as many as five emerged during the decade. In ASL poetry, which is used to communicate poems to the deaf, many different features can signal rhyming, including the shape, movement, and orientation of the signer's hands, as well as facial expressions and body language.

Poetry also served as a vehicle for minorities to express their unique viewpoints. Maya Angelou first rose to prominence in 1969 with the publication of the autobiographical *I Know Why the Caged Bird Sings* and the book's subsequent National Book Award nomination. She also published three collections of poetry during the decade, including *Just Give Me a Cool Drink of Water 'fore I Die,* for which she received a Pulitzer Prize nomination in 1972. She divided this collection into two sections: poems of love and poems of racial confrontation. In 1975, Angelou published another collection of poetry, *Oh Pray My Wings Are Gonna Fit Me Well.* In 1978, Angelou published another collection, *And Still I Rise,* which describes city life for black Americans.

Readers have praised her poetry as a forum for focusing attention on the political and social issues relevant to the African American experience. Many of Angelou's poems have been set to music; other poems have been compared to "an enormous praise-song, a totemic tribute to those gone souls and a challenge to those living and unborn."[21] Gwendolyn Brooks also published material about the African American experience; her poem "We Real Cool" is often included in textbooks for children. During the 1970s, she published several collections of poetry, with titles such as *Family Pictures* and *Black Steel: Joe Frazier and Muhammad Ali.*

Another poet, Rod McKuen, stayed true to more traditional forms of poetry and he enjoyed unparalleled commercial success, selling more than 65 million copies of his poetry collections and seeing them translated into one dozen languages. His poetry tapped into feelings common among people everywhere, that of love and hope and fear, and some have compared the atmosphere of his poetry readings to that of a rock concert. During the 1970s, McKuen published 11 collections of poetry with titles such as *Caught in the Quiet, Fields of Wonder,* and *Come to Me in Silence.*

William Stafford served as the Poetry Consultant for the Library of Congress during 1970 and 1971; in 1975, Oregon's governor named him poet laureate of the state. Stafford also contributed to the world of poetry by traveling around the globe—visiting Egypt, India, Bangladesh, Pakistan, Iran, Germany, Austria, and Poland—to help emerging poets.

MAGAZINES

Three magazines that captured the attention of a significant portion of America's reading audience—*Ms., Hustler,* and *People*—first appeared in the 1970s, but each of these magazines appealed to a considerably different set of demographics and a crossover of audience seems unlikely.

The first to debut was *Ms.,* a magazine founded by Gloria Steinem and a small group of others dedicated to the feminist movement. The very name of this magazine caused controversy as, during the early portion of the decade, debate flourished about the appropriate title for women. Heated discussions began when some women pointed out that "Mr." did not designate the marital status of a man, whereas "Miss" indicated an unmarried woman and "Mrs." designated those married or widowed—and these women demanded a title comparable to "Mr." that performed the same function for them. Although "Ms." had been suggested as a neutral feminine title 10 years earlier, it was Steinem's magazine that brought the choice to the forefront. (Many married women who were opposed to the title would claim that "MRS" was the best degree they'd ever earned and some women heading off to college would claim that they were in search of an MRS.)

In 1971, *New York* magazine inserted a mini version of *Ms.* into its publication. In January 1972, Felker, the editor of *New York* magazine, sponsored the first independent issue of *Ms.,* and, starting in July 1972, the magazine appeared monthly, funded by Warner Communications. By 1978, the Ms. Foundation for Education and Communication had begun publishing *Ms.*

This magazine was controversial on more than one front. Some despised the magazine for the feminist beliefs that it espoused, while many of those advocating feminism protested the ads that *Ms.* carried, which included bikini-clad women as an advertisement for Coppertone suntan lotion.

Nevertheless, the magazine enjoyed significant support from its advocates and subscribers, and it provided practical information to those curious about the feminist movement.

Shortly after *Ms.* debuted, a radically different type of publication began: Larry Flynt's *Hustler* newsletters, which were intended to promote his strip clubs. By 1974, the newsletter format evolved into a glossy magazine that featured raw and explicit sexual photos, along with graphic—and some say vulgar—satires and commentaries.

Hustler was not the first magazine featuring female nudity that appeared outside of Triple X bookstores; *Playboy* could stake an earlier claim. Striking differences, though, existed between the two publications. *Playboy* highlighted the nude female form as something seductively beautiful and something to be admired, and its editors would artfully prevent female genitals from appearing in photos; Flynt, meanwhile, posed his models in ways that shocked many Americans: covered with excrement or involved in male-dominated rape scenes—or, in perhaps the most appalling instance, with the upper half of the body shoved inside a meat grinder. He became especially vilified by detractors and applauded by fans in 1975, when he featured photos of a topless Jackie Kennedy Onassis.

Flynt never claimed that *Hustler* was a literary publication, but *Playboy* aspired to such a designation, and the latter publication did feature high-quality essays, thus giving rise to the tongue-in-cheek claim that one only bought *Playboy* for the articles. Although readers could not browse *Hustler* for highbrow reading, the magazine definitively altered the world of publishing. Its success during the mid-1970s pushed the acceptance of pornography in the mainstream of American pop culture—or at least at its fringes.

As more sexually explicit material appeared in print during the 1970s, a backlash occurred—even before the rawness of *Hustler* hit the shelves—in pulpits around the country. Author Paul S. Boyer quotes various religious leaders as lamenting America's "sex-drenched culture," with one warning that the country was "rapidly sinking into 'a quagmire of wickedness and lasciviousness, immorality and debauchery.'"[22] In 1972, a man named Ralph Ginzburg was sentenced to five years in prison and fined $42,000 on a pandering conviction that arose after he published *Eros,* a magazine that included reproductions of Hindu temple carvings; comic engravings, both before and after, of a seduction scene; a ribald essay written by Mark Twain; nineteenth-century ads for virility restorers; an 1897 drawing of a male chastity belt; and "Mother Goose Censored," a column where innocent words from traditional rhymes were blacked out so that the imagination could run free with bawdy replacements. During Ginzburg's sentencing, judges chastised him for his "brazenness" in marketing, which included sending material from places such as Intercourse, Pennsylvania—to incorporate their postmarks.

It is difficult to determine what made *Eros* so much more objectionable than other publications, but Boyer suggests, tongue in cheek, that his fatal error was to publish erotica with humor. One of the dissenting judges in the case—which went all the way to the Supreme Court—suggested that the pandering charge was in fact a sideways method of punishing Ginzburg for distributing legal material that judges or juries might find distasteful. The banning of *Eros* and the jailing of its publisher occurred shortly before *Hustler* began appearing in stores—which happened sans legal action, highlighting the inconsistent enforcement of obscenity laws. Meanwhile, the proximity of the initial publishing dates of *Ms.* and *Hustler* effectively illustrates the extreme nature of gender wars occurring in the United States during the 1970s.

The third major magazine that debuted in the 1970s, *People*, seems tame in comparison to her sister and brother publications and perhaps its sheer lack of controversy is what allowed it to become so popular so swiftly. First appearing on March 4, 1974, *People* quickly became a top source of popular culture news, focusing on the personal and professional lives of the country's celebrities. The first issue featured actress Mia Farrow who was appearing in the movie *The Great Gatsby*. Unlike "gossip rags" that told scurrilous secrets about stars, *People* served as a source of public relations for them, and it allowed the general American public to glimpse their favorite celebrities wearing beautiful gowns and dashing tuxedos, getting married, showing off their babies, and performing in their chosen fields of entertainment.

Another magazine launched in 1970—*National Lampoon*—was much more niche in focus and it served a smaller audience. This sharply satirical publication skewered political and pop culture figures and it served as the basis of a comedy troupe and live radio show. Although the publication was influential during the 1970s, the entire National Lampoon concept ended shortly after the decade did.

The 1970s also saw the budding of computer-based magazines, such as *Computer Graphics World* that begin in 1977. Meanwhile, teenage girls could select from a plethora of fan magazines that featured teenybopper stars such as Bobby Sherman, David Cassidy, and Donnie Osmond; they even boasted chastely exciting centerfolds.

NEWSPAPERS

The '70s was a great decade for the media, and a dreadful one for the country. As journalists scored one reportorial coup after another—My Lai, the Pentagon Papers, Watergate—the culture itself continued to unspool.[23]

Jonathan Larsen published an excellent comprehensive review of journalism from the 1960s through the 1990s. In his review, he lists significant political, economic, and moral crises from the 1970s decade, calling the country "near bankrupt" but praising the media's ability to perform its duties during the first half of the decade—not only adequately, but brilliantly. He commends Seymour Hersh and the *Dispatch News Service* for their Pulitzer Prize–winning coverage of the My Lai massacre; Neil Sheehan and the *New York Times* for their publication of the Pentagon Papers; Sydney Schanberg's reporting about the fall of Phnom Penh, again published by the *New York Times;* and the *Washington Post*'s dogged investigation of the Watergate scandal—and of the Watergate reporting of the *Los Angeles Times,* the *New York Times,* and *Time* magazine, as well.

Larsen credits the growing disconnect between the media and the White House for the significant improvement in media reporting in the 1970s. Gone were the days that a president could call up the media and simply request that a story not appear. In 1970, during one of the earliest incidents of this devolving relationship, Max Frankel, the Washington bureau chief of the *New York Times,* refused Henry Kissinger's request to keep quiet about the resumption of bombing by the United States in North Vietnam. Between that decision—and the one of the *New York Times* to publish, in 1971, three days' worth of the 47-volume war study that became known as the Pentagon Papers—the formerly close relationship between the press and the White House became even less congenial.

Not only did this relationship disintegrate, but Larsen suggests that the breakup led to even larger national crises. "The court battle over the Pentagon Papers," he writes, "had been a trauma for all concerned. Certainly the press would not regard Nixon in the same way afterward, and for his part Nixon created the plumbers to seek revenge on the man who had leaked the papers in the first place, Daniel Ellsberg, one of the many authors of the study. Thus it truly was one big story: the Vietnam war begat the Pentagon Papers and the Pentagon Papers begat Watergate."[24] By the time the Watergate hearings began in 1973, the *Washington Post* had already won its Pulitzer.

Larsen believes that the public then turned on the media, "rewarding" their quality work with mistrust. They were blamed, in effect, for being the messengers of bad news, of which the 1970s had plenty, and the average citizen began perceiving journalists as liberals living in New York and Washington, D.C., out of touch with mainstream society.

Overall, newspapers continued to grow in the 1970s, in large part because of the country's expanding population. Newspaper advertising revenue leaped from $5.7 billion in 1970 to $14.8 billion 10 years later. Unions lost labor battles, printing technologies improved, and newspapers became "big business." What Larsen saw, though, was declining quality. He cites a critical line that was crossed in 1975, when, on the front pages of the *New York Times,* there appeared an article written by Craig Claiborne about a $4,000 Parisian meal paid for by American Express. Journalists such as

Nora Ephron expressed their horror at this paid endorsement and at this shift to celebrities as news.

All was not entirely doom and gloom, however. The 1970s were also a time when young journalists entered the field, eager to make their mark on the world. As Michael Schudson points out in his article, "Watergate and the 'Rush' to Journalism," that enthusiasm for reporting existed prior to the political scandals; the reality is that the number of journalism and communication majors shot up in the mid- to late 1960s and doubled in the years between 1967 and 1972.[25]

Bob Cauthorn, former editor of the *San Francisco Chronicle,* recalls the 1960s and 1970s as glory days of journalism; in one comment, he praises the fortitude and perseverance of both writers and readers. "Trust me," he said, "people who were reading about civil rights stories and Vietnam and women's rights—these people were not reading fluff stories, you know?"[26]

THE 1970s

9
Music

INTRODUCTION

Not surprisingly, songs of the 1970s reflected movements underfoot, and a number of feminists adopted Helen Reddy's song, "I Am Woman (Hear Me Roar)," as their rallying cry. Reddy has been quoted as saying that, after joining the feminist movement, she needed to create the song that she wished she could find as an anthem. Although initial sales were mediocre, female fans began requesting to hear the song on radio stations; Reddy won a Grammy Award for this song, thanking God because "She" made this possible. In a similar manner, country singer Johnny Paycheck typified the frustrations of blue-collar workers when he sang David Allen Coe's song, "Take This Job and Shove It."

Also in the 1970s, some bands began filling up large arenas for their performances. Previously, artists put out albums or they sang in live venues, but this supersized option amplified the latter choice. Bands and artists who filled stadiums included the Beatles, the Rolling Stones, and the Who. Later on, bands such as Queen, Pink Floyd, Boston, Foreigner, Journey, KISS, and Genesis followed suit, as did some heavy metal bands.

Meanwhile, lines blurred between genres. What, for example, typified folk music and what transformed into pop? What was the difference between a softer country song and a pop tune with twang? What constituted rock? What features pushed rock into progressive rock? This decade served as a gateway to crossover tunes, wherein artists that appealed to one fan base could also begin to break onto the charts of another.

Teenyboppers worshipped young stars such as Donny Osmond, David Cassidy, Bobby Sherman, and the Jackson 5, which featured the young, talented, and sure-footed Michael Jackson. Easy listening fans could enjoy the

Carpenters, the Commodores, and Barry Manilow, while those in search of a funkier beat snapped their fingers in time with the tunes of Stevie Wonder.

Technologically speaking, advancements were being made, even if their value was not yet recognized. In 1970, for example, James Russell invented a way to record digital sounds, such as music, on a photosensitive platter; these sounds could be repeatedly played back. Russell, however, could not interest the music industry in his invention. Twenty years later, CD manufacturers, including Time Warner, needed to pay a $30 million patent infringement settlement to the company that had employed Russell when he invented the device.

FOLK MUSIC

All music is folk music. I ain't never heard a horse sing a song.[1]
—Louis Armstrong

The original folk singers were balladeers who told rhythmic stories, often of human frailty, that were set to music. Folk songs shared the struggles and triumphs, the joys and sorrows, of the "common folk." These songs were passed along orally; as generations passed, the music evolved and it isn't unusual to hear several versions of the same ancient song. Sometimes, words were misunderstood; other times, folk singers localized and personalized the songs for their intended audiences. During the 1960s and 1970s, men and women identified as "folk singers" often wrote their own music, which differs from the more primitive songs that were entirely oral, but contemporary singer-songwriters held true to the spirit of the folk song as they sang heartfelt stories that resonated.

Singers such as Bob Dylan, Woody Guthrie, Paul Simon and Art Garfunkel, and Joan Baez, who performed folk songs in the 1960s, inspired music of the 1970s. The influence of folk music can be heard in many 1970s songs, such as "Ohio," the Vietnam War ballad written by Neil Young and performed by Crosby, Stills, Nash and Young; the spirituality seeking song, "My Sweet Lord," written and sung by former Beatle George Harrison; and the music of Fleetwood Mac and Bruce Springsteen.

SINGER-SONGWRITERS

In a world of celebrity worship, it can be hard to fathom how someone could walk away from the money, fame, and success that stardom offers—but that's exactly what Cat Stevens, a pop/folk singer, did in the 1970s. Born with the name of Stephen Demetri Georgiou to a Greek father and a Swedish mother, he gained a steady following during the 1960s. Near the end of that decade, though, a bout of tuberculosis and a lukewarm reception to some of his new music sent Stevens into a funk—and also on a spiritual quest. Becoming a vegetarian, he embraced "flower power" and he wrote songs that reflected his search for truth and meaning in his life. In 1970, Stevens had two hit songs—"Mona Bone Jakon" and "Tea for the Tillerman," the second of which reached number one on music charts in the United States. Thereafter, Cat Stevens toured as a lead act, complete with magicians, backup singers—and even wild animals.

In 1971, Stevens released a successful album, *Teaser and the Firecat,* which included a song called "Peace Train." Many embraced this song, with its tone of gentle longing, as a plea for the Vietnam War to end; Stevens, though, saw the symbolism of the train's journey as something much deeper, stating that the locomotive was rolling along the edge of darkness without a known destination. Perhaps this reflected his search for truth.

Over the new few years, Stevens continued his pursuit of the sacred, rejecting life as a Buddhist monk, Zen, Christianity, and various New Age options. Dissatisfied with what he felt about each of those and frustrated with a life without a fulfilling sense of spirituality, he nevertheless churned out three more highly successful albums: *Catch Bull at Four* (1972), *Foreigner* (1973), and *Buddha and the Chocolate Box* (1974).

Then, his brother David visited Jerusalem and gifted Stevens with a translation of the Koran. Within its pages, Stevens found what he called the "true religion," one that answered his questions about life's purpose. While studying Islam, he released two more albums, *Numbers* in 1975 and *Izitso* in 1977; after officially converting to Islam and choosing a new name, Yusaf Islam, he recorded one last album as Cat Stevens, *Back to Earth.* Marrying and focusing on his religion, he then turned his back on his stardom.

Cat Stevens was part of a trend during the 1970s wherein singers wrote their own songs, often from a first-person perspective. These songs tended to be introspective and were often called "confessional" in tone and content. Carole King experienced significant success in this genre, with her 1971 album, *Tapestry,* selling 11 million copies and garnering four Grammy Awards: Album of the Year; Best Pop Vocal Performance, Female; Record of the Year (for the song, "It's Too Late"); and Song of the Year ("You've Got a Friend"). King wrote or co-wrote every song on *Tapestry;* some had already been successfully performed by other singers, including Aretha Franklin with "You Make Me Feel Like a Natural Woman" and the Shirelles with "Will You Still Love Me Tomorrow?" *Rolling Stone* called *Tapestry* an "album of surpassing personal intimacy."[2]

Another singer-songwriter, James Taylor, also experienced success during the 1970s. In 1970, he released his second album, *Sweet Baby James;* in large part because of the hit song, "Fire and Rain," its success brought attention back to his first album and its single, "Carolina in My Mind." In 1971, he released *Mud Slide Slim and the Blue Horizon,* winning a Grammy Award for performing Carole King's song, "You've Got a Friend." Taylor continued to release albums during the 1970s, with another significant hit

Folk singer Cat Stevens, known for such hits as "Morning Has Broken" and "Peace Train," appears in a photo from the 1970s. Near the end of the decade, Stevens converted to Islam and gave up his singing career. Courtesy of A&M Records/Photofest.

with "How Sweet It Is (To Be Loved by You)." His greatest hits album, released in 1976, sold more than 11 million copies. In 1977, he released *JT*, winning a Grammy Award for the single "Handy Man."

Carly Simon, another singer-songwriter, married James Taylor in 1972, shortly after launching her solo career with an album, *Carly Simon*; this album included a top-10 hit, "That's the Way I've Always Heard It Should Be." The featured song on her next album, *Anticipation*, also garnered significant attention for Simon. In 1972, she released a highly successfully album, *No Secrets*, featuring her signature song, "You're So Vain"; this song admonished an unnamed former lover for his vanity, leading to decades of speculation about who had inspired this song. Simon continued releasing albums on a regular basis throughout the 1970s, including a greatest hits collection, with "Nobody Does It Better" serving as her biggest hit besides "You're So Vain." Another top 10 hit was "You Belong to Me." She also sang backup on several of James Taylor's albums.

Still other well-known singer-songwriters of the 1970s include Harry Chapin, best known for his singles, "Taxi" and "Cat's in the Cradle." Jackson Browne released albums steadily through the decade, with "Doctor My Eyes" his first hit single and "Running on Empty" his biggest. Jim Croce became well known for "Time in a Bottle" and "Big Bad Leroy Brown," while Gordon Lightfoot released such songs as "If You Could Read My Mind," "Sundown," and "Wreck of the *Edmund Fitzgerald*." Joni Mitchell became known as the "female Bob Dylan" for her body of work, although she did not use that label.

Not all folk singers turned into celebrities. Other singer-songwriters of the folk tradition performed in front of smaller, more intimate venues, including Steve Goodman and John Prine. Goodman, whose wife said that part of his talent lay in extracting meaning from the mundane, opened for singer Kris Kristofferson in 1971. That same year, his first album came out. Titled *Gathering at the Earl of Old Town*, it referred to the Chicago facility known as the Old Town School of Folk Music.

Singer and songwriter Paul Anka was impressed with Goodman and he helped him produce a self-titled album, *Steve Goodman*, with Buddah Records. This album contained Goodman's song, "The City of New Orleans," which was later recorded by Arlo Guthrie, the son of Woody Guthrie. This song is now considered a folk standard. Goodman recorded several other albums during the decade and other singers besides Guthrie recorded Goodman songs; these included country singer David Allen Coe, who had a top 10 country hit with "You Never Even Called Me by My Name" and "Banana Republics," sung by Jimmy Buffett. Goodman also produced an album for friend and folk singer John Prine titled *Bruised Orange* (1978).

Prine emerged on the folk scene in 1971 with his highly acclaimed self-titled debut album. This album contained the song "Illegal Smile," a humorous take on a financially strapped man's illicit bit of pleasure; the song doesn't mention the specific cause of this smile. The album also contained songs such as "Hello in There," later sung by both Joan Baez and Bette Midler; "Paradise," a signature song for environmentalists; and "Angel from Montgomery," a song eventually performed by Bonnie Raitt. These songs caused some to compare Prine to Bob Dylan; at one of Prine's first appearances, Dylan showed up, unannounced, and backed up Prine on the harmonica. Other albums of Prine's include *Sweet Revenge* (1973) and *Common Sense* (1975).

COUNTRY MUSIC

One show consistently delivered country music to television audiences throughout the 1970s. Named *"Hee-Haw"* after a sound that donkeys make, the show began in 1969. Featuring celebrity guests who performed country music tunes, *"Hee-Haw"* interspersed corny comedy shticks, often performed by women in scanty and stereotypically rural outfits, in between songs. Hosted by musicians Roy Clark and Buck Owens, the show was cancelled by CBS in 1971 after executives determined that, although the program showed respectable ratings, it appealed to less affluent demographics. Producers therefore syndicated the program throughout the 1970s and beyond; this show is one of the most successfully syndicated television programs in American history.

The list of well-known country music performers and bands that appeared on the show is quite lengthy. Bands included Alabama, a group that received its first recording contract in 1977 and went on to become one of the genre's most successful groups; the Bellamy Brothers, whose 1976 song, "Let Your Love Flow," became an international hit; the Nitty Gritty Dirt Band, perhaps best known for their 1970 rendition of "Mr. Bojangles"; and Riders in the Sky, who combined both country singing and comedy into their act.

Individual performers ranged from rising stars to those in the prime of their careers—and even those, such as Roy Acuff, who were already country and western legends. By the time that Acuff appeared on *Hee-Haw*,

"Hee-Haw" hosts Roy Clark and Buck Owens discuss their instruments on an episode of their popular country music show that was set in fictional "Kornfield Kounty." Courtesy of Gaylord/Photofest.

he had been singing on the Grand Ole Opry radio program, which aired on Saturday nights in Nashville, Tennessee, for more than 30 years. In 1974, the radio program moved to the 4,400-seat Grand Ole Opry House, which was adjacent to the country music theme park, Opryland USA.

Other well-established country music stars appearing on *"Hee-Haw"* include Johnny Cash, the "Man in Black" who sold more than 50 million albums; Conway Twitty, who had 55 singles reach number one on various music charts; and Roy Rogers, known as the "King of the Cowboys," and who, along with his second wife, Dale Evans, appeared in more than 100 movies and who hosted their own television show from 1951–1964.

Perhaps *"Hee-Haw"* became so successful because the show hosted a wide spectrum of country subgenres—including outlaw country—that became popular in the 1970s. Led by such singers as Waylon Jennings, Johnny Cash, Johnny Paycheck, Merle Haggard, David Allen Coe, Willie Nelson, and Kris Kristofferson, the term outlaw country arose from a song, "Ladies Love Outlaws," sung by Jennings in 1972. In 1976, Jennings and Nelson recorded country's first platinum album, which was titled *Wanted: The Outlaws!* Singers who subscribed to the outlaw country movement often wore their hair long and dressed in faded denims and leather. They often drank hard, got into brawls, and, in some cases, even spent time in prison. They brought a raw hardness back into country music.

After releasing "Ladies Love Outlaws," Jennings's career continued with *Lonesome, On'ry and Mean,* and *Honky Tonk Heroes,* both released in 1973 and both huge hits. Other albums included *The Ramblin' Man* and *This Time* (1974); *Dreaming My Dreams* (1975); and *Ol' Waylon* (1977), which included another duet with Nelson. In 1978, the two coproduced an album called *Waylon and Willie* that contained their biggest hit: "Mamas, Don't Let Your Babies Grow Up to Be Cowboys." Jennings then released *I've Always Been Crazy* (1978) and a greatest hits album in 1979. Nelson, meanwhile, also released a flurry of solo albums in the 1970s, including *Shotgun Willie* (1973), *Phases and States* (1974), *Red Headed Stranger* (1975), and *Stardust* (1978). A chart-topping song was "If You've Got the Money, I've Got the Time."

Meanwhile, Merle Haggard could genuinely claim to be an outlaw. Sent to prison for 15 years in 1957 on a burglary charge, he continued his rebellious ways inside of prison, planning escapes that he never attempted and running a gambling ring from his cell. He also attended three of Johnny Cash's concerts at San Quentin; years later, when Haggard was an established singing star, the story goes, he complimented Cash's singing at San Quentin. When Cash said that he didn't recall Haggard performing there, Haggard told him that he didn't; he was in the audience. By the 1970s, Haggard had his own hits on the country chart, including "Someday We'll Look Back," "Carolyn," "Grandma Harp," "Always Wanting You," and "The Roots of My Raising."

Kris Kristofferson released a solo album, *Kristofferson,* in 1970; this album contained new songs but ones performed in the 1960s, as well. The reception was lukewarm, but, when the album was rereleased the following year, under the title of *Me & Bobby McGee,* people bought the album—and Kristofferson's other 1971 album, *The Silver Tongued Devil and I,* was very successful and established him as a recording artist. He won several Grammy nominations in 1972 and he continued to release albums. Meanwhile, other recording artists performed his songs, including Janis Joplin's rendition of "Me and Bobby McGee" in 1971, Joe Simon with "Help Me Make It through the Night," and Patti Page with "I'd Rather Be Sorry," among others.

In 1971, George Jones, a veteran country music singer, and his new wife, Tammy Wynette, became two of country's biggest stars, selling out concerts across the country. Jones, who had previously sung in a honky tonk style, switched to singing smooth ballads, and, in 1972, Jones had a solo hit with "We Can Make It," a song celebrating his marriage to Wynette. Shortly thereafter, their duet "The Ceremony" made the charts. Although the two were finding musical success, their marriage was sometimes described as a soap opera as Jones fought alcoholism and drug abuse; Wynette filed for divorce in 1973, but she quickly withdrew her petition. Their personal life continued to be played out in their songs, with their next hit titled, "We Gotta Hold On." Jones also sang "The Grand Tour," a song about a broken marriage, and "These Days (I Barely Get By)." Shortly after he recorded the latter song, Wynette left Jones again, and, this time, they divorced. Continuing as a singing duo, they still made the country music charts.

Singer Charlie Pride has the unique distinction of finding success in two competitive fields: country music and in professional baseball. Playing in the Negro Leagues, he realized that he wasn't going to make the major leagues and so he focused on his music. In large part because of the success of "Kiss an Angel Good Morning," he won the Country Music Association's Entertainer of the Year Award in 1971; that year and in 1972, he was its Top Male Vocalist, as well.

Other male country music stars of the decade included Charlie Rich, Entertainer of the Year for 1974; Mel Tillis, recipient of that award in 1976; Boxcar Willie, Don Williams, and Hank Williams Jr. Meanwhile, female stars chalked up their own musical successes, with Loretta Lynn receiving fame as the "Coal Miner's Daughter," a hit song released in the 1970s. Lynn used that title for her 1976 biography, and, in 1980, Sissy Spacek starred in a film based on Lynn's life, also with that title. Lynn penned songs that detailed the challenges of women's lives, including "Wanna Be Free" from 1971, which showed divorce in a positive light; "The Pill," a 1974 song that promoted birth control; and "When the Tingle Becomes a Chill," a 1976 song about sexual dissatisfaction. Lynn's own challenging marriage was often gossip column fodder, as well.

Lynn's younger sister, Brenda, who went by the stage name of Crystal Gayle, also forged a country music career. Known for her waist-length curtain of shining dark hair, she released her fourth album in the 1970s; her

1977 hit single, "Don't It Make My Brown Eyes Blue," played internationally, became a number one hit on U.S. country charts and reached number two on the pop charts, as well. Gayle was the first female country artist to have an album reach gold and she won a Grammy Award for Best Female Country Vocal Performance in 1977; that year and the next, she was the County Music Association's Female Vocalist of the Year.

Barbara Mandrell also boasted a list of number one country hits, earning millions of dollars from record sales around the world. Her most recognizable songs include "Sleeping Single in a Double Bed," "Standing Room Only," "Years," "One of a Kind Pair of Fools," "I Was Country When Country Wasn't Cool," and "If Lovin' You Is Wrong (I Don't Want to Be Right)." In 1979, she won the Country Music Association's Female Vocalist of the Year Award.

Yet another female star deserves mention: Dolly Parton, who incorporated many traditional elements of folk music into her songwriting. After singing duets with Porter Wagoner for many years, she began to record as a solo artist and "Joshua," in 1971, became her first number one hit. In 1974, Parton had five singles in a row become number one: "Jolene," "I Will Always Love You," "Please Don't Stop Loving Me," "Love Is Like a Butterfly," and "The Bargain Store." In 1975, she won the Country Music Association's Female Vocalist of the Year Award, and, in 1976, she starred in her own syndicated television program, "Dolly." Her 1977 album, *Here You Come Again,* sold more than 1 million copies and her songs appeared on country and pop charts simultaneously; by this point, her songs were deliberately crafted for crossover appeal to gain pop chart success. For her 1977 album, she also won a Grammy Award.

Post-1970s, Parton sang duets with Kenny Rogers. He also had a significant number of crossover hits on the country and pop charts; perhaps he served as the most successful "crossover artist" of the decade, as he found fans in both genres and opened the doors for other easy listening artists to follow this route.

After singing in pop bands in the 1960s, Rogers had his first solo hit in 1976; called "Love Lifted Me," it was followed by a major hit on the country charts, "Lucille." The latter song won the Country Music Association's single of the year award—and it also reached number five on the pop charts. Rogers followed this dual success with "Love or Something Like It," "The Gambler," "She Believes in Me," "You Decorated My Life," and "Coward of the County." He also sang duets with Dottie West that hit the charts, including 1979's "Every Time Two Fools Collide."

POP AND ROCK

April 10, 1970—For pop and rock fans in the United States—and throughout many other countries around the world—shock, anger, and sadness reverberated after Paul McCartney announced that the Beatles had broken up.

In December 1970, McCartney sued the other three Beatles—John Lennon, Ringo Starr, and George Harrison—to officially dissolve the group. Throughout the 1970s, rumors circulated that the group was getting back together, but that reunion never happened.

To understand the effect that their breakup had on a large segment of America, it's important to understand the influence that they once had. According to Judith L. DiGrazia of the Yale-New Haven Teachers Institute in *The Sixties: Notes of Discord*, "Their wittiness and unabashed faith in themselves reaffirmed young people's beliefs in themselves as well. The Beatles represented a complete and entirely 'youthful change in clothes, hair styles, social customs and music.' They re-established rock music as the unifying force of the youth movement."[3] The dissolution of the Beatles, then, was something much bigger than the breakup of a band; it was, for a significant demographic of America, the shattering of the symbol of youth as a force with which to reckon.

"The King of Rock 'n' Roll," Elvis Presley, performs at his January 14, 1973, concert "Aloha from Hawaii," which was broadcast to millions of Americans and an estimated 1.5 billion viewers worldwide. For the concert, Presley wore a white eagle jumpsuit. Courtesy of Photofest.

That said, after the Beatles broke up, fans could still listen to the "King of Rock 'n' Roll," Elvis Presley. It would be very difficult, if not impossible, to pigeonhole Presley's style of singing. Influenced by the blues, soul music, and gospel, he incorporated elements of country and rock 'n' roll to create his unique brand of entertainment. Already a musical superstar by the advent of the 1970s, his "Aloha from Hawaii" concert aired on NBC on January 14, 1973, the first performance broadcast live by satellite; it reached 1.5 billion viewers. Performing a wide variety of hits, including "Burning Love," "Blue Suede Shoes," and "Suspicious Minds," and ending with "Can't Help Falling in Love," Presley completed his show by dramatically flinging his cape into the audience.

Music fans suffered a second loss, though, when Elvis Presley was found dead in his bathroom on August 16, 1977, at the age of 42. He was rushed to the hospital, but it was too late to save Presley. People talked about where they were when they heard the news of his death, much as they did when John F. Kennedy had died almost 14 years earlier. During his career, Presley had 94 gold singles and more than 40 gold albums, and, even though he stopped recording new rock and pop songs during the 1970s, he still sold out concert venues and his death created a gaping hole in the world of music.

The dissolution of the Beatles and the death of the King, though, opened up a vast field of opportunity for aspiring rock singers to ascend to the height of stardom. In 1969, a struggling singer released an album, *Empty Sky*, in hopes of finding commercial success—but the reception was lukewarm and nothing about its sales would indicate the level of success that Reginald Dwight and songwriter Bernie Taupin would reach during the 1970s. By this time, Dwight was using his musical pseudonym, Elton John, and he became known throughout the world for his music, but also for his flamboyant style of dress—which included extraordinarily high and extravagant platform shoes and oversized, glittery and glamorous glasses—and his melodramatic concert performances. Blessed with the ability to sing poignant ballads, John could also rock and roll.

His first top 10 single, "Your Song," hit the charts in 1970, followed by a Billboard 200 album later that year, called *Tumbleweed Connection*. Thereafter, John had a steady row of hits on the musical charts, including "Levon," "Rocket Man," "Honky Cat," "Crocodile Rock," "Daniel," "Bennie and the Jets," "Goodbye Yellow Brick Road," "Candle in the Wind," and "Saturday Night's Alright for Fighting." Overall, the album titled *Goodbye Yellow Brick Road* brought significant acclaim to John.

In 1974, Elton John collaborated with John Lennon, a partnership between an emerging rock star and an established rock legend. Elton John performed "Lucy in the Sky with Diamonds," a Beatles song, and John Lennon's "One Day at a Time"; he and his band were also featured on Lennon's "Whatever Gets You thru the Night" record. The duo performed these songs along

Singer Elton John, who began his climb to rock superstardom in the 1970s, appears at a concert during the decade. Although in relatively conservative attire in this photo, he would become well known for his flashy and outrageous outfits. Courtesy of Photofest.

with "I Saw Her Standing There" at Madison Square Garden. This was Lennon's last live performance; a deranged fan killed him in 1980.

In 1975, John released *Captain Fantastic and the Brown Dirt Cowboy*, an album containing autobiographical material that detailed how he and Taupin struggled to find musical success. His best song on the album, it is generally conceded, is "Someone Saved My Life Tonight," referring to a friend persuading John not to marry his fiancée; in 1976, John revealed that he was bisexual. This album reached number one on the charts, as did his greatest hits album. John recorded the song "Tommy" for the movie of the same name, and he filled stadiums throughout the world wherever he performed.

Other hit singles included "Sorry Seems to Be the Hardest Word" and "Don't Go Breaking My Heart." In 1977, John announced his retirement and some suggested that he suffered from negative feedback resulting from his admission of bisexual preferences. Despite his announcement, he continued to record, but without significant success; in 1979, though, he became the first Western pop/rock star to tour the Soviet Union.

Rock musicians and bands that found success in the 1970s also included Peter Frampton, Bob Seger, Bruce Springsteen, Rod Stewart, Meat Loaf, Billy Joel, Chicago, the Eagles, and Journey. Frampton had played rock 'n' roll in concerts prior to his breakout album, but it was clearly his 1976 *Frampton Comes Alive!* album that propelled him to stardom. Selling more than 6 million copies, the record included such hit singles as "Do You Feel Like We Do," "Baby, I Love Your Way," and "Show Me the Way." His follow-up album, *I'm in You,* sold nearly 1 million copies, but it is perhaps better remembered for its cover; Frampton was in a cheesecake pose, wearing shiny pink pants and a patchwork quilt shirt that is completely unbuttoned.

Bob Seger formed his Silver Bullet Band in 1974, and the group steadily produced albums throughout the 1970s. Seger's themes often focused on blue-collar workers, particularly in the Midwest. His album, *Night Moves,* with a title track of the same name, helped Seger get significant air time play; other songs of note include "Hollywood Nights," "We've Got Tonight," "Turn the Page," and "Old Time Rock and Roll."

Even better known for his songs of working-class trials, tribulations, and occasional triumphs is Bruce Springsteen. Part folk singer and part rocker, his 1975 hit, "Born to Run" quickly made Springsteen a household name; the song has become a rock classic, often played on radios on Fridays to signal the beginning of the weekend. Years later, *Rolling Stone* magazine called the release of this song one of rock's most important moments. Other songs from the album were "Thunder Road" and "Jungleland."

Featured on *Time* and *Newsweek* after this album's release, Springsteen and his E Street Band toured across the country, playing these songs and new ones that Springsteen was writing. In 1978, they released *Darkness on the Edge of Town;* this album contained "Badlands" and "The Promised Land." This album's tone was different, darker than his previous one, causing fans to debate which version of Springsteen they preferred.

Meanwhile, British rocker Rod Stewart had a mammoth hit in 1971; called "Maggie May," the Rock and Roll Hall of Fame later listed this song as one of the world's 500 most influential rock tunes. That album also contained a harder rock song, "Every Picture Tells a Story (Don't It)," which garnered significant attention. In 1975, Stewart moved to the United States, creating such hit songs as "This Old Heart of Mine," "Tonight's the Night," "The First Cut Is the Deepest," and "The Killing of Georgie," the last of which detailed the killing of a gay man. As the decade progressed, he continued to churn out hit singles, including "You're in My Heart," "Hot Legs," "I Was Only Joking," and "Do You Think I'm Sexy?"

Billy Joel has sold more than 100 million albums and won six Grammy Awards during his musical career, kick started by his first big hit, "Piano Man," released in 1973. Other highly successful singles include "Just the Way You Are," "My Life," "Big Shot," and "Honesty." His song, "Only the Good Die Young" stirred controversy, as it featured a worldly male attempting to seduce an innocent Catholic female; once, when asked not to play this song at a concert, Joel responded by playing it twice.

A rock singer who went by the moniker of Meat Loaf released an album in 1977—*Bat Out of Hell*—that still sells copies at a regular pace today;

worldwide, it is estimated that 34 million copies have been purchased. Featuring songs such as "You Took the Words Right out of My Mouth," "Heaven Can Wait," "All Revved Up with No Place to Go," "Two out of Three Ain't Bad," and "Paradise by the Dashboard Light," the entire album has become a classic and songs still receive significant attention today.

Chicago named their albums in a practical manner, using the appropriate Roman numeral to indicate how many albums they had released, so far. Hits of the 1970s include "Saturday in the Park," "Just You and Me," "Feelin' Stronger Every Day," "I've Been Searching So Long," the Grammy Award–winning "If You Leave Me Now," and "Baby, What a Big Surprise."

The Eagles, a composite band led by singer Glenn Frey, found tremendous success in the 1970s, most notably with their 1976 album, *Hotel California*; this album contained hit singles such as "New Kid in Town," "Hotel California," "Wasted Time," and "The Last Resort." Other hits of the decade included "Best of My Love," "One of These Nights," "Take It Easy," "Lyin' Eyes," "Witchy Woman," and "The Long Run."

In October 1977, the progressive rock band, Journey, hired a new lead singer; Steve Perry brought a new style to the band, upsetting some fans but delighting more. In 1978, the group released an album called *Infinity*, featuring the song "Lights" written by Perry. This song appeared on many radio stations and elevated Perry to rock star status.

Finally, a quartet from Sweden, ABBA, reached a global market, recording two of the decade's biggest pop hits: "Waterloo" and "Dancing Queen."

PROGRESSIVE ROCK

The 1970s opened with the deaths of three promising young rocks stars, including Jimi Hendrix, electric guitarist extraordinaire, who died on September 18, 1970, at the age of 27. The left-handed Hendrix simply played a right-handed guitar upside down, dazzling fans with his riffs and shocking many with his version of the "Star-Spangled Banner." Janis Joplin, a gravelly voiced singer who sang powerfully emotional ballads, died three weeks later, on October 4, also at the age of 27. In 1979, Bette Midler played a character based on Joplin in *The Rose*, winning an Oscar for her performance. Next was Jim Morrison of the Doors, who died on July 3, 1971, at the age of 27. He is perhaps best known for his haunting song, "Light My Fire." Joplin's death was clearly attributed to a heroin overdose, while Morrison appeared to die of heart failure; Hendrix's cause of death was more uncertain, although drugs appeared to play a role. Radio stations continued to play their music, though, and the deaths of Hendrix, Joplin, and Morrison in quick succession surely contributed to their cult status that continues even today.

Meanwhile, several bands of the 1960s continued with their concerts and studio recordings in the 1970s, including the Rolling Stones, the Who, and Black Sabbath. Rolling Stones was led by the campy and dramatic singer Mick Jagger and hard-living guitarist Keith Richards, who struggled with drug addiction throughout the decade. Their albums during the first half of the 1970s received lukewarm reviews and members of the group pursued individual musical opportunities as the band struggled to regain its momentum of the 1960s. Coming back together for an album in 1978, *Some Girls,* the hit single "Miss You" reached number one on U.S. charts, and the Rolling Stones were back in business. They continued to regain momentum and celebrity status, post-1970s.

The Who, featuring guitarist Pete Townsend, vocalist Roger Daltrey, bass player John Entwistle, and drummer Keith Moon, were well known for their extremely energetic live performances that included plenty of Townsend's improvised riffs. During the 1970s, they recorded hit singles such as "Won't Get Fooled Again." In 1978, they returned to their harder rock roots, releasing *Who Are You.* Although this album reached platinum status and served as their comeback album, the entire band was derailed when Keith Moon died of a drug overdose on September 7, 1978. The other members continued to play together as a band, but the group's identity basically dissolved after Moon's death. In retrospect, perhaps band members wished that they had disbanded, for, on December 3, 1979, their concert in Cincinnati, Ohio, served as the impetus for the most deadly rock event ever, as 11 fans were crushed to death in an uncontrollable throng.

Meanwhile, Black Sabbath, fronted by singer John "Ozzy" Osbourne, continued their trademark heavy metal play. In 1971, *Paranoid* sold more than 4 million copies, their most commercially successful album yet; the most popular song, "Iron Man," fueled sales. The band continued to churn out successful albums that sold more than 1 million copies—including *Master of Reality* (1971), *Black Sabbath, Vol. 4* (1972), *Sabbath Bloody Sabbath* (1973), and *We Sold Our Soul for Rock 'n' Roll* (1975). Late in the decade, Osbourne and Black Sabbath parted ways; in the 1980s, he became notorious for biting off the head of a bat during a concert and of a dove during an executive level meeting.

The 1970s also witnessed the explosion of several new superstar rock bands. These bands included Aerosmith, AC/DC, KISS, Led Zeppelin, Blue Oyster Cult, Queen, and Van Halen. Aerosmith, fronted by singer Steven Tyler and guitarist Joe Perry, formed in 1970; Tyler became well known for his passionate live performances, which included lifting and dancing with the microphone stand and carrying a bottle of Jack Daniels on stage. Their debut album, *Aerosmith,* received respectable attention with "Dream On" regularly playing on radio stations, and other hits such as "Train Kept a Rollin'" added to the success of this record. It was their 1975 album, though, that catapulted them to international stardom. *Toys in the*

Attic included such hits as "Sweet Emotion," "Walk This Way," and a remixed version of "Dream On." Their next album, *Rocks,* included songs such as "Back in the Saddle" and "Home Tonight"—and these two albums are considered some of rock's best. Touring stadiums throughout the country, Aerosmith's song "Come Together" became a classic rock anthem. Band members were heavily using drugs, though, and they faded out at the end of the decade, not to return for several years.

Australia's AC/DC began playing music in 1973, and, within two years, they were traveling all over Europe, serving as the opening act for such established rock stars and bands as Alice Cooper, Thin Lizzy, Cheap Trick, Nazareth, and many others. AC/DC first reached U.S. radio in 1977 and their 1979 album, *Highway to Hell,* launched them into the top ranks of rock bands of the decade.

KISS, a band that played an intriguing hybrid of rock and glam music, formed in 1973 with lead singer Gene Simmons and guitarist and vocalist Paul "Ace" Frehley serving as the best known band members. Easily recognizable by their face paint worn during concerts, which included stark white all over with black and red embellishments, their live performances included fire breathing, smoke, and lasers. In 1975, they recorded their breakthrough album, which eventually achieved quadruple platinum status; on this album, they added a guitar solo to their song, "Rock and Roll

Members of the rock 'n' roll band KISS don their customary black, white, and red face makeup. They are, clockwise from top left, Peter Criss, Paul Stanley, "Ace" Frehley, and Gene Simmons. Courtesy of Photofest.

All Nite," creating a classic rock anthem. A rock ballad from this same album, "Beth," reached number seven on rock charts. In 1977, a Gallup poll listed KISS as America's favorite band.

Led Zeppelin, led by singer Robert Plant and guitarist Jimmy Page, enjoyed significant success during the 1970s, releasing one of rock's all-time best songs in 1971: "Stairway to Heaven." Meanwhile, Blue Oyster Cult released two of the decade's hard rock favorites: "Don't Fear the Reaper" and "Godzilla."

The British band Queen released two albums, the second quite successfully, before they first toured America, and "Few bands embodied the pure excess of the '70s like Queen. Embracing the exaggerated pomp of prog rock and heavy metal, as well as vaudevillian music hall, the British quartet delved deeply into camp and bombast, creating a huge, mock-operatic sound with layered guitars and overdubbed vocals. Queen's music was a bizarre yet highly accessible fusion of the macho and the fey."[4] They found significant success with their 1975 album, *A Night at the Opera;* this album included "Bohemian Rhapsody," which became a hit single in many countries. Their 1976 album, *A Day at the Races,* contained the hit "Somebody to Love," which reached number 11 on U.S. singles charts; their 1977 album, *News of the World,* included "We Will Rock You" and "We Are the Champions," songs that are still played at international sporting events.

Debuting their first album in 1978, lead guitarist Eddie Van Halen of the band Van Halen dazzled the rock world with his skill and innovation with his electric guitar, setting a new standard for rock guitarists, nationwide. Employing a variety of techniques, some self-taught, that created animal and machine sounds from his instrument, he displayed a creativity that was astounding. Lead singer David Lee Roth understood the nuances of showmanship and the band established themselves as forerunners in the 1970s rock world. Within three months, their first album had gone gold; five months later, it reached platinum and eventually sold more than 6 million copies. Single hits from the album include "You Really Got Me," "Jamie's Cryin'," and "Runnin' with the Devil." The following year the band released *Van Halen II;* their song, "Dance the Night Away," hit the Top 20 Singles list.

REGGAE AND DISCO

Reggae

Seldom does one single artist or band represent a movement in the way that Bob Marley and his band, the Wailers, did for Jamaican reggae in the United States in the 1970s. This form of reggae borrowed from American soul music, merging it with traditional African and Jamaican folk music, and incorporating elements of *ska* music, which is Jamaican folk music influenced by rhythm and blues, creating a unique fused sound. The music relied upon bouncy rhythms and an ensemble of musical instruments, most notably the electric guitar and electric bass.

Themes of reggae songs included love and sexuality, political and social commentary, and the Rastafari movement. The latter combined politics and religion, advocating that the former emperor of Ethiopia, Haile Selassie I, was the Messiah promised in the Bible.

Bob Marley and his band released *Catch a Fire* in 1973, following it up with *Burnin'*; the latter contained songs such as "Get Up, Stand Up" and "I Shot the Sheriff," later recorded by Eric Clapton. After releasing these two albums, the group broke up, with band member Peter McIntosh continuing to record, but under the name of Peter Tosh; Bunny Livingston became Bunny Wailer. Bob Marley kept recording, as well, under the name of "Bob Marley & the Wailers," releasing his first international hit in 1975: "No Woman, No Cry." In 1976, he released *Rastaman Vibration*, an album that stayed on the top 10 of Billboard charts in the United States for a month. In December 1976, Marley, his wife, and his manager were shot inside of his home; the shootings were suspected to be politically motivated. Two days later, the injured Marley performed at a preplanned concert intended to reduce political tensions in Jamaica. Bob Marley & the Wailers set off on a world tour in 1978, releasing an album of love songs, *Kaya*, to coincide with their tour.

Post-Wailers, Peter Tosh released "Legalize It," a song that received significant attention—and a radio ban. He often chose darker, more serious music than Marley, with songs such as "Equal Rights" focusing on the plight of blacks in South Africa. On April 22, 1978, Marley and Tosh appeared back to back in a Jamaican concert; Tosh selected his most militant songs to perform, interspersing them with antigovernment speeches. Although fans applauded his sentiments and his forthrightness, the press and government condemned his words and viewpoints.

Other reggae performers included Burning Spear, Toots and the Maytals, and Jimmy Cliff. Burning Spear combined political anger against repression with a focus on spirituality, with hits such as "Joe Frazier (He Prayed)" in 1972. Cliff's most popular album in the United States was released in 1975: *Follow My Mind*. International hits by Toots and the Maytals were "Funky Kingston" in 1973 and "Reggae Got Soul" in 1976.

Disco

Disco has been called one of the "most glitzy and celebrated fads in American popular cultural history" as the "established sensibilities of rock and pop, which emphasized sincerity, emotion, and rebellion, gave way to the enchantment of dance floor rhythms, which colonized popular imagination as an alluring dreamscape of pleasure and sexual utopia. In disco, the boundary between commercial fabrication and real experience became blurred."[5] Disco became so deeply engrained in American pop culture that even classic music icons such as Beethoven and Mozart found themselves posthumously associated with the disco movement, with songs such as "Rock Me, Amadeus" playing on the radio.

Disco as music is deeply intertwined with disco as a dance form and more information about the dance is included in Chapter 10 of this book. Disco songs were upbeat, in direct contrast to many of the darker rock songs or introspective first-person folk songs written during the 1970s. The music pulsed at quick and steady rhythms, with between 110 and 136 beats per minute, and it fused funk and soul with rhythm and blues, Motown, jazz, and swing. Lyrics were teasing and often distinctively sexual.

One of the most popular disco songs, by Van McCoy, urged listeners to "do the hustle." McCoy later stated that "The Hustle" was a last-minute addition to his album, *Disco Baby*. He needed one more song to complete his album, and, recently introduced to the group participation of the hustle dance, he jotted the words to the song in one hour. McCoy won a Grammy Award for this song and it was his only song to reach the Top 40.

Yet another disco classic is "Disco Inferno" by the Trammps, while KC and the Sunshine Band provided discothèques with plenty of singles for dance aficionados, including "Get Down Tonight," "That's the Way (I Like It)," "I'm Your Boogie Man," "Shake Your Booty," and "Keep It Comin', Love."

Women who recorded popular disco songs were identified as "disco divas," with Donna Summer surely serving as the queen. In 1975, Summer released a 17-minute version of a song that she wrote: "Love to Love You, Baby." Complete with suggestive moans, the song reached number one on dance charts and quickly became gold. Many radio programs refused to air this song because of its sexually suggestive background sounds.

In 1977, Summer incorporated techno sounds into "I Feel Love," an innovative use of electronic enhancements in music. The following year, she released "Last Dance," another disco hit for which she received her first Grammy. Later that year, she released a live album, *Live and More*, which featured her first number one pop single, "MacArthur Park." In 1979, she released the album for which she is perhaps most famous: *Bad Girls*. This album boasted two number one singles, "Bad Girls" and "Hot Stuff." She sold more than 7 million copies and the album reached number one on the charts.

Gloria Gaynor had two disco hits of significance: "Never Can Say Good-bye" (1974) and "I Will Survive" (1979). The latter song reached number one on the Billboard Hot 100 list and served as an anthem for the feminist movement, as well as the gay movement. Anita Ward's "Ring My Bell" perhaps served as disco's closing hymn, receiving prominent air play in 1979 before the disco movement began to self-destruct.

As far as a disco group goes, the Bee Gees dominated the scene, in large part because their songs served as background music on the soundtrack of *Saturday Night Fever*, the ultimate disco movie. Three singles—"Stayin'

Alive," "How Deep Is Your Love," and "Night Fever" reached number one; a song they wrote for Yvonne Elliman for the movie, "If I Can't Have You," also reached number one. More than 30 million copies of this album sold, but this unprecedented success also had a backlash; as popular as disco was during much of the decade, by the end of the 1970s, few people admitted to being swept into this manic music form—and the Bee Gees suffered from this reversal.

THE 1970s

10
Performing Arts

INTRODUCTION

The 1970s served as a comeback decade for the movies. Although television had gobbled up increasing numbers of America's leisure hours, a combination of blockbuster movies and technological advances such as Panavision and Dolby sound, and more believable special effects such as those seen in *Star Wars* and *Jaws*, enticed people to return to the movie theater. Young and energetic filmmakers, including Francis Ford Coppola, George Lucas, Martin Scorsese, and Steven Spielberg, also revived the movie industry. Cynics called them "movie brats" because they were young and because they had graduated from film school. Other top directors were Woody Allen, Robert Altman, and Michael Cimino. Another movie trend of the 1970s was the film as art. Audiences were smaller for these films, which were expected to be artistically experimental.

Meanwhile, television continued to evolve to meet the needs of America. For the first time, sitcoms and other shows focused on social consciousness, tackling pressing issues of the day, often in a satirical manner. Taboo topics found their way into many of these shows, as producers continued to debate the censors about the appropriateness of their material. By 1972, for the first time, half of U.S. households owned a television set and so shows were finding a broader audience. Soap operas became increasingly popular, and this decade saw the rise of the television miniseries, the made for TV movie, and cable.

Disco dominated the dance scene from the middle of the decade until its end, when it suffered a significant backlash. Broadway saw the rise of more African American musicals and endured a spate of controversy over material called sacrilegious.

FILMS

The image of John Travolta as Tony Manero is burned into our public consciousness. Decked out in a three-piece white leisure suit with his shirt collar wide open, his hand points toward the heavens as the lighted disco floor glares defiantly below him. Tony, a disaffected, disillusioned youth from Brooklyn, New York, sees the disco as the only way out of a dead-end life that includes a low-paying repetitive job at the local paint store; his boss, already devoured by cynicism, provides no encouragement. Tony is both cocky and vulnerable, and, as two film critics point out, has a "high powered fusion of sexuality, street jive, and the frustration of boy-man who can't articulate his sense of oppression."[1]

Strutting through the swirling lights of the disco, though, Tony swaggers with confidence and people move aside in silent tribute to watch him dance.

He and his dance partner—a woman named Stephanie who has ambitions beyond what Tony can yet comprehend—win a highly competitive dance contest that confers prestige in Manero's world, but even that doesn't bring joy because he knows that the Hispanic couple who competed against them was better. Tony isn't totally without hopes or dreams, though; spurred on by Stephanie, he longs to move to Manhattan—or, more accurately, to escape to Manhattan—where he vaguely perceives that a better life may exist. As the movie winds down, Tony stumbles toward his dream and we want to believe that, somehow, he will "make it."

Saturday Night Fever and its lead character were tapping into something deep in our culture, something that perhaps couldn't have been well articulated at the time. Manero reflected the uncertainty and ambivalence that many Americans felt in a decade filled with political scandals, oil embargoes, financial stagflation, and gender wars. Americans were dissatisfied with the country's political leaders and the economy, and they were no longer certain of the direction they needed to take; they knew something better existed, but, like Manero, they weren't necessarily certain how to get there—or even sure if they could. *Saturday Night Fever* is more sad than hopeful, more poignant than redemptive. Even so, the image that still resonates is of Tony Manero in his blazing moment of glory on the disco floor—and so, somehow, we know that hope remains, that Manero has triumphed over despair, however briefly—and that, perhaps, he will again.

This same sense of ambivalence and uncertainty about the future also helps explain the abundance and popularity of disaster films made during this decade—ones where all hope seems lost, but then the hero somehow manages to salvage the situation. These films gave moviegoers the sense that they, too, could find their way.

Salvaging the situation, though, didn't necessarily mean triumph; sometimes mere survival was the yardstick used during these dark times.

John Travolta and Karen Lynn Gorney in perhaps the most memorable scene from the movie Saturday Night Fever. *The film made disco the dance craze of the decade. Courtesy of Paramount Pictures/Photofest.*

"Americans lamented the decline of heroism and the heroic; defining themselves instead as survivors—of incest, of cancer, of the Vietnam War, and of the sinking ships, burning buildings, shark attacks, zombie invasions, and other disasters and tragedies that reflected the siege mentality and were staples of Hollywood in the era."[2] If that wasn't enough of a reason to explain the popularity of the disaster movies, a journalist uses dark humor to provide another. "For sheer contentment," he writes, "there is nothing to beat the sight of constant catastrophe happening to others."[3] This theory can make a person squirm. On the one hand, taking vicarious pleasure in another's misfortune can feel quite wrong if we like to think of ourselves as compassionate; on the other hand, disaster movies can be among the most absorbing, so there must be some truth to the comment.

This discomfort didn't stop filmmakers in the 1970s from making disaster films, of course, or people from flocking to them. Disaster and horror films of the 1970s include *Towering Inferno; Earthquake; Poseidon Adventure; Airport; Jaws; Amityville Horror; Alien;* and the *Exorcist.* Each could be defined as a successful movie in that large numbers of viewers paid to watch them in the theater, and many could even be labeled with the emerging term of "blockbuster." (If there is any doubt that America longed for the disaster film and turned some into blockbusters, note that *Jaws* was the first movie ever to make more than $100 million for its studio!) As a practical note, the 1970s probably saw more successful disaster films than previous decades because technology now permitted movie producers to create credible-looking disasters that would cause audiences to scream, rather than to laugh at the poor quality of the special effects.

The first well-known disaster movie of the decade was *Airport,* released in 1970, with a stellar cast of Burt Lancaster, Jean Seberg, and Dean Martin. In this movie, the manager attempts to keep his airport open during a snowstorm; meanwhile someone is attempting to blow up an airplane. As a rule, disaster movies have large casts with multiple subplots and personal and dramatic interactions occurring among characters—and *Airport* followed that formula. In that movie—and others of the genre— these personal dramas are interwoven along the main thread of the plot, which involves characters attempting to prevent or escape from a disaster; sometimes they're also forced to cope with the disaster's aftermath. Some disaster films use nature as the enemy and force of reckoning, while others point toward technology and human error as the source of disaster. From a psychological standpoint, either can be effective.

In 2004, a group of cinema buffs voted *Airport* as the fourth-best disaster film of all time. Two other 1970s movies—*Poseidon Adventure* and *The Towering Inferno*—ranked first and third, respectively. In the *Poseidon Adventure,* starring Gene Hackman, a tidal wave turns a luxury liner upside down, and, to survive, passengers must work together to find their way to the top. Some succeed; others do not—and many do not even try. As one woman is dying after saving another person from drowning, she passes on a pendant that she wants her grandchildren to have and she tells potential survivors that life matters, very much. In contrast, in Paul Newman and Steve McQueen's *Towering Inferno,* people do want to survive and don't need encouragement; in fact, some may value life too much.

Although each of these movies—*Airport, The Towering Inferno,* and *Poseidon Adventure*—thrilled and entertained moviegoers, they didn't necessarily change their behavior patterns outside the theater. The disaster film *Jaws,* however, did have such an effect, causing many beach goers to fear entering the water as "'formerly bold swimmers now huddle in groups a few yards offshore,' while 'waders are peering timorously into the water's edge.'"[4] This movie's effect spread even further as posters advertising *Jaws,* the movie, were supplemented by political and social parodies using the

Jaws theme; the State of Liberty was menaced by the CIA; Americans by tax bites, inflation, the energy crisis, and unemployment; Uncle Sam by a Soviet submarine; and Gerald Ford by recession, Ronald Reagan, and an ineffective Congress. In a satiric twist that reveals much about how Americans feared the potential effects of the feminist movement, Gloria Steinem is attacked by male chauvinism using *Jaws* symbolism—but, in this case, the attacked person bites back.

Surely the fact that *Jaws* was in production during the Watergate scandal explains part of this fearful appropriation of symbolism. Furthermore, it coincided with the fifth anniversary of Chappaquiddick, and news programs were quick to point out that the mechanical sharks swam through the same waters that flowed over the young campaign worker who died in mysterious circumstances; by the time *Jaws* reached the theaters, Ted Kennedy had removed himself from the presidential race.

Political fears were subtly revealed in *Jaws,* but other films faced the Vietnam War issue directly; these include *Coming Home, The Deer Hunter,* and *Apocalypse Now.* Each film—and others like them—presented a unique twist to the challenges presented by the war; still there are similarities among the films. Here is writer Richard Pells's take on the likenesses: "These movies offered a vision of an America drenched in loneliness, conspiracy and corruption, psychic injury and death. Yet despite their melancholy view of American life, the films themselves were made with wit and exceptional exuberance."[5] The first movie explored the changing relationships between the men who fought in Vietnam and the women left behind; the second involves three friends who were drafted, captured, and imprisoned, and must break all rules to escape; and the third focuses on a special forces officer sent into the jungle to capture and kill the U.S. military leader who has created his own renegade army.

Other films tackled social issues, such as divorce and child custody (*Kramer vs. Kramer*); intolerable work conditions and the resistance to union organization (*Norma Rae*); care of those with psychological problems (*One Flew over the Cuckoo's Nest*); and Native Americans and their challenges (*Billy Jack*), among others. Still other movies were inspiring, sentimental and/or nostalgic. These include *American Graffiti, Grease,* and *Rocky.* Comedies that continue to air long after the decade ended include *The Rocky Horror Picture Show* and *Animal House.* No listing of 1970s movies would be complete, though, without mentioning *The Godfather* (I and II) and *Star Wars.*

Many movie reviewers and film experts consider *The Godfather* and its first sequel as masterpieces; they are considered cultural phenomena. Directed by Francis Ford Coppola, the original film features an all-star cast, including Marlon Brando, Al Pacino, and James Caan. The movie brought about public awareness of the Mafia, and much of what we know about the subculture came from these movies. Americans added phrases such as "going to the mattresses" and "sleeping with the fishes" to their repertoire of linguistics, as well as "I'll make him an offer he can't refuse," and "leave the gun—take the cannoli."[6] When we first meet the Godfather, he is immaculately dressed, receiving visitors in his darkly impressive office while others celebrate his daughter's wedding outside in the sunshine. We immediately know that he is powerful, a force with which to reckon. The first movie focused on the attempted assassination of the leader of the Corleone family and his family's response. In the second movie, which stars Robert DeNiro, as well, we watch the maturation of the upcoming Godfather of the Corleone family. *The Godfather* and its sequel won the Academy Award in 1972 and 1974.

Although gangster movies were not new in or unique to the 1970s, there was a growing recognition of and interest in different racial and ethnic groups during this decade. The Godfather films focused on an immigrant Italian family, albeit an atypical one, and so perhaps the emerging social value of honor-

Marlon Brando appears as Don Vito Corleone in the Academy Award–winning movie The Godfather, *directed by Francis Ford Coppola. This 1972 movie was based on Mario Puzo's novel of the same name. Courtesy of Paramount Pictures/Photofest.*

ing and understanding ethnic differences helped fuel the movies' successes. Moreover, the male dominance and control that exists in mob narratives resonates with some men in our culture and the emerging feminist movement left many Americans grasping for a more traditional power balance in terms of gender. Moreover, the Corleones held tight to traditions, which might provide comfort to viewers in shifting and unsettling times.

Family ties were extremely important to the Corleones. In another blockbuster movie series that began in the 1970s, though, the *Star Wars* trilogy, the lead character finds himself bereft of family and he must create new ties with which to sustain himself. The 1977 science fiction film opens with Luke Skywalker, a orphaned young man living with his aunt and uncle, longing for adventure. His uncle needs him at home, though, and so he stays. Soon, disaster strikes Luke's homeland, and all ties are broken. Luke meets up with adventurer Han Solo and together they attempt to rescue Princess Leia from the clutches of the evil Darth Vader, whose dark empire intends to take over the galaxy.

Star Wars examines the concepts of good and evil and juxtaposes the notions of technology and humanity. Surrounded by combative robots and other mechanical creatures who will do whatever the dark empire bids

In 1977, George Lucas directed his blockbuster film Star Wars, *starring Mark Hamill (Luke Skywalker), Carrie Fisher (Princess Leia Organa), and Harrison Ford (Han Solo). The movie opened with these words scrolling across the screen: "A long time ago in a galaxy far, far away ... " Courtesy of Lucasfilm Ltd./Twentieth Century Fox Film Corp./ Photofest.*

them, the humans triumph—although even they also rely upon a couple of their own robotic friends, plus the deep wisdom and intense tutelage of Jedi Master Obi Wan Kenobi—thereby saving a planet from destruction. In the movie, good clearly wins out against evil—and, although the ending provides a hint that victory is only temporary and that evil will rise again—it's quite understandable why moviegoers of the challenging 1970s would appreciate the opportunity to simply sit back and cheer for the victory of goodness and humanity.

One final movie theme or genre should be explored—that of "blaxploitation films." In 1971, a man named Melvyn Van Peebles produced an independent film called *Sweet Sweetback's Baadasssss Song,* a movie described as an "angry, violent screed about the racist persecution of a poor black everyman."[7] In *Song,* a pimp named Sweet Sweetback becomes celebrated as a cult figure after killing two white police officers who have abused their authority in the black community. Van Peebles's film cost $500,000 to produce—and then grossed $20 million within the first few months of release. In 1971, Hollywood was suffering financially and this skyrocketing success caused studios to focus on creating more blaxploitation movies. They made about 40 during the first half of the 1970s, and three—Van Peebles's *Song,* plus *Shaft* and *Superfly*—became quite successful. In all three movies, black heroes fight against and beat the white system.

These films starred black actors and deliberately targeted black audiences. These actors expressed sexuality and they served as heroes who survive the system and escape the ghetto. Ironically, these films were frequently produced and directed by white professionals, although both *Shaft* and *Superfly* had African American directors. Despite that appropriation of black expression by white-run studios, these films allowed a greater black presence in the theater and created new stars such as Jim Brown, Ron O'Neal, Richard Rowntree, Tamara Dobson, and Pam Grier. And, while blaxploitation movies with female stars are comparatively rare, they did "activate feminine narratives concerning racial loyalties and black pride."[8] As the genre developed, critics pointed out how later films focused on the sexual and aggressive features of the genre to the degree that they overshadowed development of black identity. As more movies were made, they became more formulaic and stereotypical. By 1976, the movement crashed for two reasons. One, the market was so targeted that it became difficult for studios to make a profit, even though blacks comprised 12 percent of the country's demographics; two, a segment of the black population began protesting the pimp and/or junkie connotations of the (anti)heroes of these movies. During the latter part of the decade, students and filmmakers gathered on college campuses, most notably UCLA, and they attempted to broaden the perception of the black American experience through their movies.

Never a dude like this one!
He's got a plan to stick it to The Man!

STARRING
RON O'NEAL
AS PRIEST

See
and hear
CURTIS
MAYFIELD
play his
Super Fly
score!

One of the three most successful blaxploitation films of the 1970s, Superfly *debuted in 1972 and was directed by Gordon Parks Jr. This poster advertised the film.* © *Warner Bros. Courtesy of Warner Bros./Photofest.*

TELEVISION

Sitcoms

Groundbreaking is a word frequently used to describe new television shows, to the degree that the term loses meaning and emphasis. One show that does deserve this label, though, is *All in the Family,* which first aired on January 12, 1971, and starred Carroll O'Connor as Archie Bunker; Jean Stapleton as his wife, Edith; Sally Struthers as their grown daughter, Gloria

Stivic; and Rob Reiner as her husband, Mike. Because Mike is a college student, he and Gloria live with Archie and Edith, and they face the challenges that intergenerational families do whenever they reside together.

In the pilot program, Archie and Edith's 22nd anniversary is approaching, and so Gloria and Mike decide to plan a surprise Sunday brunch; Archie does not appear grateful for their efforts and misunderstandings ensue. From this plot summary, it's easy to infer that a series of slapstick twists and turns will then tumble over one another to the sound of canned laughter, and that all will be solved within the confines of 30 minutes.

That, however, didn't happen. Instead of dealing with trivial disagreements that could be quickly resolved during the brunch, Archie and Mike argued passionately about prejudice, politics, and religion, weighty and controversial topics, indeed.

The show's focus on social issues was radically different from previous sitcoms and author Josh Ozersky discusses the prevailing philosophy of television producers prior to the airing of Norman Lear's *All in the Family.* "TV networks," he writes, "were content to program innocuous entertainments for a general audience and to vary them only as necessary." Shortly thereafter, he summarizes those programs as, "three pastoral comedies, two Westerns, a liver-spotted handful of aging-star vehicles, and a pair of ludicrous sitcoms—one about two cute children in the care of an English valet, and the other about a housewife with magic powers."[9] NBC's head of audience research, Paul Klein, labeled this philosophical approach as providing the "least objectionable programming," or LOP.

Logic was as follows: to obtain the advertising dollars needed to pay for production costs and the salaries of those running television stations—and to also make a profit—a program, according to Ozersky, "by necessity must appeal to the rich and poor, smart and stupid, tall and short, wild and tame, together."[10] Television executives concurred with this reasoning and they shied away from provocative notions; Ozersky quotes one anonymously. "Suddenly every new idea becomes a threat to you. It means you have to act on it, one way or another. You can't afford to be reckless. So you try to push the ideas down, make them go away or, if possible, make them someone else's responsibility."[11]

Besides being innocuous, sitcoms of the 1960s—some of which carried over from the 1950s' Ozzie and Harriet era of television—employed significant elements of fantasy and implicitly asked its viewers to not question the impossibility of their premises. These shows include *Green Acres; Beverly Hillbillies; Mr. Ed; My Mother, the Car; Lost in Space; Flying Nun; Johnny Quest; Flintstones; Gilligan's Island; Bewitched; Get Smart; Batman;* the *Munsters;* the *Addams Family;* and *I Dream of Jeannie.*

On the cusp of the 1970s, though, Norman Lear and his partner Bud Yorkin (Tandem Productions) decided to smash through the blandness that had served as entertainment on television. Using the British show *Till Death Do*

Us Part as his model, Lear created a script wherein the Bunker family would bring social issues such as racism, sexism, abortion rights, homosexuality, and menopause to prime TV in a comic fashion. Persuading ABC to air the program, though, proved impossible. Taking his pilot to CBS, Lear then needed to compromise with William Tankersley, the head of the station's standards and practices department who believed in the 1960s model of programming of appealing to all and offending no one. Surprisingly, though, Tankersley and Lear came to an agreement, wherein Lear would remove scenes such as the one when Mike came downstairs while still zipping up his pants; meanwhile Lear was allowed to keep all politically controversial material in his script—and thus the show aired in January 1971.

O'Connor's character, Archie Bunker, was key in the show's premise. Archie works as a foreman on the docks and he drives a cab on the side. His world view is narrow and bigoted, and he calls people "wops," "yids," "coons," and "Hebes"; when reminded that Jesus was, in fact, Jewish, he responds with, "Only on his mother's side." He calls his son-in-law "that no-good, lunk-headed Polack" and "Meathead." He nicknames his wife "dingbat" and, whenever she talks too much or says something that upsets him, Bunker tells her to "stifle"—and yet, despite all these intolerant and

Cast members of the groundbreaking comedy All in the Family. *Clockwise from the top: Rob Reiner (Mike Stivic), Sally Struthers (Gloria Stivic), Carroll O'Connor (Archie Bunker), and Jean Stapleton (Edith Bunker). The show aired from 1971–1979. Courtesy of CBS/Photofest.*

hurtful statements, O'Connor portrays a man who, deep down, loves his family and is even tender-hearted.

Jean Stapleton provides a perfect foil for Archie; in her role as Edith Bunker, she is patient and tolerant, and her sunny nature defuses situations. Sally Struthers in the role of Gloria Bunker Stivic must mediate between her conservative and bullheaded father and her liberal and passionate husband; Rob Reiner as Mike Stivic is earning his sociology degree while living in the Bunkers' household and his opinions are nearly always polar opposite of his father-in-law's. Their next-door neighbors, the Jeffersons, also play an important role in the show. George Jefferson is as biased toward the white race as Archie is about the black; George's wife, Louise (or Weezie) is open-minded and warm-hearted—and the best friend of Edith. Their son Lionel rounds out the family; a friend of Mike's, he makes low-key and witty observations about his family's situation.

Viewer reactions to Archie's character varied widely. Some proffered that, because Archie was the butt of most jokes, the show exposed bigotry as ridiculous. Many people applauded the show for promoting tolerance but some studies indicated that other viewers enjoyed watching Archie Bunker because they agreed with what he was saying.

All in the Family was revolutionary and the *Washington Post* credits the show for paving the way for another new show, *Sanford and Son*. The article indicated that, pre-Bunkers, viewers might have refused to watch a show about an irascible and aging black junk dealer, but, perhaps now, the show had a chance.

Debuting a year after *All in the Family, Sanford and Son* was set in Watts, the site of a recent race riot. The plot and humor frequently centered on conflicts between the father, Fred Sanford (Redd Foxx), and the grown son, Lamont (Desmond Wilson). Fred's character was outspoken and somewhat manipulative; if not given what he wanted, he would clutch his chest and talk of having "the big one," a heart attack that would send him to heaven to reunite with his deceased wife, Elizabeth. Lamont played a straightforward character attempting to reason with his curmudgeonly father as he blusters his way through various get-rich-quick schemes that invariably failed. Other characters include Aunt Esther, who clucked about Fred's behavior while clutching her Bible; and Hispanic neighbor Julio Fuentes, whose eccentric behavior adds to the comic confusion at the junkyard.

Another new show that year that relied upon humor focusing on the behavior of black Americans was the *Flip Wilson Show*. This was America's first successful variety show hosted by an African American, and it was Redd Foxx who helped Clerow "Flip" Wilson first appear on the *Tonight Show,* the popular late-night talk show hosted by Johnny Carson that was known for springboarding young comics to public recognition and success. After receiving national exposure on the *Tonight Show,* Wilson was offered his own show wherein he shared jokes and humorous stories and portrayed characters such as the wildly dressed Geraldine Jones. Wilson partially based Geraldine on the Butterfly McQueen character (Mammy) in *Gone with the Wind,* making Geraldine unrefined but honest, flirtatious without being trashy, demanding—and receiving—respect from her off-screen boyfriend, Killer. Wilson also hosted well-known guests on his show.

The program won two Emmys its first year—for the best variety show and for the best writing in a variety show—relying upon outrageous humor for its success. According to J. Fred Macdonald, it "became riotously funny to joke about skin color, hair texture, race riots, poverty, welfare checks, and minority social customs. Inhibitions disappeared, and writers and comedians seemed to ignore racial sensitivities."[12] Meanwhile, Norman Lear was creating yet another successful television show: the *Jeffersons,* an *All in the Family* spin-off featuring the Bunker family's black neighbors.

Successful as these producers were, another duo provided them with competition for the title of top television producers: Mary Tyler Moore and her husband, Grant Tinker (MTM Enterprises). The pilot of their breakout program, the *Mary Tyler Moore Show,* featured Mary as a single woman working at a television studio in Minneapolis. Originally, Mary was to be a divorcee, but CBS feared that viewers wouldn't separate Mary's new character from the one she played in the 1960s' *Dick Van Dyke Show*—and would therefore assume that Mary left the beloved Van Dyke. Therefore, Mary was portrayed as a single woman who'd just suffered through the breakup of a longtime romance.

Although this idea does not seem daring today, it was of significance then because of the feminist resurgence that was occurring in the country. The show debuted in September 1970, shortly after the August 26, 1970, "Women Strike for Equality" demonstration, wherein women marched in protests across the country—most notably in New York—to both honor the 50th anniversary of the ratification of the Nineteenth Amendment granting women the right to vote and to protest the continuing oppression of women.

According to author Bonnie J. Dow, the *Mary Tyler Moore Show* is acknowledged as the first successful program that portrayed the influence of the women's movement. Although Mary was not the first working woman to appear on television, she was the first to "assert that work was not just a prelude to marriage, or a substitute for it, but could form the center of a satisfying life for a woman in the way that it presumably did for men."[13] Moreover, her profession was not one where she must be subservient to men or where she must put the needs of others before her own. Mary was novel because she had a position of authority, she was unmarried, and she lived alone. She had personal freedom.

Another strong female served as the lead of an early 1970s sitcom; yet another spin-off from *All in the Family,* the title was simply *Maude.* Played by Bea Arthur, Maude was the strong-willed, determined, and opinionated foil to Archie Bunker; her viewpoints were liberal and she seldom shied from sharing them.

Her character—and her show—illustrates the point made in an editorial published in *Time* magazine in 1972: "TV has embarked on a new era of candor, with all the lines emphatically drawn in. During the season that began last week, programmers will actually be competing with each other to trace the largest number of touchy—and heretofore forbidden—ethnic, sexual and psychological themes. Religious quirks, wife swapping, child abuse, lesbianism, venereal disease—all the old taboos will be toppling."[14] Maude was already divorced from her fourth husband when the plotline began; she lived with her current husband, Walter, and her divorced daughter. In the series, Walter and Maude deal with his alcoholism, and they decide to abort their child conceived late in life.

Lear also produced other successful television comedies. These include *One Day at a Time,* which debuted in 1975 and featured a recently divorced professional mother who was raising two headstrong teenaged daughters, and *Mary Hartman, Mary Hartman,* a quirky satire of soap operas that first aired in 1976. None of the three major networks wanted to handle the controversial characters of this last show and so the show was immediately sold to syndication. Viewers appreciated the humor and it was only because the star's show—Louise Lasser—decided to leave the show that it was cancelled in 1977.

Finally, no 1970s sitcom listing would be complete without mentioning *M*A*S*H,* a show set in a field hospital in Korea in the Korean War. Doctors and nurses use humor, sometimes dark, sometimes absurd, to deal with the horrors of war. Although Alan Alda is generally considered the star, it was the interactions of the various characters that brought richness and texture to this ensemble show. One of the most memorable may be the crossdressing Max Klinger, played by Jamie Farr; this character hoped that this charade would label him unsuitable for duty and would therefore get him sent home. The show debuted on September 17, 1972, and outlasted the decade. Some consider this show the finest ever produced for television.

From the mid-point of the decade on, though, viewers seemed to tire of socially responsible sitcoms and a degree of fantasy returned to television shows such as *Mork and Mindy, Charlie's Angels,* and the *Love Boat.* Nostalgia also reigned, as evidenced by *Little House on the Prairie,* starring Michael Landon and telling the story of a pioneer family in Minnesota; the *Waltons,* starring Richard Thomas and focusing on an idealized version of family life during the Great Depression; *Happy Days,* starring Ron Howard and Henry Winkler, and the ensemble show, *Brady Bunch.*

Soap Operas

In 1970, another television genre was reaching fruition: the soap opera. That year, 20 million people watched one or more of the 19 serial shows wherein plotlines continued from show to show and situations were not resolved within one episode. At the beginning of the decade, soap operas aired from 11:30 A.M. to 4:30 P.M., with each show lasting 30 minutes, Monday through Friday. On January 6, 1975, *Another World* expanded to one hour; shortly thereafter, *Days of Our Lives* and *As the World Turns* followed suit.

Although soap operas were traditionally considered programming for housewives, a study indicated that 30 percent of early viewers of *All My Children*, a soap opera that rose to prominence in the 1970s, were either males or younger viewers. Moreover, it might be assumed that viewers of "soaps" expected good deeds to be rewarded and evil ones punished; in fact, results of a 1979 *Soap Opera Digest* survey showed a reality that was much more complex. The favorite character selected by viewers was Karen Wolek of *One Life to Live*, played by Judith Light—and her character definitely did not embody the traditional and passively "good" characteristics of women.

Previously, soap opera viewing might have been considered a guilty secret; by 1976, though, this genre was so popular that *Time* magazine devoted a cover story and photo to *Days of Our Lives*, with the headline reading, "Soap Operas: Sex and Suffering in the Afternoon." University level courses were taught on the genre and the 1970s saw the creation of many new ones. Here are two examples:

All My Children (Agnes Nixon, ABC): This show premiered on January 5, 1970, as a half-hour program and dealt with social issues ranging from child abuse to Vietnam War protests. Highlights include the Emmy Award won by Mary Fickett in 1972; in her role of Ruth Parker Brent, she criticized the Vietnam War after her on-screen son was drafted. This was the first Emmy awarded to a daytime actor. In 1974, *All My Children* aired an episode wherein Brent's son, Phil, was shot and then dragged away by a young Vietnamese boy; this was the first war scene aired on daytime television.

Also in 1973, Erica Kane (Susan Lucci) underwent an abortion because she did not want a swollen body to affect her modeling career, an option now legal because of the recent *Roe vs. Wade* decision. Fan mail supported Erica's choice—one that was made against the advice of her soap opera husband—but the writers still had the character suffer from septicemia, so the character did not escape punishment for her decision. In 1974, when Margo Flax (Eileen Letchworth) got a facelift in real life, Nixon worked it into plot, exploring the physical and psychological effects of cosmetic surgery.

Ryan's Hope (Claire Labine and Paul Avila Mayer, ABC): This show originated on July 7, 1975, and it featured a working-class Irish Catholic family living in the Riverside district of New York: the Ryan's. As with *All My Children*, writers focused on social issues of the day and relationships of young people. Johnny Ryan (Bernard Barrow) owned a bar; his wife, Maeve (played by Helen Gallagher) helped, as did their children. Some fans objected to frequent recasting of characters, which probably affected ratings; the recurrent hiring and firings of writers added to the situation. Prior to 1979, the show's creators, Claire Labine and Paul Avila Mayer, had maintained ownership of *Ryan's Hope*. In 1979, though, they sold the show to ABC and it lasted for another decade. *Ryan's Hope* won an Emmy Award for

Outstanding Daytime Drama in 1976–1977 and 1978–1979; writers received Emmys four times during their initial decade, as well: 1976–1977, 1977–1978, 1978–1979, and 1979–1980. Lead actress Helen Gallagher, known for her singing of "Danny Boy," won two of her three Outstanding Lead Actress Emmys in the 1970s: 1975–1976 and 1976–1977.

Variety Shows

Flip Wilson created the first successful variety show featuring a black American. Other successful variety shows of the 1970s include:

Sonny and Cher (CBS): Debuting on August 1, 1971, this show featured a married couple who sang duets, hosted guests, and bickered. Cher became well known for her outrageous outfits and she even exposed her belly button, a first in television history. Personal troubles marred their success; by 1973, reports of shouting matches, missed performances—and even a black eye—appeared in the press. At the end of the 1973–1974 season, with the show still rated eighth on television overall, Sonny filed for divorce and the show ended. Each performer created a variety show without a partner, but both shows flopped—causing the divorced couple to try, once again, to perform on television together. So, on February 1, 1976—with Cher pregnant with the baby of her estranged rocker husband, Greg All-man—the new show debuted. Problems quickly cropped up, though; producers didn't think that Cher, a recent divorcee, should wear outlandish costumes; legal battles prevented skit routines from being revamped; and the quality of new writing was uneven.

Donny and Marie (ABC): Greater contrast could not exist between Cher and Marie Osmond—at least, clothing-wise, and in many other ways, as well. Donny and Marie were a brother-sister team from a large Mormon family; the boys of the family performed together as the Osmond Brothers and Donny was the most popular. Donny and Marie's first television special aired in November 1975; it was so successful that their variety show began appearing in January 1976. The most popular segment of the show was called "A Little Bit Country, A Little Bit Rock & Roll"; Marie would perform country vignettes, while Donny would provide the rock & roll. They also bantered with one another on screen; Marie was often given the humorous lines and Donny would respond with, "Cute, Marie. Real cute."

Saturday Night Live (Dick Ebersol and Lorne Michaels, NBC): "Hi. I'm Chevy Chase—and you're not." Hearing punch lines such as these, teenagers and young adults flocked to the late-night antiestablishment comedy show. Originating on October 11, 1975, this show featured satiric skits that thumbed figurative noses at convention and often mocked politicians and other top public figures. Stars included Chevy Chase, John Belushi, Dan Aykroyd, Jane Curtin, Gilda Radner, Garrett Morris, Bill Murray, and Laraine Newman. Ongoing skits focused on the Coneheads, Land Sharks, and Samurai Deli. The show featured a different celebrity guest host each week, and a guest band—some quite popular, others cutting-edge —performed on the show. Although the show has seen countless changes, most specifically in talent, it still airs today.

News

News reporting evolved during the 1970s; for the first time, a news program—CBS's *60 Minutes*—successfully competed against other prime-time programming. This show featured thought-provoking and controversial interviews and viewers responded to its quality.

Moreover, despite pressure from the Nixon administration, television stations—most notably CBS—aggressively reported on the Watergate scandal and subsequent presidential resignation; horrifying and mind-numbing updates of the Vietnam War also caused anxious viewers to tune in for details. Meanwhile, morning news shows continued to gain acceptance. Starting in 1976, presidential debates became an anticipated ritual.

The Miniseries

In 1977, ABC aired the eight-part miniseries *Roots*. Based upon a book written by Alex Haley, the series shared a broad yet intimate look at an African American family whose ancestor Kunta Kinte was kidnapped, sold into slavery, and brought to the United States against his will. He becomes maimed as the result of several attempts to escape, but he finally settles down on his owner's plantation, marrying the cook and having a daughter—who is eventually sold to another owner. Viewers watch 200 years of historical events unfold through the eyes of Kinte, played by LeVar Burton, and his descendants.

Television executives compressed this series into the shortest number of days possible, fearful of not garnering enough audience. But, nearly half of the population of the United States at the time, 100 million people, watched the conclusion of the series while 130 million viewers watched at least part of this historical drama. This miniseries was so successful that it helped launch ABC into first-place ratings and revenues for the first time, and it spurred an interest in many Americans to search for their own roots.

At the time of the airing, speculation arose about how the series would affect race relations in the United States. *Time* summarized observations this way: "Many observers feel that the TV series left whites with a more sympathetic view of blacks by giving them a greater appreciation of black history"—and yet, "the same article reported that white junior high school students were harassing African Americans and that black youths assaulted four white youths in Detroit while chanting, 'Roots, roots, roots.'"[15] Postairing, many also speculated about the degree of truth portrayed in the miniseries. Haley himself called it "faction," or a blend of fact and fiction.

Overall, *Roots* was the impetus of the successful television miniseries, helping to solidify it as a viable format for television.

Made for TV Movies

Many of the made for TV movies were designed to appeal to female viewers, many of whom—because of a purchase of a second television set—gained control over what they viewed. One of the first successful and well-done made for TV movies was *Duel.* Produced by Steven Spielberg and starring Dennis Weaver, this 1971 movie eventually appeared in European cinemas. Overall, these movies tended to have lower budgets and fewer actors; many focused on melodramatic subjects, leading to a derisive nickname of "disease of the week" movies; plots were often written to reach cliffhangers at the time television executives needed to break for commercials.

Cable Television

The notion of cable television providing a deluxe—or extra—service for additional pay was first introduced in November 1972, when Service Electric first aired Home Box Office (HBO) in the Wilkes-Barre, Pennsylvania, area. Only a few hundred households had subscribed by the time the channel had aired, but it quickly gained more subscribers. By 1975, 3,506 cable systems existed, serving nearly 10 million subscribers; these viewers could select from numerous channels, as compared to three or four channels available to viewers of broadcast-only television.

In 1975, HBO aired the well-touted Joe Frazier-Muhammad Ali heavyweight boxing match. The following year, Ted Turner's WTBS Atlanta channel broadcast throughout much of the country via cable television, as did the channel eventually known as the Family Channel. Viacom's Showtime debuted in March 1978—and ESPN, which began airing sports programming around the clock, first appeared in 1979 under the name of Sports Programming Network. Its popularity was quite high, even from its inception, reaching more than 57 million homes. The year 1979 also saw the debut of the children's cable channel, Nickelodeon, and the Movie Channel—and Ted Turner's supernews channel, Cable News Network (CNN), was only a year away.

The most obvious transformation wrought by cable was the plethora of programming choices; shows and channels were becoming both more abundant and more niche. Parents could, for example, allow their children to watch Nickelodeon or the Family Channel, safe in the knowledge that sex and vulgar language would not be part of the programming. Sports lovers no longer needed to wait for a specific time to watch athletic activities, and movie fans could enjoy films in the convenience of their own homes, day or night. Another change was subtly taking place. Satellites made possible live shows from around the nation and the world, transforming television into a "now" medium.

DANCE

Disco

Disco music tends to be upbeat with a regular rhythm, typically with 110 to 136 beats per minute. Disco dances range from choreographed line dances, often created for one particular song, to freestyle movements that fit the beat of the music being played. Although I stand by this definition of disco, dances performed at discothèques often overflowed with pulsating—even manic—energy that no technical definition of the dance or music could ever capture. Proponents of the dance form often suggested that, if this music didn't propel you to dance, then you'd better check your pulse because you may be dead. Dance floors were frequently crowded; colored lights flashed, often around a disco ball, which was a large silvery sphere hanging from the ceiling that was covered with tiny square mirrors. Men and women alike wore flashy outfits, including tight spandex pants, glittery tops, and platform shoes—and the music thumped throughout the room in an insistent bass beat.

Disco was not for the shy or claustrophobic, and, as writer Barry Walters points out, it was also not intended as something to enjoy while home alone. Disco was a public form of music and performance. "Unlike rock's bedroom confessionals," Walters writes, "disco is designed to be heard in clubs on a loud sound system while one dances in a crowd."[16]

It is difficult to separate disco as dance from disco as music, as the beat of the music fueled the dance—and the two are so intertwined that the same word—disco—is used to describe both the songs and the corresponding dance steps. Disco in the 1970s first became popular in the middle of the decade with people dancing to songs such as "Rock the Boat" by the Hues Corporation and "Rock Your Baby" by George McCrae. Donna Summer's music epitomized the disco scene later in the decade, with songs such as "Love to Love You, Baby"; "Hot Stuff"; "Heaven Knows"; "Dim All the Lights"; and "Last Dance."

Naming the first disco song ever created is difficult, and perhaps impossible. Various musical genres contributed to the culmination of the sounds and steps of disco, including funk and soul, rhythm and blues, and Motown and jazz. During the late 1960s, various male counterculture groups, most notably gay, but also heterosexual black and Latino, created an alternative to rock 'n' roll, which was dominated by white—and presumably heterosexual—men. This alternative was disco, and, by mid-1970s when it became mainstream, it was an amalgamation of the talents and influence of many subgenres.

In 1977, after the movie *Saturday Night Fever* debuted, dancers would disco in the style showcased in that extraordinarily popular film. In this movie, partners embodied the steps of the hustle in a couple format, borrowing heavily from salsa and swing and adapting that to the continuous disco beat. In this dance, the male spins his female partner quite frequently, drawing her close to him and then pushing her away. In the movie, characters danced to songs of the Bee Gees, including "Staying Alive" and "How Deep Is Your Love," and people all around the country attempted to duplicate those snazzy moves.

Even if you didn't have a partner at the disco, you could still participate. It was very common for groups of friends, either the same gender or mixed, to race out to the dance floor whenever they heard a favorite disco song and dance together in a freestyle manner. As author Jeremy Gilbert points out, "Despite the cultural rapacity of the Hustle and its representations, freestyle dance remained the beating heart of disco, powering its rhetorics of social, romantic, sexual and somatic emancipation. Freestyle required neither a partner or training, nor did one need inherent grace or skill. Freed from the technical and social demands of previous generations of ballroom or dancehall, anyone, regardless of gender, sexuality, age or ability could participate."[17]

Near the end of the decade, though, disco suffered from an enormous backlash. People criticized the disco scene for numerous—and often contradictory—reasons. The music was too feminine, it was meaningless, and the disco lifestyle was too connected with sex and drugs. People who had eagerly participated in the trend often seemed embarrassed about their previous enthusiasm and tried to distance themselves from that part of their lives. On July 12, 1979, Comiskey Park in Chicago even hosted a "Disco Sucks" night where hundreds of disco albums were placed in crates and set on fire as the crowd applauded.

Salsa

As previously noted, disco derived many of its steps from the Latino dance form of salsa. It isn't surprising, then, to also note an upswing of interest in salsa during the 1970s, particularly in New York City. Salsa itself is a mixture of various dance styles, including rhumba, mambo, and cha-cha. This interest in salsa can be attributed to Cuban musical stars, such as Celia Cruz and Tito Puente, who had recently immigrated to the United States.

DRAMA

The 1970s witnessed an upswing of African American musicals, including *Raisin,* which won the Tony Award for best new musical; Virginia Capers won a best actress award for her performance. In this play, an extended family waits for an insurance check after the death of a family member and each has a different reason for wanting that check. According to a *New York Times* review, the conflict "created by the potential uses of the insurance money made available by the father's death (escape from their slum home, a medical education for the daughter or a liquor store for the feckless son) becomes powerful and poignant" as the cast moves from acting to singing and back again.[18]

In 1975, *The Wiz,* a play based on Frank Baum's *Wizard of Oz,* won seven Tony awards and it ran for 1,672 glittery and high-energy performances. The cast urbanized the story; the most popular song was *Ease on Down the Road,* sung by characters as they danced down the Yellow Brick Road. The following year, *Bubbling Brown Sugar* celebrated the Golden Years of Harlem, receiving six Tony nominations, and a new production of *Porgy and Bess* appeared on stage. In 1978, Nell Carter won the Best Actress in a Musical Tony for *Ain't Misbehavin'.*

In 1970, for the first time ever, the Equity Council allowed someone—the New York Public Library—to tape performances for archival purposes; at the end of that year, an off-Broadway strike over pension fund issues affected 17 shows. In 1975, nine Broadway shows shut down over a musicians' strike that lasted 25 days.

A rock opera—*Jesus Christ Superstar*—caused controversy. Created by Tim Rice and Andrew Lloyd Webber, it first appeared in 1970, highlighting personal struggles between Jesus and Judas Iscariot. The play in fact opens with Judas confronting Jesus, telling him that his popularity is getting out of control. Mary Magdalene then massages Jesus with ointment, furthering angering Judas, who doesn't think that Jesus should hang around with a former prostitute. The play first appeared on Broadway on October 12, 1971, receiving mixed reviews, along with criticism from Andrew Lloyd Webber. Some religious groups also condemned the play, aghast at Jesus's portrayal as man, not God; the omission of the resurrection, they said, was sacrilegious. In 1976, the opera began a national tour in the United States, which continued until 1980.

In 1975, *A Chorus Line* by Michael Bennett first appeared on Broadway. This play featured a group of 25 desperate dancers vying for eight spots on a chorus line and it ran for 6,137 performances, becoming the longest-running show in Broadway history; it received the New York Drama Critics Award, the Pulitzer Prize, and nine Tony Awards, as well. All this was accomplished with no real scenery, except mirrors, and no costumes except for leotards and a "few spangles for the finale."[19] This, contrary to what worked for most plays, was truly an ensemble with no discernable star.

The following year, Stephen Sondheim's *Pacific Overtures* debuted. The casting director sought out 35 Asian actors, but not one—other than a single Eurasian—auditioned. Seeking out new talent, the overwhelming majority of actors in this play were therefore new to Broadway.

In 1979, Andrew Lloyd Webber and Tim Rice premiered *Evita*, which shares the rise of power of Juan Peron as president of Argentina and the significant role played by his wife in these events. It should be noted that both *Evita* and *Jesus Christ Superstar* were inspired by musical albums. In *Evita*, the lyrics were partially based upon *Evita: The Woman with the Whip*, which drew upon stories told by her enemies and victims. After the play appeared, a more sympathetic biography of Evita was written.

The play *Evita* illustrates how mediums blended together and borrowed inspiration from one another in the 1970s. A biography inspired songs—that inspired a play. In another such example, a 1979 play *The Elephant Man* told the real-life story of Joseph Merrick, a man who suffered from a disease that horribly deformed his face. Shortly after that play appeared, a character on a popular television discovers that he, too, has the disease.

THE 1970S

11

Travel

INTRODUCTION

On the cusp of the 1970s, many experts believed that more Americans than ever before would travel during the decade. Factors for this enthusiasm included the advent of the first jumbo jet—the Boeing 747—that was anticipated in 1970; the increase in ship cruise options; and the lower airfares being predicted. Furthermore, American Express announced that it expected travel to Europe to double.

Lower airfares did occur because of a rate war among airlines, and, once the 747 became available for commercial flight, Boeing dramatically slashed ticket prices, making international travel much more feasible. To compete with the glamorous nature of the Boeing 747, cruise ship operators ramped up their advertising and their special deals.

High travel expectations in the 1970s dimmed, though, for a variety of reasons, including an oil embargo that caused gasoline prices to increase significantly and an overall sluggish economy with rapid rates of inflation, high unemployment figures, and slow growth that caused the average American's budget to tighten; extras such as vacations were often the first line item to be slashed.

On a more positive note, although space travel did not continue at the fever pitch of 1969, Americans did make significant strides in space voyages and research. The 1970s saw automobile innovations, including the first American-made, fuel-efficient subcompact car. The jumbo jet was a success story and the founding of Amtrak saved a disintegrating passenger railway system from possible extinction.

SPACE TRAVEL

In the modern quest for knowledge, it is easy to forget that over the span of human existence, it has only been a mere wink of an eye since the time we revered these celestial wanderers as gods. Now, we revere the moon and planets not because they represent deities, but because they propel human imagination, compelling us to make exciting explorations on a grand scale in pursuit of scientific knowledge.[1]

When the 1970s began, the country had recently celebrated the successes of extraordinary, seemingly superhuman undertakings in space—and those accomplishments were, for America, quite exhilarating. John Glenn had walked on the moon, broadcasting his historic step for all mankind throughout the world, and people's imaginations flourished, anticipating lunar colonies—or ones on Mars—as the answer to overpopulation, pollution, or any number of other social ills. Possibilities seemed endless as astronauts literally reached for the stars and flew through the heavens.

Science magazine further fueled the elation when, in January 1970, it dedicated an entire issue to the analysis of Apollo 11 lunar samples. This was the first time that this magazine had devoted all of its pages to a single topic, and this attention from the well-respected *Science* seemed to reinforce that the world—led by the efforts of the United States of America—was on the verge of a new galactic age. This flush of success was not limited to the scientific, either; this moon landing was, for the United States, also a political coup.

Author John M Logsdon, in *Decision to Go to the Moon: Apollo and the National Interest*, discusses the political motivations of the "space race" occurring between the United States and the Soviet Union.[2] He argues that President Kennedy deliberately created the goal to reach the moon before the Soviet Union as a method of enhancing our country's prestige, internationally speaking, and so he ordered the acceleration of this outer space feat. Our technology accomplished this goal efficiently and effectively, and one cannot underestimate the sense of personal pride that Americans took in beating our Cold War enemy to the punch.

Astronauts also served as heroes for most Americans; in a time when many questioned the "establishment," those who succeeded as astronauts had, as Tom Wolfe defined the phenomenon, the "right stuff." To qualify, these men needed superb physical stamina and health; they underwent a battery of psychological tests, as well, ranging from the Wechsler Adult Intelligence Scale to the Doppelt Mathematical Reasoning Test and from the Bender Visual Motor Gestalt Test to the Edwards Personal Preference Schedule, so that America could boast of the strongest and best astronauts in the world.

Hopes for an expansion of the space program quickly faltered in the 1970s, though, as economic troubles and other concerns—ranging from the Vietnam War to feminist and civil rights struggles—took precedence.

Although the practicality of dealing with urgent and pressing issues made sense, surely the American psyche took yet another hit when the triumphs of the space program lost momentum—and when the first Apollo launch of the decade nearly turned tragic.

On April 11, 1970, NASA launched Apollo 13, hoping to land on the Fra Mauro highlands of the moon. Fifty-five hours later, an oxygen tank exploded on board, putting the entire crew in extreme danger. Aborting their mission, astronauts Jim Lovell, Jack Swigert, and Fred Haise used the resources located on their lunar lander to survive, including its oxygen, radio, and engines. Four days later, the rocket reentered Earth's orbit; on April 17, they landed safely.

According to NASA, although this barely averted disaster reminded us of the dangers of space exploration, the successful landing also "reinforced the notion that NASA had a remarkable ability to adapt to the unforeseen technical difficulties inherent in human spaceflight."[3] Whether that statement genuinely reflected the sentiments of the American public or whether NASA was attempting to recover some of its damaged reputation, the near destruction of Apollo 13 was not the end of the program. The following summer, Alan Shepard led Apollo 14 into space. Shepard was America's first space traveler, but an ailment had prevented him from participating in space flight since 1961; because of a successful surgery, though, he could command the Apollo 14. When he did, he walked on the moon's Fra Mauro highlands.

Apollo 15's astronauts explored the moon's mountains using a Lunar Rover. They discovered a rock dating back 4.5 million years, nearly the estimated age of the moon; they named the rock "Genesis." Apollo 16 explored the moon's highlands using new technology known as the ultraviolet camera and spectrograph. Apollo 17 furthered the knowledge of the moon's origins significantly, thanks to Harrison H. "Jack" Schmitt, the first scientist to also serve as an astronaut. He also advised NASA on how humans could successfully live in outer space. All told, 12 astronauts walked on the moon during six lunar landings. After Apollo 17, though, budget cuts caused this particular space program to cease operations.

Soviet cosmonauts also landed on the moon, starting in 1970; they also created automated rovers. In 1971, they attempted the world's first space station, Salyut 1, but all three cosmonauts died after the cabin suddenly lost pressure. In 1973, the Soviets succeeded in a similar scientific mission, as the Cold War continued to be waged in outer space.

Exploration of Mars also occurred in the 1970s, and NASA's Mariner 9 began photographing the planet in 1971, revealing "towering volcanoes, giant canyons and winding valleys that appeared to be dry riverbeds."[4] In 1976, two Viking landers touched down on Mars, gathering data; an attempt was made to find microbial life, but nothing was discovered. Mariner 10, employing gravity assist, used the pull of Venus to direct itself toward Mercury; using this strategy, three successful "flybys" occurred. Meanwhile, Soviets succeeded in a Venus landing, discovering temperatures of 900 Fahrenheit. The U.S. Pioneer 10 and 11 flew by Jupiter and Saturn, while Voyager 1 and 2, both launched in 1977, began a space tour that would ultimately lead to the outer solar system.

Perhaps the most remarkable accomplishment, diplomacywise, happened in 1975 when a U.S./Soviet cooperative effort created the Apollo-Soyuz Test Project (ASTP). Through this initiative, the two countries studied launching and docking protocol; after spacecraft launched from each of the countries, the crews met in space for two days, conducting more experiments. NASA carefully recorded each step of this project for posterity.

SKYLAB

America's first experimental space station. Designed for long duration mission, Skylab program objectives were twofold: To prove that humans could live and work in space for extended periods, and to expand our knowledge of solar astronomy well beyond Earth-based observations.[5]

Using Apollo and Saturn technology, NASA created a space platform from which trained scientists and astronauts could gather information; they would, while in space, examine the sun, photograph the earth, and study weightlessness. The creation of Skylab cost less than $3 billion and the space station was ready for a test run by 1973.

Skylab suffered from technical difficulties, though, during its unmanned experiment flight on May 14, 1973. Just 63 seconds after blasting off, atmospheric drag ripped off a shield intended to protect Skylab's workshop. NASA, understandably enough, spent 10 days repairing Skylab before the first of three sets of three men lived in its workshop space while orbiting Earth. All three flights were successful and these nine men lived in Skylab for a total of 171 days during 1973 and 1974. Each group stayed longer than the one before, with the three trips lasting 28, 59, and 84 days, respectively.

These men continuously pointed a sophisticated observation device, called the "Apollo Telescope Mount," at the sun to gather their data. The crew, who were both scientists and astronauts, carefully selected targets on the sun to observe, and then they watched for its active regions; once detected, they filmed those areas to record the radiation released during the flare-ups.

These men conducted nearly 300 scientific experiments while in space, trying to determine how humans adapted to zero gravity; they also continued to study Earth and sun. For the first time ever, refueling successfully occurred in space, and, on July 11, 1979, five years after the project had ceased operations and the men had safely returned home, pieces of Skylab fell back down to Earth.

THE AUTOMOBILE
Legislation

In 1965, consumer advocate Ralph Nader published *Unsafe at Any Speed,* which listed a substantial number of charges against the car manufacturing industry and its alleged unwillingness to spend money on safety features in cars. He asked why thousands of Americans continued to die in accidents that could be prevented using already existing technology. The car manufacturing industry and Nader clashed furiously over his claims; meanwhile a public outcry arose, demanding that these safety features be installed in cars. Ironically, when the National Safety Council mounted seat belt education campaigns in both 1972 and 1973, no significant changes in behavior were noted.

Nevertheless, largely in response to these demands, the federal government passed significant safety-related legislation in the automobile industry in the latter part of the 1960s—and during the 1970s. One area of concern was the cars' bumpers, as this feature protects passengers from injury in low-impact accidents. Effective September 1, 1972—for 1973 models—bumpers needed to withstand minimal impacts without damage to headlights or fuel systems. In October 1972, Congress passed an act that caused the creation of a federal bumper standard.

The notion of passive restraint systems in cars was amply debated, as well, while mandates and legislation flip-flopped frequently. The National Highway Traffic Safety Administration set a deadline of 1974 for passive restraint systems in cars; after industry executives lobbied Richard Nixon, the deadline was extended until 1976. When that deadline loomed, Gerald Ford's transportation secretary agreed to cancel that requirement after car manufacturers agreed to voluntarily install safety air bags in selected cars. In 1977, Jimmy Carter's transportation secretary reversed that decision and gave car manufacturers a new deadline of 1984 to include passive restraints or air bags.

Car manufacturers experimented with safety air bags, even before legislation definitively required them to install them in selected cars. The Oldsmobile Toronado came equipped with that feature in 1973. That same year, General Motors built 1,000 Chevrolets with air bags for testing purposes; in the first recorded air bag fatality, an infant in the front seat of a car died after an air bag deployed during a wreck. In 1974, General Motors offered air bags as an option in selected Cadillacs, Oldsmobiles, and Buicks from 1974 through 1976. Hoping to sell 100,000 cars with air bags during that three-year period, sales were a disappointing 10,000, and so General Motors abandoned the project.

In 1975, Volvo conducted an experiment to determine the safety of putting young children in front seats with air bag safety features, using pigs in place of the children; 8 of the 24 pigs died and all but 3 of the surviving pigs were injured. This experiment helped lead to the conclusion that children should stay in the back seats of cars that came equipped with air bags.

Two significant technological improvements occurred during the decade; the first was Chrysler's invention of the electronic ignition in 1972. *Popular Mechanics* named this as one of the top inventions of the second half of the twentieth century; the electronic ignition, it wrote, led to "electronic control of ignition timing and fuel metering, harbingers of more sophisticated systems to come … electronic control transmission shift points, antilock brakes, traction control systems, steering and airbag deployment."[6] Four years later, Volvo introduced cars with catalytic converters that greatly reduced harmful emissions into the environment. The following year, California passed strict new legislation that limited the acceptable levels of the three most harmful emission types.

Oil Crisis Effect

Prior to the oil crisis of 1973, American car manufacturers focused significantly on improving performance of their vehicles, each trying to outdo previous efforts, surpass domestic competitors, and prevent the imported cars from securing more of a market share in the United States. During the early part of the 1970s, the "muscle car" remained popular. "Generally defined by their oversized engine, large bodies, and elaborate ornamentation, so-called muscle cars such as the Pontiac GTO (developed by John DeLorean), the Mercury Eliminator, and the Plymouth Road Runner, were true 'kings of the road' beginning in the 1960s and lasting until the early 1970s. For better or worse, their like will probably never be seen again." These cars appealed to teenagers, as well as adults, and were frequently the models of cars that, according to author Michael L. Berger, "were/are frequently seen as a contributing factor to, if not the cause of, some socially unacceptable behavior. Even when the car is not seen as a contributor to negative behavior, there still is considerable concern for the safety of teenagers in such vehicles."[7] What the fussing of worried mothers and the rising cost of insuring these vehicles could not alter, the oil crisis did; the rapidly increasing gas prices caused muscle cars to become significantly more expensive to operate—and significantly less socially acceptable in an era concerned with the environment—and so their popularity waned.

American Subcompact Cars

American Motors Company (AMC) premiered the Gremlin, the first American subcompact, on April 1, 1970. AMC created this vehicle to compete with imported cars from Japan and Germany, and this company beat the efforts of Ford Motor Company and General Motors to offer a subcompact car; these two companies didn't debut their versions—the Ford Pinto and the Chevrolet Vega, respectively—until September 1970.

Although the car's appearance received some criticism, the Gremlin had one important factor going for it—the price. A two-seated Gremlin cost $1,879, while the hatch-backed four seater cost $1,959. Furthermore, the car boasted a decent miles per gallon rate, which would become an important factor during the oil crisis. Because of its six-cylinder engine, the car's performance was called sprightly. Perhaps to combat the criticism of its appearance—and certainly to capitalize on America's love of denim—the 1972 Gremlin came in a "Levi edition," which included copper rivets and soft-brushed denim-colored nylon in the interior.

Starting with 1971 models, Americans could choose from three domestic subcompacts: the Gremlin, the Vega, and the Pinto. *Motor Trend* named the Chevy Vega as car of the year in 1971; as author Patrick Foster points out, "a four cylinder subcompact, a product type that would have been laughed out of the showrooms ten years earlier, as car of year was certainly a sign that the auto market itself was changing."[8] The Ford Pinto, though, was in the news for less happy reasons.

Numerous Pintos were involved in car fire fatalities, in large part because of its fuel tank placement that seemed to make it especially vulnerable in rear-end collisions. Ford received significant criticism because of the 27 fatalities, and it was alleged that Ford Motor Company memos indicated that it would rather pay the expenses of lawsuits than spend the money to fix the problem;[9] more recently, though, a 1991 law review paper suggested that, because more than 2 million Pintos were built, this car was no more dangerous, percentagewise, than many others of this era.[10] Regardless, the Pinto was perhaps the most controversial car of the 1970s for this reason.

Although the creation of the American subcompact car preceded the oil embargo crisis of 1973, and was in fact built to challenge the success of smaller imported cars, appreciation of these fuel-efficient vehicles increased as gas prices skyrocketed. Foster writes that "small cars and fuel economy were going to become the most popular topics of social conversation in a country that had never thought much about either."[11] As a comparison, large cars got only about 8 miles per gallon, while compacts could get as much as 35 miles per gallon. Gas prices climbed from 30 cents per gallon to 60 cents during the embargo, and lines at gas stations stretched down the block.

More by coincidence than by deliberate preplanning, in 1974, Ford Motor Company was ready to introduce a smaller Mustang with a more fuel-efficient four-cylinder engine at an affordable price of $2,895. Although this model was enthusiastically received, 1974 was a bad year for the automobile industry. Sales were down 3 million units from 1973 and no relief was in sight. In 1975, manufacturers modified designs to make them look more compact—perhaps to give the impression that they were more fuel-efficient. Chevrolet introduced the Monza, a line of subcompact cars that were more substantial than the Vega, but still economical and fuel-efficient. The oil crisis also led to a brief interest in the Hybrid Electric Vehicles, but that enthusiasm died once the panic over oil abated. Postcrisis, car manufacturers enjoyed a couple years of rebounding sales—but another, albeit less severe oil crisis, occurred in 1979, which once again focused interest on the smaller, more fuel-efficient subcompact car.

Imported Cars

Imported cars, generally still called "foreign cars" during the 1970s, sold well during the decade; sales figures of imported cars in 1970 saw an increase of 200,000 units over the previous year. In 1970, more than half a million German Volkswagens sold in the United States, as did nearly 185,000 Toyotas from Japan. American consumers still tread somewhat cautiously when buying a Japanese product, though, as "the phrase 'made in Japan' was considered a put-down, with extreme negative connotations as to the quality of workmanship and materials."[12] Meanwhile, sales of American-made cars and light trucks fell. As just one example, sales figures from 1970 were $1 million less lucrative than sales from 1969. Although most of this particular drop could be attributed to a 67-day strike at General Motors during 1970, a pattern existed wherein imported cars were chipping away at the market share of domestic products. On February 3, 1975, because of sluggish sales, one-third of the workforce in Detroit's auto industry lost their jobs. By the end of the 1970s, Japanese manufacturers outproduced their American counterparts.

Cars were also used as diplomacy tools. During each of the three peace summits between the United States and the Soviet Union, Richard Nixon gifted Leonid Brezhnev with a car. In 1972, he gave the Soviet leader a Cadillac limousine, valued at $10,000. The following year, Brezhnev received a Lincoln Continental, also valued at $10,000. In 1974, the year that Nixon's domestic political situation was quite shaky, he gave a Chevy Monte Carlo, a car that retailed at $5,578. Although that lesser gift might seem to indicate a falling of Nixon's fortunes or a falling out in the relationship, Brezhnev in fact requested that car as a gift after *Motor Trend* named it the car of the year.

PLANES, TRAINS, AND TRUCKS
Boeing 747: Jumbo Jet

It was late at night, Jan. 21, 1970—a day the world had anticipated for years. With 336 passengers aboard, the giant Pan American World Airways 747 hurtled down the runway at New York's John F. Kennedy airport, took off gracefully, climbed smoothly, then turned east toward London and into the history books. *Thus began the jumbo-jet age.*[13]

The success of Boeing's jumbo jet known as the "747" actually began with a failure several years prior. In the mid-1960s, Boeing lost its bid on a U.S. Air Force contract for a very large plane but, through that process, the company identified a market for a jumbo-sized jet. Furthermore, Boeing could use research material collected for the bidding process to design such a plane and it began work on the project in 1966.

The first test flight was scheduled for February 9, 1969. The Federal Aviation Administration (FAA) warned Boeing that these planes must be substantially quieter than ones currently flying; this requirement marked the first time that federal authorities imposed noise criteria on airlines.

Boeing's first jumbo jet weighed 355 tons and cost $20 million to build. Capable of carrying 490 passengers on a 6,000-mile flight, the flight speed of the test run was anticipated to be 300 mph, and the maximum speed was gauged at 625 mph. The plane was two and a half times the size of current commercial planes, with three times the seating capacity and twice the cargo space. The plane was 60 percent wider than current models, and, at 231 feet in length, it was 70 feet longer than its predecessor, the Boeing 707. Because of the increased size of this plane, airports needed to modify their facilities to accommodate the jumbo jets, and, because of safety concerns related to flying on such a massive plane, insurance companies mulled over how to modify their policies.

The jumbo jet's test flight was scheduled to last four hours, but it was cut short by an hour and 15 minutes because of wing flap difficulty; all otherwise progressed well. The take-off was quiet and the landing was smooth, as well. Appearancewise, the 747 resembled the 707, except for the "hump-like cockpit that gives the plane's fuselage a vague resemblance to a reptile."[14] To ensure safety, no passengers flew on this test run; to approximate the weight of passengers, 176 barrels, each containing 55 gallons of water, were placed on seats. One observer commented that this plane looked as thought it was filled with beer kegs.

The plane's advent was anticipated with awe. "The jumbo jet is so big," one photo caption read, "it's a sort of a flying movie theater; the supersonic transport will be so fast, you may get to Paris before the movie ends."[15] An average jumbo jet would contain 12 lavatories, with plumbing available for 17; the communication system between the cabin and cockpit would operate with touch tone phone and between 12 and 18 stewardesses would be assigned to each flight. Meanwhile, experts talked about the psychological effect these huge planes would have on residents living near the airports.

On June 3, Boeing's jumbo jet successfully flew to Paris, its first overseas test. More than 2,000 Parisians toured the plane and its six movie theaters, spiral staircase leading to the upstairs lounge, and six different decorating schemes.

Not all reports were entirely enthusiastic, though. According to an article in the *Chicago Tribune*, "The faint of heart have looked on the advent of jumbos and the supersonics with all the unbridled optimism of a kamikaze pilot making a post-mission social engagement. No one has ever questioned what a single 747 crash would do in terms of air line reputation and public acceptance of aircraft some cynics say are just too big to fly."[16] To combat these concerns, the article continues, Boeing considered no safety detail too small to investigate.

Boeing received clearance for public use of its 747 on December 30, 1969. In January 1970, the 747–100 began service with Pan American.

Deregulation

The United States Airline Deregulation Act of 1978 was a dramatic event in the history of economic policy. It was the first thorough dismantling of a comprehensive system of government control since the Supreme Court declared the National Recovery Act unconstitutional in 1935. It also was part of a broader movement that, with varying degrees of thoroughness, transformed such industries as trucking, railroads, buses, cable television, stock exchange brokerage, oil and gas, telecommunications, financial markets, and even local electric and gas utilities.[17]

During the latter part of the 1970s, airline companies struggled beneath the weight of hefty regulations. The system of the era has been described as both inflexible and cumbersome; as just one example, lengthy Civil Aeronautics Board (CAB) hearings were required for two affiliated airlines to receive permission to wear similar uniforms.

CAB determined what prices airlines could charge and what routes they could take. Following their belief that consumers would not pay full price if they only needed to travel a short distance, they set lower prices for short-haul markets and higher prices for long-haul markets. Opponents of this philosophy stated that this policy inhibited the growth of air travel—and therefore of the entire airline industry.

In 1978, Congress voted to deregulate the airlines, which allowed the companies to determine their own pricing structures and to openly compete with other companies. Consumers hoped for lower prices and better service as airlines attempted to woo them; overall, studies indicate that deregulation accomplished those goals. However, before deregulation, airline tickets were generally fully refundable and consumers changed flights without penalty, so the decision contained both advantages and disadvantages.

Amtrak

> Sometimes regarded as an outmoded, vestigial form of transportation, doomed to extinction, the nation's passenger railroads, like the fabled Phoenix, have started to rise again from the ashes of the past to become a key element in the nation's balanced transportation system of tomorrow.[18]

Passenger train usage began to decline during the 1930s, as increasing numbers of people purchased automobiles. It dropped even further in the 1950s, when long-distance travelers had significantly more options that involved flying to their destinations, and when improved highways systems made driving easier and more pleasant. In October 1967, the U.S. Postal Service began transporting first class mail by truck and plane, relegating only second and third class mail to the passenger trains. In the face of such fierce competition, many passenger train systems folded.

Shortly after the postal service withdrew its first-class contracts with the railways, a young attorney named Anthony Haswell formed a lobbyist group, the National Association of Railroad Passengers, to persuade the federal government to solve the problem of declining railway passenger transportation. It lobbied Congress, the Department of Transportation, and the Federal Railroad Administration.

Concurrent with the lobbyist group forming, two major railway systems—the Pennsylvania Railroad and the New York Central Railroad—merged on February 1, 1968, to create the Penn Central Railroad system. This mammoth new railway system was expected to solve many of the railway's problems. Instead, on June 21, 1970, the Penn Central railroad system filed for bankruptcy—the largest bankruptcy to date. The failure of this system was agonized over and analyzed in depth. According to authors Joseph R. Daughen and Peter Binzen, causes of the failure included "over-regulation, subsidized competition, big labor featherbedding, greed, corporate back stabbing, stunning incompetence, and yes, even a little sex."[19] In more prosaic terms, when the Penn Central Transportation Company crashed, it had 100,000 creditors and more than 118,000 stockholders, and the railway system simply collapsed beneath these demands.

Although Congress recognized the need for a solution to the passenger railway crisis, it was not united in the specifics. The collapse of the Penn Central, though, deepened the state of emergency, and, on October 14, 1970, Congress passed the Rail Passenger Service Act to revitalize passenger railroads in the country. On October 30, Richard Nixon signed the bill that authorized the National Railroad Passenger Corporation (NRPC) to operate the railroad system. Eight presidential appointees plus key members from the Federal Railroad Administration and the Department of Transportation spearheaded the planning; their goal was to operate a quality system while maintaining freedom from regulation.

The law created a quasi-public corporation—originally to be named Railpax, but changed to Amtrak. The name Amtrak stood for "American Travel by Track" and the advertising firm of Lippincott & Margulies designed the red, white, and blue inverted arrow that came to symbolize Amtrak.

Private rail companies had until May 1, 1971, to either merge with Amtrak or decide to remain independent. Private railroad systems kept control of the more lucrative freight service, causing many policymakers to assume that passenger service would eventually fade from American culture. To join the NRPC, private passenger railways could pay a fee in cash, or provide equipment and services based on half of the company's losses for 1970, or purchase an agreed-upon amount of common stock in the new corporation. In exchange, the company no longer bore the financial burden of running a passenger service. Almost all services opted to join NRPC, but four chose to remain independent: Southern, Rio Grande, Rock Island, and Georgia Railroad.

Prior to the grand opening, Amtrak issued press releases, promising many great things for the future. Promises included clean cars, precise adherence to schedules, quality meals, and an overall pleasant travel experience. On May 1, 1971, half of the country's railways made their final private enterprise journey and the first train of Amtrak, clocker number 235, left New York's Penn Station at 12:05 A.M., heading to Philadelphia. Initially, Amtrak used 184 trains, covering 314 destinations along 21 key routes, each route traveling between two major cities. Even-numbered trains were to travel north and east; odd-numbered were assigned routes to the south and west. Because Amtrak absorbed old railway systems, though, it also kept a few numbering systems that clashed with the new organizational chart, including those from the Santa Fe Railroad and some of the Empire Corridor routes.

On the first day of operations, 184 trains covered 23,000 miles. Although that may sound impressive, that figure was half of the area covered by private enterprises just the day before, and many locales had no service, whatsoever. Other problems existed, including technical incompatibility as equipment from several companies attempted to merge. Amtrak had begun its operations by leasing older coach and sleeper cars from freight railroads in the eastern portion of the country, connecting them with newer equipment from companies on the West Coast, leading some to label the first few years of Amtrak as the "Rainbow Era."

By 1974, Amtrak had purchased much of its own equipment, painting it with a consistent color theme. It also spruced up the image of its employees, as engineers began wearing "blue bush jackets with brass buttons"; ticket sellers were "resplendent in double-breasted red vests, white visors and multicolored sleeve garters, looking as if they should be dealing out chips at a poker table"; and female passenger representatives were wearing "side-slit red gowns over blue panty hose, skirts and cardigans, red hot pants."[20] Throughout the 1970s, Amtrak attempted to improve its image and its service; as the decade progressed, other private railway systems—ones that had previously declined to merge with Amtrak—became part of the system, as well.

Trucks

Starting in 1977, the trucking industry saw a movement toward deregulation, resulting in easier entry into the industry and relative freedom for companies to set their own rates. Although many positive benefits arose from this movement, safety sometimes suffered. Truckers often communicated by CB (citizens band) radios, which consisted of a microphone, speaker system, and control box; they were relatively easy to set up and to use. By 1977, the airwaves became so crowded that 17 additional channels were set up, for a total of 40. Channel 19 became known as the most popular for truckers. Four-wheel-drive trucks gained in popularity, with several light trucks premiering with this feature, including the 1970 Range Rover and the AMC Eagle 4 x 4.

12

Visual Arts

INTRODUCTION

In 1971, portrait painter Andrew Wyeth created the first of more than 240 portraits of his neighbor, Helga Testorf. This project lasted 15 years and Wyeth kept the sketches and paintings a secret from everyone, including his wife, as he focused on the study of light and how it affected the appearance of Helga. Wyeth sometimes focused on the light hitting Helga's reddish hair; other times, he emphasized a shadow on her body. He painted her while indoors and out, throughout the seasons, and he sometimes painted her nude or asleep. Although the Helga series has intrigued untold numbers of spectators since Wyeth first made the work available to the public, this was not the typical type of visual art being produced during the 1970s. What was typical in the 1970s, though, can be somewhat hard to define.

Although some decades and some generations of artists can be pigeonholed into specific emerging artistic movements, no major movement surfaced in the world of painting or sculpture during the 1970s. Instead, many established artists continued their work from the 1960s in the fields of abstract painting, pop art, and earthwork sculpting, developing compelling—and sometimes controversial—works of art and stretching the limits of artistic expression. The 1970s served as a decade wherein artistic mediums blended and merged, as painters used film, music, and video to complement their work, and as performance art came to the forefront as a form of legitimate social expression.

Improved technology served as the impetus for a controversial art form—one that some critics say wasn't really a form of art, at all. Starting in the early 1970s, graffiti artists began using the newly invented aerosol spray cans of paint to scrawl text and create sketches on public properties. Although graffiti certainly wasn't new, the 1970s saw an explosion of graffiti's colors and designs, especially in subways. The United Graffiti Artists formed in 1972; in 1975, the association displayed an exhibition of graffiti in New York, thus causing some to label this type of work as "urban folk art" rather than random vandalism. Graffiti artists usually developed a "tag," which could be a visual or textual symbol, to identify themselves to their followers—and to their competitors.

Street photographers were capturing gritty portraits of everyday life, especially in New York, while war photojournalists were memorializing even bloodier scenes from Southeast Asia. Meanwhile, a new brand of photography was coalescing, wherein selected photographers who were taking photos of celebrities became famous themselves. Photographic technology improved during the 1970s, as digital photography allowed people to create prints from negatives; prior to this, the majority of photographers used slide or chrome film, which required the use of a slide projector for viewing.

In 1972, the Women's Caucus for Art was founded, which promoted artistic opportunities for both females and minorities. The following year, the National Endowment for the Arts began a program with a goal to make the arts available to everyone in the country, using public broadcast television as a communications medium. In 1974, the Dia Art Foundation began funding visual arts presentations; and in 1975, the Indian Self-Determination and Education Assistance Act allowed Native Americans to spend educational resources to teach their youth about the visual arts from their own heritage.

ABSTRACT PAINTING

Abstract art does not contain recognizable subjects; it does not attempt to replicate real world objects; and it does not endeavor to represent their physical shapes. Some abstract art is geometric and patterned, while other examples are more fluid and unregimented. An early practitioner of abstract art, Wassily Kandinsky, believed that abstract art was capable of capturing the spiritual, rather than the physical, realities of the world.

By the time the 1970s arrived, several experimental art forms of the twentieth century had merged into the genre generally known as abstract act. The richness of the multitude of artistic movements inherent in the abstract form allowed painters from the 1970s to select from and play around with a wide range of philosophies and styles, including Cubism. French artist Georges Braque and Spanish artist Pablo Picasso first experimented with this art form in about 1908, after being influenced by the work of painter Paul Cezanne. The name of this artistic movement comes from painter Henri Matisse's comment that a painting of Braque's consisted of "petits cubes," or "little cubes."

Advocates of Cubism believe that an artist can capture the essence of an object by showing it from multiple angles within the same painting. To accomplish this effect, the artist breaks up the representation of the actual object and then reassembles it in an abstracted form, following Cezanne's advice to express nature via three forms: the cylinder, sphere, and cone. In one of the earlier examples of this art form, Picasso's *Girl with Dark Hair*, viewers can see the front of her face as well as the side, all at the same time. Perhaps Cubism mimics the way in which the human brain actually processes visual data, as a number of glances at an object merge to create an overall perception. Italian artists influenced by Cubism became part of the Futurist movement, wherein technological force and movement inspired their paintings. In turn, Futurism contributed its own facets to the overriding concept of abstract art.

Another art form, Neoplasticism, started shortly after the birth of Cubism. Adherents do not attempt to replicate real objects; rather they attempt to study the vertical and horizontal lines and primary colors that underlie the objects. This movement focused on pure form, spiritual harmony, and order.

Expressionism developed most extensively in Germany, focusing on the extremes of color and symbolic imagery, with the artist intending to evoke emotions rather than to make impassionate observations. The paintings are said to reflect the artists' moods and are often sinister and dark in their ambiance. Closely related to this movement is Fauvism, wherein color is believed to serve as an emotional force.

The school of Abstract Expressionism began in the 1940s in the United States, with Jackson Pollock its best-known advocate and practitioner. Abstract Expressionism, in many ways, was more of an attitude than a precisely defined style. Its advocates valued individuality, spontaneous improvisation, and freedom of expression; some of them emphasized the physical act of painting, while others focused on the exploration of color. They believed that inspiration could be found from the unconscious mind, and that a spontaneous approach to their work would serve them well in this pursuit. Abstract Expressionism served as the first art form of significance that developed most fully in America and then spread to other parts of the world; prior to this, painters in the United States learned techniques and philosophies that were first developed in Europe.

Most American artists of the 1970s chose to either continue experimenting with the multiple possibilities inherent in Abstract Expressionism or to join in with an art form that was newer and quite different: Pop Art.

POP ART

One of the best-known examples of Pop Art is Andy Warhol's red-and-white Campbell's Soup can, created in 1964; another is his silk screens of the deceased movie star, Marilyn Monroe, also created during the 1960s. Pop art incorporates popular cultural and consumer icons and objects, including advertisements, household goods, and television features to make its artistic statement. This movement began in Britain during the 1950s, made its way to the United States in the 1960s, and continued to influence the art world throughout the 1970s and beyond. When it first appeared in the United States, "pop was the rock-and-roll of art (and rock was still an angry toddler). Like rock, it reset the culture clock, rewrote the rules, recast the performers."[1] Author Marco Livingstone, in *Pop Art: A Continuing History*, suggests that the acceptance of Pop Art as a legitimate movement occurred more quickly than that of any other art form in our country's history.[2] Although the death of the movement was predicted as early as 1965—a rapid rise-and-crash that seemed fitting for an art form that celebrated the built-in obsolescence of modern consumerism—the form continued to reinvent itself well past its anticipated demise.

The early popularity of the art form was said to serve as a reaction against the Abstract Expressionist movement, in which artists applied paint rapidly to express feelings, sometimes dripping—or even throwing—paint on the canvas. This intense—and some say highbrow—type of art was "emotional, intuitive, spontaneous, autographic, personal, serious and morally committed—in short, a 'hot' or romantic style." Meanwhile, Pop Art focused on features of everyday life, and was "unemotional, deliberate, systematic, impersonal, ironic, detached, non-autographic and amoral— a 'cool' or classical style."[3] Although some artists kept working in the Abstract Expressionism style during the 1960s and 1970s, pop moved to the forefront of the art world.

Some critics accused pop artists of plagiarism, of merely copying items available in the commercial world; author John Walker suggests, however, that a close, point-by-point comparison of an object in reality and of its counterpart in a piece of art proves them to be quite different. "Artists," he writes, "are often said to 'reflect' the world around them in their art. This particular optical metaphor is unsatisfactory because it implies a passive mirroring of appearances. The word 'refraction' has also been used, but even better is 'translation' because it indicates that something of the original has been preserved but also that an active process of transformation from one language into another has occurred."[4] The meaning of an object, Walker says, can be changed by its juxtaposition to other objects, and it therefore becomes recontextualized.

Warhol, the unofficial spokesperson of Pop Art, worked with a group of assistants in a studio called the "Factory," specializing in art that used a silk background and that had varieties of a master image imprinted upon it in multiple fashions. Some critics say that he attempted to critique middle-class America through his art, while others claim that his work celebrates pop culture in the United States. Starting in 1970, he focused more frequently on portraits, usually of friends or figures of pop culture, and his work, in fact, began to more closely resemble Abstract Expressionism—or it at least blended aspects of the two forms.

One critic points out Warhol's uncanny ability to discern the trends of the moment—which, during the 1960s and 1970s, included symbols of consumerism and celebrity—and to then re-create them in his art. By doing so, he not only reflected the fads of popular culture, he reinvented them, illuminating elements for historians. Although Warhol's work rebelled against what had previously been considered art, many museums, worldwide, embraced his art and showed his paintings and silk screenings in special exhibitions.

[Pop Art] is an involvement with what I think to be the most brazen and threatening characteristics of our culture, things we hate, but which are also powerful in their impingement on us.[5]

Another American pop artist of note was Roy Lichtenstein, who created his first well-known piece of art in 1956: his print of the 10-dollar bill.

Pop artist Andy Warhol served as the quintessential celebrity artist of the decade. Shown here in 1990, he is appearing in a documentary of his life and work. Courtesy of Aries Films/Photofest.

He then experimented with Abstract Expressionism for three years; after returning to the field of Pop Art, he created a painting of Disney characters Mickey Mouse and Donald Duck—the type of comic strip art for which he became famous.

Although comic strip art became a significant focus of Lichtenstein, cartoons did not turn into his sole center of attention. He also painted people and his "depictions of characters in tense, dramatic situations are intended as ironic commentaries on modern man's plight, in which mass media—magazines, advertisements, and television—shapes everything, even our emotions."[6] He also created paintings using dots, attempting to prevent any brush strokes from appearing; he preferred to have these paintings appear machine-made.

When asked what he thought of being called a "pop artist," Lichtenstein replied that he preferred to think of his work as a parody, also stating that, "If people use the word 'pop' to differentiate it from art, then I would not like the idea too much. It is inevitable I am going to be called a pop artist. The name is going to stick, no matter what I think."[7] It is somewhat ironic that Lichtenstein, who has been called a master of incorporating stereotypes in art, would be saddled with a label that could be perceived as stereotypical.

Swedish-born pop artist Claes Oldenburg, who is known for his large-scale outdoor pieces, has spent most of his life in the United States. In 1969, he set up *Lipstick (Ascending) on Caterpillar Tracks* on the campus of Yale University, which was a "25-foot-tall phallic-shaped cosmetic mounted on what looks like a battle vehicle" that "evokes both male and female sexuality, while unmistakably referencing the Vietnam War."[8] This particular piece of art became a focus of student protests. In 1976, he installed *Clothespin* in downtown Philadelphia; since then, he and his spouse Coosje van Bruggen have created and placed more than 40 large-scale pieces of art in urban areas throughout the United States and world. Oldenburg chose to create such colossal pieces because this intensified the presence of the object; he selected outdoor urban locales because he saw the city as his tablecloth.

Yet another pop artist of note is James Rosenquist, who first received significant attention for his 1965 painting, *F-111*. This 51-panel piece of art fills an entire room, containing seemingly unconnected images, including a sweetly beautiful child under a hair dryer, a mushroom cloud, and tangled strands of spaghetti. During the 1970s, yet another pop artist, Jasper Johns, created artwork that corresponded with the text of writer Samuel Beckett; other pop artists of the era include Jim Dine, Red Grooms, Philip Guston, Keith Haring, Robert Indiana, Peter Max, Mel Ramos, Larry Rivers, Edward Ruscha, and Wayne Thiebaud.

Closely related to Pop Art was the school of Photorealism, in which painters sought to create such precise detail in their work that it appeared to be a photo. The subject matter of Photorealism was often mundane, similar to what might appear in a random photo. Labels such as Superrealism and Hyperrealism were also used, and this form of art harkens back to the Illusionism of earlier, prephotography centuries. Artists associated with these movements include John Salt, Richard Estes, and Chuck Close.

Some artists took the notion of realism even further, using their own bodies as the medium for expression in an art form called performance art. Performance artists incorporated other many art forms in their work, including music, song, storytelling, video, and sculpture. Performance art took on political overtones during the 1970s, often serving as a venue for feminist, gay and lesbian, and minority messages. Although enthusiastically received by some audiences, other critics and spectators questioned how performance art differed from theater and other visual performances.

SCULPTURE

During this decade of environmental concerns, many sculptors focused on art that used nature as the backdrop for their work. These pieces of art are generally huge in scope as the sculptor uses elements of the natural world, either as they were found or rearranged to make a particular statement. Whatever choice the artist makes, his or her landscape is not permanent, as wind and erosion take their toll, and the degrees of light or darkness affect the appearance of the art. This art form served as a significant departure from the more formalized pieces found in galleries and private homes.

Various terms have been used to describe the earth-related sculptures that flourished during the 1970s; the definitions are somewhat fluid. Although closely related, they are not entirely interchangeable. The phrase *environmental art* generally covers several specialties: earth art, land art, earthworks, art in nature, eco art, and restoration art. Becoming more specific, earth artists, land artists, and earthwork artists tend to search the environment for opportunities to change its shape for aesthetic and symbolic reasons. Eco-art focuses more on the restoration of the earth and is often connected to a political agenda, with artists wishing to heal or restore the land. Alan Sonfist's *Time Landscape,* in which he planted trees from precolonial times at a busy intersection in New York, also qualifies as eco-art. Finally, art in nature projects are usually more temporary in form, and they generally involve the rearrangement of ice, leaves, sticks, dirt, and so forth in an artistic fashion. It is ironic, of course, that many environmental artists who used nature as their palate in fact changed—and some might say destroyed—part of the environment to make their statements about the land.

One of the best-known examples of an earthworks project is Robert Smithson's *Spiral Jetty.* Created in Rozel Point, Great Salt Lake, Utah, in April 1970,

Smithson incorporated the mud, black basalt rocks, algae, and salt crystals already available to craft a 1,500-foot long and 15-foot wide counterclockwise coil in the reddish waters of the lake. Smithson was said to be inspired by the Great Serpent Mound, a Native American burial ground located in southern Ohio. Water submerged the *Spiral Jetty* two years after Smithson completed his work; in 2002, the water level subsided and visitors could once again see the massive coil. Other examples of Smithson's land art during the 1970s include *Partially Buried Woodshed* in Kent, Ohio; *Amarillo Ramp* in Tecovas Lake, Texas; and earthworks crafted in Holland.

Although Spiral Jetty is significant in size, Michael Heizer created a larger piece in 1968; naming his project *Nine Nevada Depressions,* he crafted large and swirling trenches in the desert that seem to appear randomly over a region of 520 miles. Heizer liked to call this type of work, which involved removing dirt and land, "un-sculpture" or "sculpture in reverse." The following year, he blasted out 240,000 tons of rock in a Nevada mesa to create *Double Negative.* In 1970, he began buying up land in the Nevada desert for $30 an acre to fulfill his vision of sculpting giant abstract figures that would echo the work of ancient Olmecs, Mayans, Incas, and Aztecs. In 1971, he began to build *Complex 1* of this ambitious art scape.

Yet another project of significant size is James Turrell's earthwork located around an extinct volcano, the Roden Crater, in Arizona. Situated along the edge of the Painted Desert, Turrell began this project during the 1970s and it continued to evolve well past the decade's closure. The artist speaks of working with light and space, and he recalls an early memory of his Quaker grandmother encouraging him to greet the light. He has, over the ensuing years, carved out rooms and tunnels and chambers into the red and black cinders of the Roden Crater, and he said the following of his vision: "I wanted to build these spaces that engage celestial events, kind of making music with a series of light."[9]

Most earthworks followed the philosophy of minimalist thinking, in which simple arrangements, using plain, often readily available materials, formed the basis of the art. The minimalist movement also influenced other prominent sculptors who used metal as a substance of choice.

Walter de Maria crafted an outdoor metal sculpture in 1977. *The Lightning Field* consists of 400 polished stainless steel poles, each sharpened to a point. From east to west, the poles stretch out for a mile, each row consisting of 25 identical poles. From north to south, the poles are laid out for a kilometer, in rows of 16. The peaks of the poles form a perfectly even plane. Located in the high desert of southwestern New Mexico, visitors are encouraged to walk throughout the spaces of the sculpture, especially at dawn and at sunset. Weather conditions affect the appearance of *The Lightning Field,* changing the optical effects of sunlight on metal. Meanwhile, Richard Serra, a former steelworker, crafted large-scale artistic pieces using steel. He also splashed molten lead in the spaces between walls and floors, calling these his "Splash" projects; in 1975, Serra won the Skowhegan Medal for Sculpture. Other sculptors of note who created indoor metallic pieces are Alice Aycock and Donald Judd.

George Segal crafted more traditional sculptures, sometimes out of metal and sometimes out of marble. According to a PBS special about his life and work, Segal "developed a method of casting from live models that became his trademark. He used medical bandages soaked in plaster to wrap models who were often his friends and family. The resulting white plaster figures are realistic and hauntingly provocative."[10] During the 1970s, Segal began casting work in bronze and much of his work appeared outdoors.

The PBS program points out another way in which Segal's work changed the concept of sculpting: "He took sculpture off the pedestal. And he brought the figures and the environment into the everyday world. So if he did two figures on a bench, it was a real bench and it was set in a real space … that was part of the intimacy of the work."[11] One of his best-known sculptures of this type is called *Three Figures on Four Benches*, crafted in 1979 and placed by the justice center in Cleveland, Ohio. This sculpture is so intimately connected with everyday life that people sit on the benches next to the life-sized marble figures.

Lynda Benglis was often more concerned with process art, wherein the act of creation was seen as important as the final result—and yet, the results are clear and tangible and artistic. Benglis, a feminist sculptor, will perhaps never live down the notoriety of when she posed nude with a phallic symbol to advertise a 1974 art show, but her work is more important than that. In 1971, she began experimenting with more malleable materials such as wax and foam, as they allowed her to experiment with process and form. During the 1970s, she also experimented with the use of intricate knots in her art.

Another feminist sculptor, Judy Chicago, is perhaps best known for *The Dinner Party*. This elaborate sculpture depicts a ceremonial banquet table with 39 exceptionally large china plates resting on exotic textiles. Each plate contains a butterfly image and the runners on the table share imagery and stories of the 39 women being celebrated.

PHOTOGRAPHY

Photography is one of the great art forms of the past 50 years—perhaps the greatest. It also demonstrates the seemingly endless roads photographers travel to express the issues of annihilation, alienation, bizarre kinds of terror and longing for community that insistently gnaw at our society.[12]

During the 1930s, a group of photographers aligned themselves with the social realism movement and they focused on capturing the hardships of society with their cameras. Not satisfied with simply observing and recording the world around them, they hoped that their work would serve as an instrument of change in society. Perhaps one of the best-known social realists of the 1970s was Allan Sekula, who focused on people in the midst of economic or political struggles. As one example, Sekula photographed factory workers as they were leaving their shift at General Dynamics, preserving the dull monotony of the moment. In 1972, he created a series of slides from these photos, calling his collection the "Untitled Slide Sequence." In 1973, he exhibited another series of photos with the name of "Performance under Working Conditions."

Sekula urged photographers to examine their purpose in creating documentaries and he used many of his own experiences to create his art. In 1974, he shot a series of photos that he named "This Ain't China," focusing on the working conditions in a restaurant where he was once employed. Starting in 1978, he began work on "School Is a Factory," photographing night school students who were attending the classes that he taught, and documenting the working conditions of a generation that Sekula believed was detached from their lives. Sekula was virulently antiwar and he staged photos to symbolically express his viewpoints, such as the one of a man publicly slinking on his belly while wearing a straw hat and carrying a toy gun.

Sekula often employed a street photography approach to his work, capturing real-life moments as they randomly occurred in urban locales. Some street photographers used panoramic cameras to create large-scale photos, and their work, by definition, captured everyday life in the streets. Street photography interested artists around the globe, many of whom came to New York for their work because of the challenges and possibilities inherent in such a crowded and diverse venue. Photographers Robert Frank and William Klein were said to dominate street photography during this era; Frank published his second book of photography in 1972, titled *Lines of My Hand* and he then focused on creating montages with words and images directly scratched on the photos' negatives. Klein spent much of the 1970s also experimenting with film documentaries.

The 1970s saw the end of the career of Diane Arbus, whose poignant and quirky photos combined facets of street photography with studio posing. Well known for her ability to show the humanity in those she photographed, Arbus's career and life was cut short by her suicide in 1972.

Photographer Scott Mutter took a different approach in his work, creating what he called "surrational images" that seem to defy the laws of science. His photo montages were deliberately staged to look as though they could potentially be real; he mixes images in a startling fashion but keeps enough reality for viewers to accept them as "real" photographs. He searches for metaphors to create his photographic montages as he superimposes several images to create a single unifying picture.

The 1970s also witnessed the work of war correspondents who photographed scenes in Vietnam, including Dick Swanson. He spent five years there working for *Life* magazine. After marrying a woman from Vietnam, he was transferred to Washington, D.C. in 1971; he continued to travel between the two countries for the next four years and he returned to Saigon in April 1975, to help his wife's family escape before the city fell.

In retrospect, Swanson said that the tragedy of Vietnam was "stupe-fying" and a place where he learned the "ugliest of litanies—napalm, defoliation, refugees, search and destroy, Rolling Thunder, pacification, step-ons and body count. Their photographs showed combat was not the glorious thing we'd all been led to believe. It was one human being killing another indiscriminately. The legacy of their photographs is the only thing that makes their deaths meaningful."[13] Swanson also reiterates the very real danger that photojournalists faced in Vietnam, listing several who died during the war: Larry Burrows, Kent Potter, Sawata, Henri Huet, Sean Flynn, and Dana Stone.

Finally, in an era that celebrated the celebrity, it isn't surprising that photographers who snapped pictures of celebrities might find themselves accorded with some of that same status. Annie Leibovitz is a prime example of this phenomenon; according to a *USA Today* article, ever since Leibovitz "burst upon the scene in the 1970s," her "camera has become the defining depicter of the 'in' scene."[14] She began her career at *Rolling Stone* magazine in 1970, becoming the chief photographer in 1973. She first took black-and-white photographs for the magazine, but, in 1974, the magazine switched to color and Leibovitz adapted her craft. Assignments included taking photos of John Lennon of the Beatles and serving as the official photographer for the Rolling Stones' 1975 world tour.

In 1979, Leibovitz also took a now-famous photo of singer and actor Bette Midler lying in a bed of roses. "Leibovitz makes a habit of studying her subject thoroughly before a photographic shoot and arranges poses based on her research. 'She stages a scene that has many references to the character of the sitter. She packs the picture with visual elements,' comments Sylvia Wolf of the Whitney Museum."[15] Because Leibovitz focused her work on celebrities and pop culture, she received some criticism for creating commercial work. "Others, however, point to her imagination and creativity in posing her subjects and stress the importance of her photographs as documents of popular culture."[16] In her work, she would always strive to capture the essence of the celebrity's public persona.

Cost of Products in the 1970s

FOOD

Eggs: 61 cents a dozen

Milk: 33 cents a quart

Bread: 24 cents a loaf

Butter: 87 cents a pound[1]

Tomatoes: 58 cents a pound

Sugar: $2.50 a pound

Bacon: $1.25 a pound

Cereal: $1.10 a box

Black-eyed peas: 40 cents per pound

Soft drinks: 25–30 cents a bottle

Chocolate bar: 15–20 cents

Hot dogs: 77 cents per pound

Tuna fish: 49 cents for 6.5 ounce can

Round steak: $1.30 a pound

WOMEN'S CLOTHING

Athletic shoes: $9.50–$40

Warm-up suit: $20–$48

Running shorts: $4–$8

Dress shoes: $15

Sandals: $9–$11

Polyester shirt jacket: $17
Turtleneck: $9
Polyester slacks: $11
Fleece robe: $11

MEN'S CLOTHING

Slacks: $10–$14
Knit shirt: $5–$8
Sweater: $10–$25
Dress shoes: $11–$18
Leather work shoes: $15–$26
Leather coat: $70
Sport coat: $85–$95
Suit: $115–$165

JEWELRY

Costume jewelry: $3–$10
"Filled" silver jewelry: $6–$40
Mood ring: $2–$250
Diamond tie tac: $95
14 k and 28 k gold bracelets, men and women: $265–$2,160
1/2 caret diamond engagement ring: $295
3/4 caret diamond solitaire: $575
3 diamond engagement set, 1 1/2 carets total: $1,250
10 caret diamond cluster ring: $6,500

HOUSEHOLD ITEMS

Postage stamp (1970): 6 cents
Postage stamp (1979): 15 cents
Carpeting: $6–$9 per square yard
Electric can opener/knife sharpener: $9.99
AM/FM clock radio: $30–$40
Electric calculator: $50–$60
Canister vacuum: $24
Eureka vacuum cleaner: $38 and up
Portable air conditioning unit: $88–$158

FURNITURE AND APPLIANCES

Microwave oven: $178–$450

Refrigerator: $169–$449

Oven: $129–$198

Washing machine: $199–$276

Dryer: $99–$170

Dishwasher: $138–$249

Trash compactor: $138

Freezer: $199–$299

Twin mattress and box springs: $150

Sofa: $198–$248

Dining room table and four chairs: $225

19-inch black-and-white television: $86

18-inch color television: $238

RECREATION

Stereo with 8-track player: $99.99–$129.99

Gallon of gas (1970): 36 cents[2]

Gallon of gas (1975): 57 cents[3]

Gallon of gas (1979): 86 cents[4]

Original version of Apple Computer (Apple 1): $666.66[5]

10-speed bike: $75

International Ice Revue tickets: $4.50–$8.50 per person

3 days, 2 nights hotel and theater package: $60 per person

BetaMax VCR: $1,295

Notes

INTRODUCTION AND TIMELINE

1. Thomas D. Elias, "Professors Agree Pop-Culture Studies Are Window to Past: Field Merits Serious Review, They Say," *Washington Times,* April 6, 1999, 2.

2. Dolores Barclay, "Pet Rocks to Punk Rock," *Los Angeles Times,* December 25, 1979, J3.

3. http://reason.com/0004/fe.jw.rebel.shtml

4. http://www.cedmagic.com/history/betamax-sl-7200–1976.html

5. http://www.gigfoot.net/lol/facts/640.html

6. http://www.fas.org/nuke/guide/usa/bomber/b-1a.htm

7. http://www.equalrightsamendment.org/viability.htm

8. http://www.pbs.org/wgbh/amex/carter/filmmore/ps_crisis.html

CHAPTER 1

1. Paul Krugman, *Peddling Prosperity: Economic Sense and Nonsense in the Age of Diminished Expectations* (New York: Norton, 1994), p. 57.

2. Brian Trumbore, "The Arab Oil Embargo of 1973–1974," BuyandHold.com, 2002, http://www.buyandhold.com/bh/en/education/history/2002/arab.html, (accessed July 14, 2006).

3. Stephanie Slocum-Schaffer, *America in the Seventies* (Syracuse, N.Y.: Syracuse University Press, 2003), p. 44.

4. Kit Sims Taylor, *Human Society and the Global Economy* (Bellevue, Wash.: Bellevue Community College, 2001), http://online.bcc.ctc.edu/econ100/ksttext/stagflat/STAGFLTN.htm, (accessed July 14, 2006).

5. Max Heirich, *Rethinking Health Care: Innovation and Change in America* (Boulder, Colo.: Westview Press, 1998), p. 5.

6. Gary S. Belkin, *The Politics of Health Care Reform: Lessons from the Past, Prospects for the Future* (Durham, N.C.: Duke University Press, 1994), p. 2.

7. Eli Ginzberg, *The Road to Reform: The Future of Health Care in America* (New York: Free Press, 1994), p. 16.

8. Robert D. Johnston, *The Politics of Healing: Histories of Alternative Medicine in Twentieth-Century North America* (New York: Routledge, 2004), p. 36.

9. Ibid, p. 159.

10. Slocum-Schaffer, *America in the Seventies*, p. 97.

11. Ibid, p. 37.

12. Ibid, pp. 54–55.

13. Ibid, p. 56.

14. "President, Peace Maker, Peanut Farmer," CNN.com, October 11, 2002, http://archives.cnn.com/2002/US/South/10/10/carter.profile/index.html, (accessed July 14, 2006).

15. For more information about President Carter's legacy, see "American Experience: Jimmy Carter" by PBS, http://www.pbs.org/wgbh/amex/carter/peopleevents/e_hostage.html, (accessed July 14, 2006).

16. "Jimmy Carter," The White House, 1977-1981, http://www.whitehouse.gov/history/presidents/jc39.html, (accessed July 14, 2006).

17. "President, Peace Maker, Peanut Farmer."

18. "Civil Rights and Racial Preferences: A Legal History of Affirmative Action," Maryland School of Public Affairs, 1999, http://www.puaf.umd.edu/IPPP/2QQ.HTM, (accessed July 14, 2006).

19. "Roe v. Wade," Thomson Gale, 1997, http://www.gale.com/free_resources/whm/trials/roe.htm, (accessed July 14, 2006).

20. Lionel Wright, "The Stonewall Riots: 1969," *Socialism Today*, No. 40, July 1999, http://www.socialistalternative.com/literature/stonewall.html, (accessed July 14, 2006).

21. "Stonewall and Beyond: Lesbian and Gay Culture," Columbia University, 2004, http://www.columbia.edu/cu/lweb/eresources/exhibitions/sw25/case1.html, (accessed July 14, 2006).

22. Robert Aldrich, *Who's Who in Contemporary Gay and Lesbian History: From World War II to the Present Day* (London: Routledge, 2001), p. 55.

23. *"Gregg v. Georgia,"* Oyez: U.S. Supreme Court Multimedia, 2005, http://www.oyez.org/oyez/resource/case/469/, (accessed July 14, 2006).

24. "History of the Court," The Supreme Court Historical Society: The Burger Court, 1969-1986, http://www.supremecourthistory.org/02_history/subs_history/02_c15.html, (accessed July 14, 2006).

25. David Frum, *How We Got Here: The 70's—The Decade That Brought You Modern Life (for Better or Worse),* (New York: Basic Books, 2000), p. 16.

26. Denise Grady, "Doctors See Way to Cut Suffering in Executions," *New York Times,* June 23, 2006, http://www.nytimes.com/2006/06/23/us/23inject.html?ex=1161144000&en=14d9ad94cab46b83&ei=5070, (accessed July 14, 2006).

27. Doug Linder, "The Charles Manson (Tate-LaBianca) Trial," 2002, http://www.law.umkc.edu/faculty/projects/ftrials/manson/mansonaccount.html, (accessed July 14, 2006).

28. Chris Summers, "David Berkowitz, Son of Sam," BBC News Online, http://www.bbc.co.uk/crime/caseclosed/berkowitz1.shtml, (accessed July 14, 2006).

29. "Kent State Shootings Remembered," CNN.com, May 4, 2000, http://archives.cnn.com/2000/US/05/04/kent.state.revisit/, (accessed July 14, 2006).

30. Mark Barringer, "The Anti-War Movement in the United States," *Oxford Companion to American Military History,* 1999, http://www.english.uiuc.edu/maps/vietnam/antiwar.html, (accessed July 14, 2006).

31. "The Legacy of Psychological Trauma from the Vietnam War for American Indian Military Personnel," US Department of Veterans Affairs, http://www.ncptsd.va.gov/facts/veterans/fs_native_vets.html, (accessed July 14, 2006).

32. Donald E. Messer and Bonnie J. Messer, "Day Care: A Need Crying to Be Heard," *Christian Century,* November 6, 1974, p. 1034.

33. Frum, *How We Got Here,* pp. 73–74.

34. Ibid.

35. Ibid., p. 80.

36. Messer and Messer, "Day Care," pp. 1034–37.

37. Gustav Niebuhr, "'The Family' and Final Harvest," *Washington Post,* June 2, 1993, p. A01.

38. Joanne Beckman, "Religion in Post-World War II America," Duke University, National Humanities Center, http://www.nhc.rtp.nc.us/tserve/twenty/tkey-info/trelww2.htm, (accessed July 14, 2006).

CHAPTER 2

1. Lisa Cozzens, "Brown v. Board of Education," African American History, May 1998, http://fledge.watson.org/~lisa/blackhistory/early-civilrights/brown.html, (accessed July 14, 2006).

2. Thomas R. Ascik, "The Anti-Busing Constitutional Amendment," *Heritage Foundation Policy Research and Analysis,* no. 47 (July 18, 1979), http://www.heritage.org/Research/Education/IB47.cfm, (accessed July 14, 2006).

3. Jesse Walker, "The Fever Swamps of Kansas," Reason Online, March 2005, http://www.reason.com/0503/cr.jw.the.shtml, (accessed July 14, 2006).

4. "The Biology Wars: The Religion, Science, and Education Controversy," Pew Forum on Religion and Public Life, December 5, 2005, http://pewforum.org/events/index.php?EventID = 93, (accessed July 14, 2006).

5. Priscilla Pardini, "The History of Sexuality Education," Rethinking Schools Online, 2002, http://www.rethinkingschools.org/sex/sexhisto.shtml, (accessed July 14, 2006).

6. Daniel Schugurensky, "1973: Sexism in Schools and Society Returned by Frustrated Consumers," History of Education, 2002, http://fcis.oise.utoronto.ca/~daniel_sch/assignment1/1973sexism.html, (accessed July 14, 2006).

7. Ibid.

8. David Allyn, *Make Love, Not War: The Sexual Revolution, An Unfettered History* (New York: Little, Brown, 2000), p. 206.

9. Mary E. Williams, *The Sexual Revolution* (San Diego, Calif.: Greenhaven Press, 2002), p. 151.

10. Jennifer Schaefer, "Changing Times: Tracing American Sexuality through Magazine Cover Lines on *Redbook* and *Glamour* Magazines," *University of Florida Journal of Undergraduate Research* 6, no. 2 (October 2004), http://www.clas.ufl.edu/jur/200410/papers/paper_schaefer.html, (accessed July 14, 2006).

11. Allyn, *Make Love, Not War*, p. 237.

12. Ibid., p. 230.

13. Williams, *The Sexual Revolution*, p. 154.

14. "Do You Know: LSD," Centre for Addiction and Mental Health, 2003, http:// www.camh.net/About_Addiction_Mental_Health/Drug_and_Addiction_Information/lsd_dyk.html, (accessed July 14, 2006).

15. Eric Schlosser, "Reefer Madness," *Atlantic Monthly*, August 1994, p. 45.

16. Suzanne Fields, "No Kick from Cocaine," *Jewish World Review*, August 27, 1999, http://www.jewishworldreview.com/cols/fields082799.asp, (accessed July 14, 2006).

17. "Thirty Years of America's Drug War: A Chronology," PBS Frontline, 2006, http://www.pbs.org/wgbh/pages/frontline/shows/drugs/cron/, (accessed July 14, 2006).

CHAPTER 3

1. John D. Morris, "Cigarette Maker Loses Court Test," *New York Times*, January 1, 1970, p. 43.

2. Murray Dubin, "Corporations Take New Look at Public Attitudes—and Take Heed," *Los Angeles Times*, July 11, 1973, p. C17.

3. "Best Super Bowl Commercials," Page 2, ESPN.com, 2006, http://espn.go.com/page2/s/list/sbcommercials.html, (accessed July 15, 2006).

4. "Top 100 Advertising Campaigns," AdAge.com, 2005, http://www.adage.com/century/campaigns.html, (accessed July 15, 2006).

5. Peter N. Carroll, *It Seemed Like Nothing Happened: America in the Seventies* (New Brunswick, N.J.: Rutgers University Press, 2000), p. 312.

6. "Top 100 Advertising Campaigns."

7. Steve Craig, "Feminism, Femininity, and the 'Beauty' Dilemma: How Advertising Co-opted the Women's Movement" (paper presented at the American Culture Association Conference, 1998), p. 6, http://69.28.198.79/feminist/fashion/The-Beauty-Dilemma.html, (accessedJuly 15, 2006).

8. Carroll, *It Seemed Like Nothing Happened*, p. 27.

9. Beth L. Bailey and Dave Farber, *America in the Seventies* (Lawrence: University of Kansas Press, 2004), p. 124.

10. Nancy Artz, Jeanne Munger, and Warren Purdy, "Gender Issues in Advertising Language," *Women and Language* 22, no. 2, 1999, p. 20.

11. Carroll, *It Seemed Like Nothing Happened*, p. 63.

12. Ibid., p. 207.

13. Marilyn Kern-Foxworth, *Aunt Jemima, Uncle Ben, and Rastus: Blacks in Advertising, Yesterday, Today, and Tomorrow* (Westport, Conn.: Praeger, 1994), p. 132.

14. Ibid., p. 133.

15. Ibid.

16. Ibid., p. 134.

17. Ibid.

18. Carroll, *It Seemed Like Nothing Happened*, p. 296.

19. Gail B. Stewart, *A Cultural History of the United States through the Decades: The 1970s* (San Francisco: Lucent Books, 1999), p. 72.

CHAPTER 4

1. Lawrence Biemiller, "Preserving the Wondrous Home of a Legendary Architect," January 12, 1996, http://www.iceandcoal.org/nfa/moore.html, (accessed July 18, 2006).

2. Peggy Goetz, "Architect's Legacy Encircles UCI," *Irvine World News,* July 18, 2002, http://www.irvineworldnews.com/Astories/july18/pereira.html, (accessed July 18, 2006).

3. Scott Johnson, "William Pereira," http://www.laforum.org/forum_issue_7_late_moderns/william_pereira_by_scott_johnson, (accessed July 18, 2006).

4. Biemiller, "Preserving the Wondrous Home."

5. Paul Heyer, *American Architecture: Ideas and Ideologies in the Late Twentieth Century* (New York: Van Nostrand Reinhold, 1993), pp. 228–30.

6. "Paola Soleri," PBS.com, 2006, http://www.pbs.org/wnet/egg/308/soleri/, (accessed July 18, 2006).

7. Marvin Trachtenberg and Isabelle Hyman, *Architecture from Prehistory to Post-Modernism* (Englewood Cliffs, N.J.: Prentice-Hall, 1986), p. 568.

8. Heyer, *American Architecture,* p. 128.

CHAPTER 5

1. Anne Bissonnette, "Revolutionizing Fashion: The Politics of Style," Kent State University Museum, 2000, http://dept.kent.edu/museum/exhibit/70s/hippie.html, (accessed July 19, 2006).

2. Gail B. Stewart, *A Cultural History of the United States through the Decades: The 1970s* (San Francisco: Lucent Books, 1999), p. 70.

3. Cynthia Boris, "The Partridge Family," DVD Verdict, http://www.dvdverdict.com/reviews/partridgefamilyseason2.php, (accessed July 19, 2006).

4. Jeannine Grenier-Wheeler, "David Cassidy Redux: I Think I Love You Still," June 8, 2004, starbulletin.com/2004/06/08/features/goddess.html, (accessed July 19, 2006).

5. Stewart, *Cultural History of the United States,* p. 64.

6. David Frum, *How We Got Here: The 70's—The Decade That Brought You Modern Life (for Better or Worse),* (New York: Basic Books, 2000), p. 192.

7. Bernadine Morris, "Review/Design: When America Stole the Runway from Paris Couture," *New York Times,* September 10, 1993, http://query.nytimes.com/gst/fullpage.html?res=9F0CE6DF153BF933A2575AC0A965958260, (accessed July 19, 2006).

8. Michael Jay Goldberg, *The Collectible Seventies: A Price Guide to the Polyester Decade* (Iola, Wis.: Krause Publications, 2001), p. 109.

9. "Angie Was Aggressive Outspoken and Fiercely Bisexual. Once She Had Seduced Bowie She Set about Moulding Him to Her Own Weird Image," *Daily Mail,* November 19, 1996, p. 32.

10. Ibid.

11. Roger Sabin, *Punk Rock, So What? The Cultural Legacy of Punk* (London: Routledge, 1999), p. 96.

CHAPTER 6

1. Sylvia Lovegren, *Fashionable Foods: Seven Decades of Food Fads* (Chicago: University of Chicago Press, 2005), http://www.press.uchicago.edu/Misc/Chicago/494071_1970.html, (accessed July 21, 2006).

2. Michael Jay Goldberg, *The Collectible Seventies: A Price Guide to the Polyester Decade* (Iola, Wis.: Krause Publications, 2001), p. 106.

3. "The World's Healthiest Foods," The George Mateljan Foundation, http://www.whfoods.com/genpage.php?tname=diet&dbid=6, (accessed July 21, 2006).

4. "Perrier in Six Packs," *Time*, May 16, 1977, http://www.time.com/time/magazine/article/0,9171,918972,00.html, (accessed July 21, 2006).

5. "In Season: 1970s Bistro Food," Waitrose Food Illustrated, February 2004, http://www.waitrose.com/food_drink/wfi/cooking/entertaining/0402044.asp, (accessed July 22, 2006).

6. Eric Schlosser, *Fast Food Nation: The Dark Side of the All American Meal* (New York: HarperPerennial, 2002), http://www.ecobooks.com/books/fastfood.htm, (accessed July 22, 2006).

7. Carolyn Dimitri and Anne Effland, "Milestones in U.S. Farming and Farm Policy," *Amber Waves* (June 2005), http://www.ers.usda.gov/AmberWaves/June05/DataFeature, (accessed July 21, 2006).

8. Jonathan H. Adler, "Fables of the Cuyahoga: Reconstructing a History of Environmental Protection," *Fordham Environmental Law Journal* 14, p. 89, law.case.edu/faculty/adler_jonathan/publications/fables_of_the_cuyahoga.pdf, (accessed July 22, 2006).

9. Ibid., p. 93.

10. Stephanie Slocum-Schaffer, *America in the Seventies* (Syracuse, N.Y.: Syracuse University Press, 2003), p. 130.

11. Ibid., p.132.

12. Ibid., p. 133.

13. Pagan Kennedy, *Platforms: A Microwaved Cultural Chronicle of the 1970s* (New York: St. Martin's Press, 1994), p. 31.

14. Ibid., p. 32.

15. Eckardt C. Beck, "The Love Canal Tragedy," *EPA Journal*, January 1979, http://www.epa.gov/history/topics/lovecanal/01.htm, (accessed July 22, 2006).

16. Eric Zuesse, "The Love Canal: The Truth Seeps Out," ReasonOnline.com, February 1981, http://www.reason.com/8102/fe.ez.the.shtml, (accessed July 22, 2006).

17. Beck, "Love Canal Tragedy."

CHAPTER 7

1. Dolores Barclay, "Pet Rocks to Punk Rock," *Los Angeles Times*, December 25, 1979, p. J3.

2. Judith Martin, "A Ring around the Mood Market," *Washington Post*, November 24, 1975, p. B9.

3. Ibid.

4. Alan Cartnal, "Gimmickry Jewelry Guru Just Revving Up," *Los Angeles Times*, December 14, 1976, p. OC–A1.

5. Jane Stern and Michael Stern, *Encyclopedia of Pop Culture* (New York: HarperPerennial, 1992), http://www.virtualpet.com/vp/farm/petrock/petrock. htm, (accessed July 24, 2006).

6. Ruth Barcan, *Nudity: A Cultural Anatomy* (New York: Berg, 2004), p. 188.

7. Ronni Lee Scheier, "Naked Truth of Streaking," *Chicago Tribune,* April 2, 1974, p. 14.

8. David Singmaster, "Mathematics: Rubik's Rubrics," *American Scientist,* September–October 2003, p. 468.

9. Joan Beck, "Simon Says: Make Chores as Much Fun as Pinball," *Chicago Tribune,* September 11, 1978, p. C2.

10. Carol Ting, Johannes M. Bauer, Steven S. Wildman, "The U.S. Experience with Non-traditional Approaches to Spectrum Management: Tragedies of the Commons and Other Myths Reconsidered." Prepared for presentation at the 31st Research Conference on Communication, Information and Internet Policy, Arlington, VA, September 19–21, 2003. http://quello.msu.edu/wp/wp-03-05.pdf.

11. Beth Ann Krier, "Fantasy Life in a Game without End," *Los Angeles Times,* July 11, 1979, p. H1.

12. Ibid.

13. Karen DeWitt, "Fantasy Game Finds Unimagined Success," *New York Times,* October 3, 1979, p. C16.

14. Patricia Anselt, "Genealogy Comes of Age," *Chicago Tribune,* June 19, 1976, p. F1.

15. Tom Buckley, "Curiosity about Roots of the Family Tree Is Growing," *New York Times,* May 3, 1974, p. 41.

16. "Half Million Amateur Genealogists Dig into Past to Trace Ancestors," *Los Angeles Times,* May 1, 1974, p. B10.

17. Bill Nichols, "Love Match? Chris Arrives Late—With Friend," *Cleveland Plain Dealer,* July 25, 1972, http://www.lkwdpl.org/nworth/evertcon.htm, (accessed July 22, 2006).

CHAPTER 8

1. Roland Sodowsky, "1970s AD," *Studies in Short Fiction,* Fall 1996, http:// www.findarticles.com/p/articles/mi_m2455/is_n4_v33/ai_20906637, (accessed July 28, 2006).

2. Paul Boyer, *Purity in Print: Book Censorship in America from the Gilded Age to the Computer Age* (Madison: University of Wisconsin Press, 2002), pp. 307, 309.

3. Steven Ratiner, *Giving Their Word: Conversations with Contemporary Poets* (Amherst: University of Massachusetts Press, 2002), p. 78.

4. Joyce Carol Oates, "John Updike's American Comedies," *Modern Fiction Studies,* Fall 1975, http://jco.usfca.edu/updike.html, (accessed July 28, 2006).

5. Charles Berryman, *Decade of Novels: Fiction of the 1970s Form and Challenge* (Troy, N.Y.: Whitston, 1990), p. 25.

6. Christopher Lehmann-Haupt, "Is Kurt Vonnegut Kidding Us?," *New York Times,* May 2, 1973, http://www.nytimes.com/books/97/09/28/lifetimes/vonnegut-breakfast.html, (accessed July 28, 2006).

7. Kelly Boyer Sagert, "Toni Morrison: Spinning the Silver and Gold in Our Veins," *Ohio Writer* 9, no. 2 (March/April 1995): p. 7.

8. Hilary Mantel, "Ghost Writer: Compared to So Many White Male Novelists with Their Vapid Posturing, Toni Morrison Has Lost None of Her Power," *New Statesman* 132, no. 4667, (December 2003): pp. 50ff.

9. "Author Saul Bellow Dies," Associated Press, msn.com, April 5, 2005, http://www.msnbc.msn.com/id/7397496, (accessed July 28, 2006).

10. Tracy Johnson, "Tom Robbins," Salon.com, March 9, 2000, http://archive.salon.com/people/feature/2000/03/09/robbins/index.html, (accessed July 28, 2006).

11. Leon Lad Panek, *New Hard-Boiled Writers, 1970s–1990s* (Bowling Green, Ohio: Bowling Green State University Popular Press, 2000), p. 7.

12. Lisa Maria Hogeland, *Feminism and Its Fictions: The Consciousness-Raising Novel and the Women's Liberation Movement* (Philadelphia: University of Pennsylvania Press, 1998), http://www.upenn.edu/pennpress/book/888.html, (accessed July 28, 2006).

13. Tom Wolfe, *Mauve Gloves & Madmen, Clutter & Vine* (New York: Farrar, Straus and Giroux, 1976).

14. Bill Beuttler, "Whatever Happened to New Journalism?" (master's thesis, Columbia University Graduate School of Journalism, 1984, http://www.billbeuttler.com/work50.htm, (accessed July 28, 2006).).

15. Ibid.

16. Carolyn Wells Kraus, "Hurting People's Feelings: Journalism, Guilt, and Autobiography," *Biography* 26, no. 2 (Spring 2003): pp. 283-297.

17. Joseph Parisi, *100 Essential Modern Poems* (Chicago: Ivan R. Dee, 2005), p. 6.

18. Kevin Power, "The Robert Bly Interview on His Poetry," Montgomery College Library, 19 no. 3 (1976), http://mclibrary.nhmccd.edu/lit/blypow.html, (accessed July 28, 2006).

19. David Yezzi, "Confessional Poetry and the Artifice of Honesty," *New Criterion* 16, no .10 (June 1998): pp. 14–21.

20. "L-A-N-G-U-A-G-E P-O-E-T-R-Y," Poetry Previews, 1999, http://www.poetrypreviews.com/poets/language.html, (accessed July 28, 2006).

21. Harold Bloom, *Modern Black American Poets and Dramatists* (New York: Chelsea House, 1995), p. 5.

22. Boyer, *Purity in Print*, p. 291.

23. Jonathan Z. Larsen, "On the Roller Coaster," *Columbia Journalism Review*, November 2001, http://www.newswatch.in/?p=913, (accessed July 28, 2006).

24. Ibid.

25. Michael Schudson, "Watergate and the 'Rush' to Journalism," *Columbia Journalism Review*, May/June 1992, http://archives.cjr.org/year/92/3/watergateside.asp, (accessed July 28, 2006).

26. David LaFontaine, "Old School Community Journalism Shows: It's a Wonderful Light," AUSC Annenberg Online Journalism Review, August 25, 2005, http://www.ojr.org/ojr/stories/050825lafontaine, (accessed July 28, 2006).

CHAPTER 9

1. "A Quick Guide to Folk," British Broadcasting Corporation, 2005, http://www.bbc.co.uk/music/folkcountry/guide_folk.shtml, (accessed July 26, 2006).

2. Rachel Louise Snyder, "Will You Still Love Me Tomorrow?" Salon.com, June 19, 1999, http://www.salon.com/people/feature/1999/06/19/king/index1.html, (accessed July 26, 2006).

3. Judith L. DiGrazia, "The Sixties: Notes of Discord," Yale/New Haven Teachers Institute, http://www.yale.edu/ynhti/curriculum/units/1983/4/83.04.04. x.html, 2005, (accessed July 26, 2006).

4. "Queen," Answers.com, 2006, http://www.answers.com/topic/queen-artist, (accessed July 26, 2006).

5. Sam Binkley, "Disco," *St. James Encyclopedia of Pop Culture* (Farmington Hills, Mich.: Gale Group, 2002), http://findarticles.com/p/articles/mi_g1epc/is_tov/ai_2419100348, (accessed July 26, 2006).

CHAPTER 10

1. Beth L. Bailey and Dave Farber, *America in the Seventies* (Lawrence: University Press of Kansas, 2004), p. 93.

2. Ibid., p. 158.

3. "Why Do We All Love a Disaster Movie?" *Evening Standard,* May 27, 2004, p. 25.

4. J. Hoberman, "Don't Go Near the Water," *Artforum International,* April 1994, p. 13ff, http://www.findarticles.com/p/articles/mi_m0268/is_n8_v32/ai_16109590/pg_3, (accessed July 29, 2006).

5. Richard H. Pells, "Movies and Modern America," *Span,* July/August 2005, p. 29, http://usembassy.state.gov/posts/in1/wwwhspjulaug056.html, (accessed July 29, 2006).

6. Mary Ann Mannino, "The Godfather and American Culture: How the Corleones Became 'Our Gang,'" *MELUS,* 2003, p. 218ff, http://www.findarticles. com/p/articles/mi_m2278/is_3_28/ai_110473975, (accessed July 29, 2006).

7. Thomas Elsaesser, Alexander Horwath, and Noel King, *The Last Great American Picture Show: New Hollywood Cinema in the 1970s* (Amsterdam: Amsterdam University Press, 2004), p. 117.

8. Susan Hayward, *Cinema Studies: The Key Concepts* (London: Routledge, 2000), pp. 40–47.

9. Josh Ozersky, *Archie Bunker's America: TV in an Era of Change, 1968–1978* (Carbondale: Southern Illinois University Press, 2003), pp. xviii, 2.

10. Ibid., p. 4.

11. Ibid., p. 5.

12. Ibid., p. 74.

13. Bonnie J. Dow, *Prime-Time Feminism: Television, Media Culture, and the Women's Movement since 1970* (Philadelphia: University of Pennsylvania Press, 1996), p. 24.

14. Kathryn C. Montgomery, *Target, Prime Time: Advocacy Groups and the Struggle over Entertainment Television* (New York: Oxford University Press, 1990), p. 29.

15. "Alex Haley," *Africanamericans.com,* 2005, http://www.africanamericans. com/AlexHaley.htm, July 29, 2006.

16. Barry Walters, "Disco: The Longest Night," *Advocate,* July 21, 1998, pp. 42ff.

17. Jeremy Gilbert, *Discographies: Dance Music, Culture, and the Politics of Sound* (London: Routledge, 1999), p. 14.

18. John S. Wilson, "Theater: Equity Library Presents Musical 'Raisin,'" *New York Times,* May 18, 1981, p. C12.

19. "A Chorus Line," PBS.org, 2004, http://www.pbs.org/wnet/broadway/musicals/chorus.html, July 29, 2006.

CHAPTER 11

1. Robert Reeves, *The Superpower Space Race: An Explosive Rivalry through the Solar System* (New York: Plenum Press, 1994), p. 1.

2. John M. Logsdon, *The Decision to Go to the Moon: Project Apollo and the National Interest* (Cambridge MA: MIT Press, 1970), pp. 108-109, 112-115.

3. "Launching NASA," NASA History Division, July 25, 2005, http://www.hq.nasa.gov/office/pao/History/factsheet.htm, (accessed July 29, 2006).

4. Andrew Chaikin, "Greatest Space Events of the 20th Century: The 70s," Space.com, December 30, 1999, http://www.space.com/news/spacehistory/greatest_70s_991230.html, (accessed July 29, 2006).

5. "Skylab Mission Goals," Skylab Kennedy Space Center, September 29, 2000, http://www-pao.ksc.nasa.gov/history/skylab/skylab-goals.htm, (accessed July 29, 2006).

6. Alex Hutchinson, "Top 50 Inventions," *Popular Mechanics,* December 2005, http://www.popularmechanics.com/science/research/2078467.html, (accessed July 29, 2006).

7. Michael L. Berger, *The Automobile in American History and Culture: A Reference Guide* (Westport, Conn.: Greenwood Press, 2001), p. 154.

8. Patrick R. Foster, *Super 70s: Cars of the Disco Era* (Iola, Wis.: Krause Publications, 2000), p.51.

9. Matthew T. Lee, "The Ford Pinto Case and the Development of Auto Safety Regulations, 1893-1978," Department of Sociology and Criminal Justice, University of Delaware, http://www.h-net.org/~business/bhcweb/publications/BEHprint/v027n2/p0390-p0401.pdf, (accessed July 29, 2006).

10. Gary T. Schwartz, "The Myth of the Ford Pinto Case," *Rutgers Law Review* 43 (1991). Paper first presented at the Third Annual Lecture in the Pfizer Distinguished Visitors' series, Rutgers School of Law–Newark, November 14, 1990, http://www.pointoflaw.com/articles/The_Myth_of_the_Ford_Pinto_Case.pdf, (accessed July 29, 2006).

11. Ibid., p. 103.

12. Ibid., p. 19.

13. "Boeing 747 Celebrates 30 Years in Service," Boeing.com, January 21, 2000, http://www.boeing.com/news/releases/2000/news_release_000121a.html, (accessed July 29, 2006).

14. Robert Lindsey, "Jumbo Jet Flies First Time; Flaw in Flap Noted," *New York Times,* February 10, 1969, p. 78.

15. Robert J. Serling, "Two for Tomorrow," *Chicago Tribune,* May 4, 1969, p. 102.

16. Ibid., 102.

17. Alfred E. Kahn, "Airline Deregulation," *The Concise Encyclopedia of Economics,* 2002, http://www.econlib.org/LIBRARY/Enc/AirlineDeregulation. html, (accessed July 29, 2006).

18. "Traveling by Rail: An Informal History," Amtrak Historical Society, http://www.amtrakhistoricalsociety.com/bah.htm, (accessed July 29, 2006).

19. Joseph R. Daughen and Peter Binzen, *The Wreck of the Penn Central* (Washington, DC: Beard Books, 1999), back cover, http://www.beardbooks.com/the_wreck_of_the_penn_central.html, (accessed July 29, 2006).

20. *"This* Is Any Way to Run a Railroad?" *Time,* December 21, 1971, http://www.time.com/time/business/article/0,8599,185650,00.html, (accessed July 29, 2006).

CHAPTER 12

1. Douglas Cruickshank, "Size Matters," Salon.com, 2000, http://www.salon.com/bc/1998/12/22bc.html, (accessed July 29, 2006).

2. Marco Livingstone, *Pop Art: A Continuing History* (London: Thames and Hudson, Ltd, 2000).

3. John A. Walker, *Art in the Age of Mass Media* (Boulder, Colo.: Westview Press, 1994), p. 31.

4. Ibid.

5. "Roy Lichtenstein," Artcyclopedia.com, September 2006, http://www.art-cyclopedia.com/artists/lichtenstein_roy.html, (accessed July 29, 2006).

6. "Works of Art: Roy Lichtenstein," Metropolitan Museum of Art, 2006, http://www.metmuseum.org/works_of_art/viewone.asp?dep = 21&viewmode = 0&item = 1980.420, (accessed July 30, 2006).

7. "Roy Lichtenstein Biography: 1923–1997," artelino.com, http://www.ar-telino.com/articles/roy_lichtenstein.asp, (accessed July 30, 2006).

8. Cruickshank, "Size Matters."

9. "Seeing the Light with James Turrell," British Broadcasting Company, November 2, 2000, http://www.bbc.co.uk/worldservice/arts/highlights/001102_turrell.shtml, (accessed July 30, 2006).

10. "Remembering George Segal," PBS Online NewsHour, June 14, 2000, http://www.pbs.org/newshour/bb/remember/jan-june00/segal_6–14.html, (accessed July 30, 2006).

11. Ibid.

12. "Reflecting on Modern Society; 140 Photographs at Hirshhorn Display 'Open City' in the Raw," *Washington Times,* June 22, 2002, p. D01.

13. Dick Swanson and Gordon Chaplin, "Last Exit from Saigon," Digital Journalist, http://www.digitaljournalist.org/issue9904/exit1.htm, (accessed July 30, 2006).

14. Robert S. Rothenberg, "Annie Leibovitz: Celebrity Photographer," *USA Today,* September 1997, p. 81.

15. "Annie Leibovitz," An Encyclopedia of Gay, Lesbian, Bisexual, Transgender, and Queer Culture, 2002, http://www.glbtq.com/arts/leibovitz_a.html, (accessed July 30, 2006).

16. Ibid.

COST OF PRODUCTS IN THE 1970s

1. http://www.uen.org/utahlink/tours/tourElement.cgi?element_id=29103&tour_id=15477&category_id=24007

2. http://www.1970sflashback.com/1970/Economy.asp.

3. http://www.1970sflashback.com/1975/Economy.asp.

4. http://www.1970sflashback.com/1979/Economy.asp.

5. http://oldcomputers.net/index.html.

Further Reading

Adler, Jonathan H. "Fables of the Cuyahoga: Reconstructing a History of Environmental Protection." *Fordham Environmental Law Review* 14 (Fall 2002): pp. 89–146, law.case.edu/faculty/adler_jonathan/publications/fables_of_the_cuyahoga.pdf.

Aldrich, Robert. *Who's Who in Contemporary Gay and Lesbian History: From World War II to the Present Day.* London: Routledge, 2001.

Allyn, David. *Make Love, Not War: The Sexual Revolution, An Unfettered History.* New York: Little, Brown, 2000.

Anselt, Patricia. "Genealogy Comes of Age." *Chicago Tribune,* June 19, 1976, p. F1.

Artz, Nancy, Jeanne Munger, and Warren Purdy. "Gender Issues in Advertising Language." *Women and Language* 22, no. 2, 1999, p. 20.

Ascik, Thomas R. "The Anti-Busing Constitutional Amendment." *Heritage Foundation: Policy Research and Analysis,* no. 47, July 18, 1979, http://www.heritage.org/Research/Education/IB47.cfm.

Bailey, Beth L., and Dave Farber. *America in the Seventies.* Lawrence: University of Kansas Press, 2004.

Barcan, Ruth. *Nudity: A Cultural Anatomy.* New York: Berg, 2004.

Barclay, Dolores. "Pet Rocks to Punk Rock." *Los Angeles Times,* December 25, 1979, p J3.

Barringer, Mark. "The Anti-War Movement in the United States." *Oxford Companion to American Military History,* 1999, http://www.english.uiuc.edu/maps/vietnam/antiwar.html.

Beck, Eckardt C. "The Love Canal Tragedy." *EPA Journal,* January 1979, http://www.epa.gov/history/topics/lovecanal/01.htm.

Belkin, Gary S. *The Politics of Health Care Reform: Lessons from the Past, Prospects for the Future.* Durham, N.C.: Duke University Press, 1994.

Berger, Michael L. *The Automobile in American History and Culture: A Reference Guide.* Westport, Conn.: Greenwood Press, 2001.

Berryman, Charles. *Decade of Novels: Fiction of the 1970s Form and Challenge.* Troy, N.Y.: Whitston, 1990.

Beuttler, Bill. "Whatever Happened to New Journalism?" Master's thesis, Columbia University Graduate School of Journalism, 1984.

Biemiller, Lawrence. "Preserving the Wondrous Home of a Legendary Architect." January 12, 1996, http://www.iceandcoal.org/nfa/moore.html.

Binkley, Sam. "Disco." *St. James Encyclopedia of Pop Culture.* Farmington Hills, Mich.: Gale Group, 2002, http://findarticles.com/p/articles/mi_g1epc/is_tov/ai_2419100348.

Bissonnette, Anne. "Revolutionizing Fashion: The Politics of Style." *Kent State University Museum,* 2000, http://dept.kent.edu/museum/exhibit/70s/hippie.html.

Bloom, Harold. *Modern Black American Poets and Dramatists.* New York: Chelsea House, 1995.

Boyer, Paul. *Purity in Print: Book Censorship in America from the Gilded Age to the Computer Age.* Madison: University of Wisconsin Press, 2002.

Buckley, Tom. "Curiosity about Roots of the Family Tree Is Growing." *New York Times,* May 3, 1974, p. 41.

Carroll, Peter N. *It Seemed Like Nothing Happened: America in the Seventies.* New Brunswick, N.J.: Rutgers University Press, 2000.

Cartnal, Alan. "Gimmickry Jewelry Guru Just Revving Up." *Los Angeles Times,* December 14, 1976, p. OC–A1.

Chaikin, Andrew. "Greatest Space Events of the 20th Century: The 70s." *Space.com,* December 30, 1999, http://www.space.com/news/spacehistory/greatest_70s_991230.html.

Cozzens, Lisa. "Brown v. Board of Education." African American History, May 1998, http://fledge.watson.org/~lisa/blackhistory/early-civilrights/brown.html.

Craig, Steve. "Feminism, Femininity, and the 'Beauty' Dilemma: How Advertising Co-opted the Women's Movement." Paper presented at the Southwest/Texas Popular Culture/American Culture Association Conference, Lubbock, TX, January, 1998), http://69.28.198.79/feminist/fashion/The-Beauty-Dilemma.html.

Cruickshank, Douglas. "Size Matters." *Salon.com,* http://www.salon.com/bc/1998/12/22bc.html.

Daughen, Joseph R., and Peter Binzen. *The Wreck of the Penn Central.* Washington, DC: Beard Books, 1999, http://www.beardbooks.com/the_wreck_of_the_penn_central.html.

DeWitt, Karen. "Fantasy Game Finds Unimagined Success." *New York Times,* October 3, 1979, p. C16.

Dow, Bonnie J. *Prime-Time Feminism: Television, Media Culture, and the Women's Movement since 1970.* Philadelphia: University of Pennsylvania Press, 1996.

Dubin, Murray. "Corporations Take New Look at Public Attitudes—and Take Heed." *Los Angeles Times,* July 11, 1973, p. C 17.

Edelstein, Andrew J., and Kevin McDonough. *The Seventies: From Hot Pants to Hot Tubs.* New York: Dutton, 1990.

Elsaesser, Thomas, Alexander Horwath, and Noel King. *The Last Great American Picture Show: New Hollywood Cinema in the 1970s.* Amsterdam: Amsterdam University Press, 2004.

Fields, Suzanne. "No Kick from Cocaine." *Jewish World Review,* August 27, 1999, http://www.jewishworldreview.com/cols/fields082799.asp.

Foster, Patrick R. *Super 70s: Cars of the Disco Era.* Iola, Wis.: Krause Publications, 2000.

Frum, David. *How We Got Here: The 70's—The Decade That Brought You Modern Life (for Better or Worse).* New York: Basic Books, 2000.

Gilbert, Jeremy. *Discographies: Dance Music, Culture, and the Politics of Sound.* London: Routledge, 1999.

Ginzberg, Eli. *The Road to Reform: The Future of Health Care in America.* New York: Free Press, 1994.

Goetz, Peggy. "Architect's Legacy Encircles UCI." *Irvine World News,* July 18, 2002, http://www.irvineworldnews.com/Astories/july18/pereira.html.

Goldberg, Michael Jay. *The Collectible Seventies: A Price Guide to the Polyester Decade.* Iola, Wis.: Krause Publications, 2001.

Grady, Denise. "Doctors See Way to Cut Suffering in Executions." *New York Times,* June 23, 2006, http://www.nytimes.com/2006/06/23/us/23inject.html?ex =1161144000&en=14d9ad94cab46b83&ei=5070.

Grenier-Wheeler, Jeannine. "David Cassidy Redux: I Think I Love You Still." *Star Bulletin.com,* June 8, 2004, starbulletin.com/2004/06/08/features/goddess. html.

Hayward, Susan. *Cinema Studies: The Key Concepts.* London: Routledge, 2000.

Heirich, Max. *Rethinking Health Care: Innovation and Change in America.* Boulder, Colo.: Westview Press, 1998.

Heyer, Paul. *American Architecture: Ideas and Ideologies in the Late Twentieth Century.* New York: Van Nostrand Reinhold, 1993.

Hoberman, J. "Don't Go Near the Water." *Artforum International,* April 1994, p. 13ff, http://www.findarticles.com/p/articles/mi_m0268/is_n8_v32/ ai_16109590/pg_3.

Hogeland, Lisa Maria. *Feminism and Its Fictions: The Consciousness-Raising Novel and the Women's Liberation Movement.* Philadelphia: University of Pennsylvania Press, 1998.

Hutchinson, Alex. "Top 50 Inventions." *Popular Mechanics,* December 2005, http:// www.popularmechanics.com/science/research/2078467.html.

Johnson, Scott. "William Pereira." http://www.laforum.org/forum_issue_7_late_ moderns/william_pereira_by_scott_johnson.

Johnson, Tracy. "Tom Robbins." *Salon.com,* March 9, 2000, http://archive.salon. com/people/feature/2000/03/09/robbins/index.html.

Johnston, Robert D. *The Politics of Healing: Histories of Alternative Medicine in Twentieth-Century North America.* New York: Routledge, 2004.

Kahn, Alfred E. "Airline Deregulation." *The Concise Encyclopedia of Economics,* 2002, http://www.econlib.org/LIBRARY/Enc/AirlineDeregulation.html.

Kennedy, Pagan. *Platforms: A Microwaved Cultural Chronicle of the 1970s.* New York: St. Martin's Press, 1994.

Kern-Foxworth, Marilyn. *Aunt Jemima, Uncle Ben, and Rastus: Blacks in Advertising, Yesterday, Today, and Tomorrow.* Westport, Conn.: Praeger, 1994.

Kraus, Carolyn Wells. "Hurting People's Feelings: Journalism, Guilt, and Autobiography." *Biography* 26, no. 2 (Spring 2003): p. 283–297.

Krier, Beth Ann. "Fantasy Life in a Game without End." *Los Angeles Times,* July 11, 1979, p. H1.

Krugman, Paul. *Peddling Prosperity: Economic Sense and Nonsense in the Age of Diminished Expectations.* New York: Norton, 1994.

LaFontaine, David. "Old School Community Journalism Shows; It's a Wonderful Light." *AUSC Annenberg Online Journalism Review,* August 25, 2005.

"L-A-N-G-U-A-G-E P-O-E-T-R-Y," *Poetry Previews,* 1999, http://www.poetry previews.com/poets/language.html.

Larsen, Jonathan Z. "On the Roller Coaster." *Columbia Journalism Review,* November 2001, http://www.newswatch.in/?p=913.

Lehmann-Haupt, Christopher. "Is Kurt Vonnegut Kidding Us?" *New York Times,* May 2, 1973, http://www.nytimes.com/books/97/09/28/lifetimes/vonnegut-breakfast.html.

Lindsey, Robert. "Jumbo Jet Flies First Time; Flaw in Flap Noted." *New York Times,* February 10, 1969, p. 78.

Lovegren, Sylvia. *Fashionable Foods: Seven Decades of Food Fads.* Chicago: University of Chicago Press, 2005.

Mannino, Mary Ann. "The Godfather and American Culture: How the Corleones Became 'Our Gang.'" *MELUS,* 2003, pp. 218ff., http://www.findarticles.com/p/articles/mi_m2278/is_3_28/ai_110473975.

Mantel, Hilary. "Ghost Writer: Compared to So Many White Male Novelists with Their Vapid Posturing, Toni Morrison Has Lost None of Her Power." *New Statesman,* December 8, 2003, pp. 50ff.

Martin, Judith. "A Ring around the Mood Market." *Washington Post,* November 24, 1975, p. B9.

Messer, Donald E., and Bonnie J. Messer. "Day Care: A Need Crying to Be Heard." *Christian Century,* November 6, 1974, p. 1034.

Montgomery, Kathryn C. *Target, Prime Time: Advocacy Groups and the Struggle over Entertainment Television.* New York: Oxford University Press, 1990.

Morris, Bernadine. "Review/Design: When America Stole the Runway from Paris Couture." *New York Times,* September 10, 1993, http://query.nytimes.com/gst/fullpage.html?res=9F0CE6DF153BF933A2575AC0A965958260.

Morris, John D. "Cigarette Maker Loses Court Test." *New York Times,* January 1, 1970, p. 43.

Nichols, Bill. "Love Match? Chris Arrives Late—With Friend," *Cleveland Plain Dealer,* July 25, 1972, http://www.lkwdpl.org/nworth/evertcon.htm.

Niebuhr, Gustav. "'The Family' and Final Harvest." *Washington Post,* June 2, 1993, p. A01.

Oates, Joyce Carol. "John Updike's American Comedies." *Modern Fiction Studies,* Fall 1975, http://jco.usfca.edu/updike.html.

Ozersky, Josh. *Archie Bunker's America: TV in an Era of Change, 1968–1978.* Carbondale: Southern Illinois University Press, 2003.

Panek, Leon Lad. *New Hard-Boiled Writers, 1970s–1990s.* Bowling Green, Ohio: Bowling Green State University Popular Press, 2000.

Pardini, Priscilla. "The History of Sexuality Education." *Rethinking Schools Online,* 2002, http://www.rethinkingschools.org/sex/sexhisto.shtml.

Parisi, Joseph. *100 Essential Modern Poems.* Chicago: Ivan R. Dee, 2005.

Pells, Richard H. "Movies and Modern America." *Span,* July/August 2005, p. 29.

Power, Kevin. "The Robert Bly Interview on His Poetry." *Montgomery College Library* 19, no. 3 (1976), http://mclibrary.nhmccd.edu/lit/blypow.html.

Ratiner, Steven. *Giving Their Word: Conversations with Contemporary Poets.* Amherst: University of Massachusetts Press, 2002.

Reeves, Robert. *The Superpower Space Race: An Explosive Rivalry through the Solar System.* New York: Plenum Press, 1994.

Rothenberg, Robert S. "Annie Leibovitz: Celebrity Photographer." *USA Today,* September 1997, p. 81.

Sabin, Roger. *Punk Rock, So What? The Cultural Legacy of Punk.* London: Routledge, 1999.

Sagert, Kelly Boyer. "Toni Morrison: Spinning the Silver and Gold in Our Veins." *Ohio Writer* 9, no. 2, March/April 1995, p. 7.

Schaefer, Jennifer. "Changing Times: Tracing American Sexuality through Magazine Cover Lines on *Redbook* and *Glamour* Magazines." *Journal of Undergraduate Research, University of Florida* 6, no. 2, October 2004, http://www.clas.ufl.edu/jur/200410/papers/paper_schaefer.html.

Scheier, Ronni Lee. "Naked Truth of Streaking." *Chicago Tribune,* April 2, 1974, p. 14.

Schlosser, Eric. *Fast Food Nation: The Dark Side of the All American Meal.* New York: HarperPerennial, 2002.

———. "Reefer Madness." *Atlantic Monthly,* August 1994, p. 45.

Schudson, Michael. "Watergate and the 'Rush' to Journalism." *Columbia Journalism Review,* May/June 1992, http://archives.cjr.org/year/92/3/watergateside.asp.

Schugurensky, Daniel. "1973: Sexism in Schools and Society Returned by Frustrated Consumers." History of Education, 2002, http://fcis.oise.utoronto.ca/~daniel_sch/assignment1/1973sexism.html.

Schulman, Bruce J. *The Seventies: The Great Shift in American Culture, Society, and Politics.* Cambridge, Mass.: Da Capo Press, 2001.

Serling, Robert J. "Two for Tomorrow." *Chicago Tribune,* May 4, 1969, p. 102.

Singmaster, David. "Mathematics: Rubik's Rubrics." *American Scientist,* September–October 2003, p. 468.

Slocum-Schaffer, Stephanie. *America in the Seventies.* Syracuse, N.Y.: Syracuse University Press, 2003.

Snyder, Rachel Louise. "Will You Still Love Me Tomorrow?" *Salon.com,* June 19, 1999, http://www.salon.com/people/feature/1999/06/19/king/index1.html.

Sodowsky, Roland. "1970s AD." *Studies in Short Fiction,* Fall 1996, http://www.findarticles.com/p/articles/mi_m2455/is_n4_v33/ai_20906637.

Stern, Jane, and Michael Stern. *Encyclopedia of Pop Culture.* New York: HarperPerennial, 1992.

Stewart, Gail B. *A Cultural History of the United States through the Decades: The 1970s.* San Francisco: Lucent Books, 1999.

Summers, Chris. "David Berkowitz, Son of Sam." *BBC News Online,* http://www.bbc.co.uk/crime/caseclosed/berkowitz1.shtml.

Swanson, Dick, and Gordon Chaplin. "Last Exit from Saigon." *Digital Journalist,* http://www.digitaljournalist.org/issue9904/exit1.htm.

Taylor, Kit Sims. *Human Society and the Global Economy.* Bellevue, Wash.: Bellevue Community College, 2001, http://online.bcc.ctc.edu/econ100/ksttext/stagflat/STAGFLTN.htm.

Trachtenberg, Marvin, and Isabelle Hyman. *Architecture from Prehistory to Post-Modernism.* Englewood Cliffs, N.J.: Prentice-Hall, 1986.

Trumbore, Brian. "The Arab Oil Embargo of 1973–1974." BuyandHold.com, 2002, http://www.buyandhold.com/bh/en/education/history/2002/arab.html.

Walker, Jesse. "The Fever Swamps of Kansas." Reason Online, March 2005, http://www.reason.com/0503/cr.jw.the.shtml.

Walker, John A. *Art in the Age of Mass Media.* Boulder, Colo.: Westview Press, 1994.

Walters, Barry. "Disco: The Longest Night." *Advocate,* July 21, 1998, pp. 42ff.

Williams, Mary E. *The Sexual Revolution.* San Diego, Calif.: Greenhaven Press, 2002.

Wilson, John S. "Theater: Equity Library Presents Musical 'Raisin,'" *New York Times,* May 18, 1981, p. C12.

Wolfe, Tom. *Mauve Gloves & Madmen, Clutter & Vine.* New York: Farrar, Straus and Giroux, 1976.

Woodward, Bob, and Carl Bernstein. *The Final Days.* New York: Touchstone, 1976.

Wright, Lionel. "The Stonewall Riots: 1969." *Socialism Today,* no. 40, July 1999, http://www.socialistalternative.com/literature/stonewall.html.

Yezzi, David. "Confessional Poetry and the Artifice of Honesty." *New Criterion* 16, no .10 (June 1998): pp .14–21.

Index